Postures and politics

FRANK MacKINNON

Postures and politics

Some observations on participatory democracy

University of Toronto Press

320.5
M 21

© University of Toronto Press 1973
Toronto and Buffalo
Printed in Canada

ISBN 0-8020-1928-5 (cloth)
ISBN 0-8020-6167-2 (paper)
ISBN 0-8020-0266-8 (microfiche)
LC 72-95553

Contents

Preface   vii

1   Introduction: Flourishes and participations   3

2   Must democracy be drab?   21

3   Preventive politics   44

4   Crown and Valhalla   61

5   Conflicting postures in administration   75

6   Eccentricity in administration   88

7   Collectivized postures   99

8   Meddling   111

9   Principles   130

10 Church politics   145

11 The impact of church politics   167

12 The personnel of universities   184

13 Campus politics   206

14 The politics of culture   225

15 The state and culture   242

16 Man's only unlimited asset   252

Acknowledgments   261

Notes   263

Index   271

741071x

Preface

Life in this world has endless possibilities for man. He has countless talents for thinking and doing vast numbers of things. The world he inhabits is rich in physical beauty, resources, and stimulations for his emotions. He has thus been generously endowed with assets and opportunities.

Nevertheless the view of man from heaven must be astonishing. Even by earthly standards his activities are hilarious and sad. He is capable of so much brilliance and happiness, and yet he wastes so much of his ability on stupidity and melancholy. He is such an insignificant part of the forces of nature, and yet he takes himself with a deadly seriousness that is dependent, not even on his merits and abilities, but on complicated theories which he uses as formidable weapons for self-delusion and self-destruction. Thus preoccupied, he does not take life seriously enough. History reveals him to be a repeater of mistakes, and technical growth enables him to make bigger mistakes as he increases his control over natural resources, other species, and his own kind. Unfortunately, however, he has reached the limit; he needs to make only one more big mistake to lose control and go the way of other species that became extinct because they did not adjust to one another and the world.

But, some say, man is not an animal; he is a child of God not comparable with other species. Neither zoological nor theological literature indicates that he so behaves. Some may say he has conquered the world; there is as good a case for saying the world has conquered him.

The main element in this dilemma is man; the subordinate elements are his theories and institutions. But the dilemma occurs because he has reversed these elements, and made himself subordinate to his theories. It has long been my conviction that whenever man uses the means at his disposal to relate men to men and men to nature he is at his happiest and most productive. When he relies too much on his theories and institutions he is subordinated to them; when they are unstable he is kept in continuous discord; when they become unnatural he behaves unnaturally.

Man needs theories and institutions to perform functions and establish relationships. But he tends to expand these instruments out of proportion to their significance, even turning them into 'ways of life.' Thereupon he relies too heavily on them and not enough on himself and on nature; he prides himself, not on what he is, but on what he belongs to. History indicates, for example, that every political and ideological war has been fought, at enormous cost, by men who neither knew nor hated one another as men for the destruction or defence of mere theories and institutions. Similar confrontations bedevil affairs in even the smallest communities. Man needs to communicate more as man, and his theories and institutions require adjustments which will enable him to use them without sacrificing his individuality and his relationships with others.

With man, as with all species, postures and politics are vital and distinguishing parts of his behaviour and his relationships. These are natural phenomena, and it is a tragic mistake to deprive individuals of them, or to neglect their impact in collectivities. I have attempted in this book to deal with a few of these postures and politics as they are illustrated by selected human activities in systems where there is much discussion of participatory democracy. Other activities and systems would yield similar observations.

This book is a mixture of fact, political observation, and social commentary. I have given references for some of the statements, not to indicate reading, but to call upon reliable witnesses or refer to special events. All unacknowledged statements concern matters with which I have had direct contact: every example I have seen in action; every function I have participated in; every tactic I have shared or watched, from observing lyre birds at dawn in the Australian bush to devoting delightful and fruitful days to discussing construction problems with architects. As for the institutions discussed, I have been closely involved in various capacities with every one.

Social observations often appear to be predominantly negative if problems are stressed and foibles are emphasized. This book may seem at first to follow this pattern. I do not mean it to; I intend it to be positive. The target is negativism. My aim is to advocate positive relationships among men and institutions by pointing out the prevalence and futility of negative ones and suggesting alternatives. I do not decry human foibles, but suggest that they be recognized and provided for, rather than denied and suppressed. I believe that they can be given full scope in positive ways by means of natural postures and politics, that they can be useful and enjoyable, enabling men to hate and cry less, to love and laugh more.

The discussions are organized in two kinds of chapters. The general ones deal with ideas and functions, and they offer just a few examples and illustrations. The specific chapters on institutions and culture *are* the examples and illustrations. The themes in the general chapters are developed by means of the examples discussed in the specific ones.

Many of my views science has authenticated, but I have avoided attempts to be 'scientific.' The discussions, on power for example, are *not* based on psychological testing of a sample of 641 politicians and civil servants. Nor are they dependent on data compiled from the questionnaires so popular with some social scientists. They are the results of my own experience, and largely happy experience, with people in many activities and many places.

I have made use of several phenomena well known to science which are applicable in parallel ways in political and social affairs. Indeed many basic laws of life are found in both the physical and biological sciences on the one hand and the social sciences and humanities on the other. I prefer this approach to the uncertainties of contemporary statistical methodologies unaccompanied by scientific discipline. For example, I prefer the conclusions suggested by what science says about the 'bends' and the mixing of materials discussed in chapters 3 and 13 to the airy dogmas of political ideologies that, despite some attractions, have been so often proved wrong.

Dialogue is essential to participatory democracy. This book is a contribution to that dialogue by an observer who believes in participatory democracy, but does not think that it − or indeed any other system − will work if it is put on an ideological pedestal, or if its limitations are not discussed frankly and remedied effectively. Man has become, however, very theoretical, and he tends to take dogmatic positions based on his theories, so that social action becomes a contest rather than a dialogue, a relationship among theories and institutions often rendered unintelligible by jargon and unworkable by regulation, rather than a communication among men. Man also fancies administration, and devotes much energy to entangling himself in his own red tape, often with fatal results. He is careless too, and allows many of his endeavours to waste his talents and the world's resources. It has become obvious that he can afford to do none of these things, and that alternative forms of behaviour must be found. It is to contribute to this search that I have written the book. I must confess too that I find life far more interesting, enjoyable, and rewarding than the contemporary morbidity of social commentary and the drabness of much social action would suggest. That is why I offer as solutions the ideas on which this book is based.

F.M.   *University of Calgary   June 1972*

Postures and politics

1

Introduction
Flourishes and participations

Men in communal affairs are more inclined to control than to trust one another. We talk more readily than we listen. And we expect more agreement and gratitude than we are willing to give. A discrepancy exists, therefore, between a communication and the response to it, if there is a response at all. This discrepancy is desirable, because not all of our control, talk, or expectation is sensible, and our natural resistance to them is a suitable protection. Nevertheless we must communicate with one another, and the resistance has to be diminished or overcome. We therefore use flourishes to make our communications more agreeable to ourselves and acceptable to others. These flourishes are postures and politics.

Few of our actions are carried out simply. Most of them are accompanied by much politics, that is, the mechanics and negotiations necessary to carry out actions, reconcile them with other complementary or opposing actions, and compensate for varying abilities of people. They are carried out with postures too, that is, accompanying acts providing explanation, emphasis, and the expression of sensation. Communicating, eating, love making, worshipping, and governing are direct actions accompanied by attitudes, gestures, and rituals that invite, reinforce, control, or reward the actions. These postures also accompany the expression and satisfaction of instincts like status seeking and territoriality. Postures and politics have a preventive purpose too. Because actions invite reactions in the form of unexpected as well as expected consequences, postures and politics are used to control reactions or cushion their effects.

We often forget our dependence on postures and politics, or assume wrongly that man is a purely rational animal who can perform unadorned action. In groups we may interpret such flourishes as the mechanical requirements of institutions, rather than the consequences of human peculiarities. This is why institutions grow beyond expectations. We may think we can anticipate all reactions and neglect preventives. This is why many institutions fail despite the most optimistic confidence. As individuals we sometimes think we can perform or appreciate services just as we may wish. Sooner or later, however, these services lose meaning and attraction because we perform them badly and reject them unnecessarily. Anyone can verify all this by trying to make a speech without postures or raise taxes without politics.

We may also forget how necessary postures and politics are to doing the right thing. To be right in the wrong way is usually to be wrong. And right judgments about people and actions are rarely made on the spur of the moment. There must be ample opportunity for demonstration and appraisal. In the absence of postures and politics we tend to consider ourselves right with inadequate effort and on insufficient evidence.

When we participate in an activity we need to understand the postures and politics which make that particular participation successful. An unaccompanied action, however sound it may appear to be, will not have the effect it deserves, especially if the person who performed it has personal characteristics, like a lazy disposition, a gossiping tongue, or a quick temper, that invoke negative responses in others. This fact some reformers and social workers neglect to the detriment of their causes. Specific kinds of politics are appropriate to certain participations, and he who neglects them or uses the wrong kinds will often fail in even the most laudable venture. Anyone who tries to run a university like an army, or an army like a business concern, soon finds this out. And people vary in their acceptance of other people's participation, something professors have had occasion to learn when they talk to the public as they do to their students. Some people are skilled at suiting postures and politics to the varied actions they undertake. Some are not.

The latter may consider natural postures irrational, undesirable, or irrelevant, and seek to discard them altogether. But postures cannot be abolished. They cannot even be subjugated. They are so essential that, if they are not respected, men seek alternatives, and the same postures rise again in other, and perhaps less desirable, forms. The man who discards postures which explain actions fails to make his unaccompanied actions understood. Or he becomes unable to distinguish between what are postures and what is action to the point where cherished activities and beliefs are mere postures with no action behind them. Then the wrong postures get mixed with activities to the latter's detriment.

Men have mixed, for example, religious postures with government and war, and political and bellicose postures with religion, which inefficient and sacrilegious aberrations have caused great havoc and tragedy. Making love is accompanied by natural postures in all forms of life. Yet men often assault the postures of love so that they get separated from love and become distributed unnaturally among other activities, to be replaced in love by fetishes and taboos more appropriate elsewhere. Social reform may be desirable, but many activists who advocate it fail, not because their cause is wrong, but because they cannot communicate; and others over-react to them in the absence of preventive postures. Government has neglected many of its natural postures, featured some unnatural ones, and thereupon become drab. Consequently both officials and citizens with problems are often like mixed-up animals using mating postures for hunting, or neglecting postures altogether and becoming alienated.

The results of this faulty communication are only too evident. Man deliberately kills his own kind, which unnatural vice has resulted in the wilful slaughter of more than 59,000,000 humans by other humans in 125 years.[1] He is therefore so suspicious of his kind that in 1967 he spent 7.2 per cent of the world's gross national product on 'defence,' some of which was offense, as compared with 5 per cent on education and 2.5 per cent on health.[2] This is not a very good record by any calculation. There is obviously something fundamentally wrong in the actions of men and groups of men which causes such havoc in their affairs. This havoc has even prompted some experts to predict the disappearance of the human species.

Such predictions are gloomy and reflect man's lack of confidence in himself despite all the pretensions of his theories and organizations. This is the ultimate danger. It is, warns Kenneth Clark, 'lack of confidence, more than anything else, that kills a civilization. We can destroy ourselves by cynicism and disillusion, just as effectively as by bombs.'[3]

In all this gloom there shines a concept called 'participatory democracy.' It is based on a most confident attitude of men toward themselves and other men, and many see it, rightly in my opinion, as a great light for civilization. But, like all shining lights, it is hard to define, difficult even to look at without being dazzled by its brightness and blinded by its intensity. Indeed the phrase has been bandied about to the point where it means many things to many people, and where it is in danger of becoming just a slogan.

In this book we shall consider participatory democracy to be social action, including that of a political nature, to which the people affected by that action contribute their ideas effectively, and with growing perception, and, in so doing, increase their own and other people's personal relevance and collective happiness. The concept is admirable, provided we can live up to it. Alas! we do not seem to be living up to it in view of all the complaining and violence in which we feel compelled to indulge.

Yet the thesis of this book is a confident one: that we *can* live up to participatory democracy and all its stands for, provided we recognize our inability to perform and accept direct unaccompanied action, and develop the postures and politics that facilitate both the action and other people's acceptance of it. This thesis will affirm that colour and culture are the natural endowments of man which enable him to develop his more sensible postures and politics, and do more to preserve and advance his civilization than any of his currently emphasized communal participations.

By colour we mean hue, character, or contrast of a pleasing, emotional, or informative kind in sensations or activity. Culture will be considered the means of communication of the same kind by sight, sound, form, colour, and motion that are common to all men and independent of language, creed, nationality, or other category limited by time or space. These means of communication involve art, architecture, music, literature, dance, and drama.

There is certainly no lack of participation by men in their affairs. It is the kinds of participation, the motives and principles behind them, and the degree to which they can be carried out that need assessment. We shall examine these and related subjects in later chapters, and use specific institutions and functions as examples. But we should note in this introductory chapter some general qualifications on participation. They are applicable to any system, but are especially significant in participatory democracy, which, in theory at least, correctly places so much emphasis on man's right to participate. These qualifications must be allowed for in participatory democracy. They have to be, if man is to live up to, and survive, the theoretical elevations to which he tends to raise himself.

The first qualification is the need for man to take direct responsibility for his actions and institutions. This, by and large, he does not do. He often shifts responsibility to God, and then treats it in a way completely inappropriate for a divine relationship. This shifting therefore appears a mere posture without action to back it up. Thus man uses man-declared divine auspices to bolster his institutions, whether they are good or bad, whatever their purpose, and regardless of the number of conflicting institutions so credited. He also invokes the same auspices when preying on other people's institutions. Success and failure are frequently ascribed to the 'will of God.' This careless assumption of patronage seems vain and sacrilegious.

Man also invokes more modest, but still potent, auspices in the form of man-declared great truths, natural laws, principles, and theories. An institution based on one of these is assumed to be amply fortified, and, often enough, one differently fortified is looked upon with suspicion and even hatred. Indeed all the great dogmas and political theories are splendid, which is a reason philosophers are so devoted to them and politicians so ready to extol them. They fail, or are unacceptable, because carrying them out is in the hands, not of angels or even wise men who agree, but of fallible and differing human beings who, however they laud theory, suspect it when it does not suit their convenience, and rarely trust others for long with either the interpretation of the theory or the control of practice. They also fail when men use them as mere excuses for any actions that take their fancy. Failure is often blamed on un-this, anti-that, or counter-something else. This attitude seems presumptuous.

The use of divine and theoretical auspices may be prompted, not by a real belief in the auspices, but by an instinct which seeks a stable political environment. Because he knows this, man is not as inclined to live up to the auspices as he is to claim them and criticize the assumed auspices of others. Were his claims more modest he might have better luck with his institutions and enjoy more congenial relationships with other people.

A second qualification on participation is the nature of action. How man acts is usually more important than the mere fact that he acts. Certainly all men have a stake in their institutions and collective activities, and, therefore, the right to participate in them. This right itself is not enough, however, to make the system laudable or workable. It must be lived up to, for example, recognized as a privilege of others, and not only people of one's own viewpoint either. It must be exercised with some degree of efficiency and responsibility, for example, by people who are sufficiently informed to talk, prepared to work, and honest enough to be trusted. Even then the participation is not enough; it must have the necessary flourishes to be effective.

A scrutiny of credentials is therefore necessary in participatory democracy. Two kinds of scrutiny are required: that of institutions – now very active; and that of people who would participate in institutions – which is not active enough. One is inadequate without the other. On the one hand, institutions are too important to be hamstrung by inadequate people, or by grandiose theories unaccompanied by appropriate practice. The widespread contemporary scrutiny of them has been invited by just such people and theories.[4] Criticism of governments, churches, the professions, and universities is often both the fault of the institutions themselves, which do not ask whether they are actually doing what they are supposed to do, indeed whether they are able to do it at all, as well as the fault of the public which may want more from them than it has reason to expect.

On the other hand, those who would participate in institutions need to examine not only their rights to participate and serve, which are not nearly as all-embracing as their expectations, but also their own credentials and motivations for demanding and exercising these rights. After all, it is the participation of people in institutions that invites praise or blame. Nothing will kill participatory democracy more quickly than a rising level of unjustifiable and unattainable expectations and erratic interventions on the part of unprepared people who are unaware that there can be no rights without responsibilities. Moreover participation often involves interference, and in most activities, from child raising to international diplomacy, interfering successfully involves knowing when and when not to interfere. Many people never learn. Furthermore, some people combine a massive ego and weak self-control, and take matters into their own hands impulsively, incompetently, and undemocratically, often using some ideology or issue as an excuse for their self-gratification. From an assassinator of a president to a malicious gossip in a ladies' aid, their participation is something a society can well do without.

The scrutiny is essential also because participatory democracy is not an unmixed blessing. We are inclined to assume theoretically that any kind of participation is good, and that anyone who becomes involved has a positive contribution to make. This assumption is naive and unworkable. In this context there are three general kinds of people: those who become involved and make contributions; those who become involved, perhaps in spectacular ways, but contribute little or nothing; and those who, with an unerring drive toward the wrong thing caused by an inability to handle power or their own emotions, contribute mischief to everything in which they become involved, get in other people's way, and cause the rest of society much trouble, expense, and sorrow. All three kinds are inevitable, and they can be found at any level of society or ability from cabinet ministers to members of service clubs. Far from getting all three types involved, participatory democracy should include ways of featuring the efforts of the first group, confining the second to modest responsibility, and keeping the third at their own personal work or at special harmless diversions and as far away as possible from the other two. Nobody can assess people, put them in these categories, and treat them accordingly. But society can provide institutions and activities with appropriate postures in which those in the first category can be recognized, and to which those in the other two categories may naturally gravitate or be shunted and in which they can feel important and content. The total productive effort and personal happiness in participatory democracy will be greater if the participation is recognized and unfettered but qualified in this self-regulating way.

The kind and the degree of participation are also limitations on the theory of participatory democracy. In every organization there are people who can be depended upon to do only agreeable things. The number who will do any task and stick to it until it is completed is much smaller. There are also people who are interested only if they are guaranteed money, power, substantial kudos, or a sojourn in the limelight. Others shun publicity, thanks, or reward, but they are not numerous. Many are afflicted with a tendency to mind other people's business and participate simply to indulge it. Their expressed motives may be excellent, but they may find it difficult to distinguish between charity and self-interest and between the desire to serve and the urge to dominate. There are some with a dog-in-the-manger attitude, who are possessive and jealous by nature, and do not like to see things done unless they or their organizations do them. These are often associated with venerators of the status quo, social saboteurs, and killjoys whose participation is hampered by mental inertia or selfishness.

Still other people do not know how to participate at all. Lack of experience may be a hindrance at first, but it can be overcome. A more serious deficiency is lack of perspective. There are people so absorbed in participation that they magnify issues and work out of proportion to their significance, and perhaps even create them, just to make the participation seem important, occupy their time, release their energy, and satisfy their egos. Or they may make unnecessary fuss to hide their own inefficiency. From a legislature to a ladies' auxiliary or a student organization, selective, lazy, or hyperactive participators and prima donnas, both able and incompetent, inevitably affect the quality of the work and increase the effort necessary to get it done. They confuse the right to say and do things merely as they wish, which is not socially desirable, with the right to think them out and do them properly. The best of plans will go awry if such participation is accepted as it is offered. Special attractions and obstacles are always needed to enhance the effectiveness of participation by overcoming the limitations encumbering it.

Overcoming limitations has to be accompanied by encouraging competence. Participatory democracy cannot function without competent leadership, and it must discover, promote, and empower the able and wise. It will die if leadership is submerged in a mass of uninformed and conflicting activity, or frustrated by the actions of incompetent participators. While everyone must enjoy the rights associated with opinion and action, the ablest citizens at all levels need opportunities to reveal themselves for what they are and encouragements to offer themselves for leadership. Modern democracy often forgets, in the rush of glamorous causes and sobering results, that the lack of competent leadership was a main feature of every great upheaval in the twentieth century. And it also forgets that a large proportion of all government is devoted to remedying mistakes.

The scrutiny of credentials is made more urgent by two kinds of demands for relevance. One is simply a desire for relevance; the other is a desire for relevance accompanied by a call for the abolition of what someone thinks is irrelevant. The impacts of these differ greatly. The first is usually positive and creative, and it tends to displace existing things with minimal friction. The other is often arrogant and destructive because it is as much, and perhaps more, interested in displacing than in creating, and because it bolsters what may be a doubtful innovation by assault on what may stand in its way. Scientific invention usually falls into the first category. Denominational friction almost always illustrates the second.

In using the word 'relevance' we should remember its meaning: 'bearing upon,' says the Oxford Dictionary, 'pertinent to, the matter at hand.' Relevance is often misused in social discussion, however, and frequently interpreted as what someone thinks is right, desirable, fashionable, pleasing, modern, or interesting to certain people, institutions, or causes. Indeed what someone neither likes nor wants might be relevant, and to dismiss it as irrelevant is stupid. And what someone does like or want may be of no relevance whatever to him or his activities, and the pursuit of it may be folly. Again scientific invention and denominational friction provide illustrations. The first must seek relevance and isolate and discard what is irrelevant; the second has a long history of obscuring relevance by encouraging the clash of irrelevancies.

Vague and temporary ideas of relevance are not reliable if we handle our ideas like our clothes, and tailor or change them to suit the shifting demands of fashion. Fashion is perfectly natural, and it provides variety and interest. But one of its features is dangerous in participatory democracy; it is dictatorial, not only because it says what is in vogue, but also because it demands that we discard what is not. It also obstructs change. Indeed fashion, in its ridicule of variety, is not democratic at all. Ladies, for example, could go from maxiskirts in 1915 to miniskirts in 1965 and back to maxiskirts again in 1970, but they had to do it together or incur criticism. Would a lady in a miniskirt in 1915 have been really immoral, or just out of fashion? It is only fashion which dictates whether men should have crew cuts or long hair, yet young men who wore long hair and beards in 1965 were regarded as indecent, although they looked like their great grandfathers.

The dictatorship of fashion also encourages people to accept things which are unsuited to them and to neglect their individual needs in following the crowd. Not everyone looks well in a mink coat. The dictatorship also prevents people from using things that may increase their comfort or improve their appearance. Why should a man, especially a fat one, not be able to wear Arab dress in downtown New York or Montreal in the heat of summer without being considered odd? In terms of postures some people are required by fashion to present themselves to their contemporaries in the worst possible light and incur the negative reactions which inevitably follow.

Perhaps man can indulge himself relatively harmlessly in clothes. But the same lock-step dogmatic indulgence is not harmless in the field of social action. What is relevant to some people is one thing. The insistence that it displace what is relevant to other people is something else. Reconciling the two requires a scrutiny that will balance discarding and retaining and avoid the danger that society, frightened of doing anything that is irrelevant to anyone, will ultimately find nothing relevant at all.

Relevance is qualified by man's attachment to both real and unreal worlds. His ideas and wants result from experience and imagination; both contribute to life, and there is no clear boundary between them. It is a mistake, therefore, to be too 'practical' and 'realistic' in the interest of relevance, because man is wholly neither. In the first place, relevance is easily misjudged: few great inventions and ideas were regarded at first as practical or realistic. It is also easily neglected. Man's valuable assets, from his speech to his drinking water, excite little interest in those devoted to 'relevance' of a fashionable kind. And it is easily distorted: bird watching is much more relevant than arms production. In the second place, man's imagination is far more relevant to his life than either he or his social priorities will admit. It provides both inspiration for reality and the release of instincts and emotions which have no other outlet. It is ineffective, however, if it is not given scope for its own sake, or if it is mistaken for reality. People who do not read fairy tales or dream dreams with a clear understanding that they are fairy tales and dreams will seek them in their dogmas and institutions. When institutions in turn leave nothing to the imagination they tend to get gimicky in order to remedy the deficiency, and then to expand unnecessarily without satisfying the cry to be 'turned on.' This cry is usually a plea for something to stimulate the imagination and create and sustain interest and morale. It may even be a plea for something with which to preserve sanity. Entertainments and play-acting among those who are bored with reality or live empty lives are as important to sanity as competitive louse hunting was among the suffering in a wartime prison camp.

Relevance is also qualified by the prevailing lag between man's professing of principles and his living up to them, and between his desire for things and his readiness to pay their price. Indeed a man may behave in direct contrast to his stated ideas. He can be a liberal, Christian, free-enterpriser, or whatever by profession of faith, membership, or stated allegiance, and at the same time be in fact the direct opposite in thought and action. And, however devoted to his rights, he may shirk responsibilities, and persist in calling upon an anonymous 'they' to fill his wants. Thus many institutions and services fail, not because they are unwanted or wrong, but because people do not fulfil the obligations involved. They also fail because the efforts of careless participators cancel one another out. In participatory democracy, where people come forward with all kinds of beliefs and wants as props for interventions, the scrutiny mentioned earlier becomes essential. Participation is too important to be left to dabblers committed to talk and desires but not to conviction and responsibility.

One reason is that dabblers are unstable. They are the first to change their minds, run away, or take an opposite tack when the inevitable difficulties arise in the institutions or policies which they supported or opposed with vehemence, or when they are themselves affected by the consequences of commitments which they have proved to be unable to support. Indeed, if participatory democracy should die, the first to give the lethal blows will be the vocal participators who cannot or will not participate effectively. Another reason is the tendency of unstable allegiances to cancel one another out. It is easier for people who live up to differing principles than for mere adherents to cooperate, because the latter are more concerned with being identified with something than being committed to it, and identifications conflict more readily than commitments. Democracy therefore must say in effect to the participator: what is your opinion? what kind of conviction is back of it? and how prepared are you to support it with work and responsibility? The first question alone will not serve democracy; and it is unfortunate that the other two are often resented, because it is the system itself that suffers from the resentment. Indeed, far from encouraging unstable affiliations and fickle participations, democracy can ensure firmer and more effective public effort by imposing some limitations on participation. Formal assessment of people's allegiances and desires is virtually impossible, because those who judge may themselves be unreliable, as all inquisitions have so clearly demonstrated. A remedy is the provision of ample postures and politics by which people can themselves demonstrate their degrees of reliability. Like other species, men need ample opportunity to look one another over and test one another before bestowing their trust.

It is often assumed that people who participate actively in important affairs increase automatically their own relevance, and therefore their happiness, as well as contribute to the welfare of others. This delusion is one of the greatest mistakes of advocates of participatory democracy, and, unless it is abandoned, it may well destroy the idea. It is the effectiveness, not the extent, of the activity that counts. How happy are the very active participators? their families? their associates? The busy socialite, the student activist, the energetic clubman, the messianic reformer – are they prime examples of relevance and the pursuit of happiness? and how do they affect the relevance and happiness of others? As a matter of fact many men whose participations resulted in enormous wealth or power have led irrelevant and unhappy lives. Judging the extent of relevance and happiness is difficult. But there is evidence from society's problems that the discontents of the more hyperactive seekers of relevancy and happiness are caused as much by their own weaknesses as by social conditions. It is a mistake therefore to get those involved who should not be involved, because their inadequacy only makes them unhappy when they cannot and do not succeed, frustrates other people, and makes social conditions worse. Indeed the more excitable of them may endanger a highly organized society in crisis when they lose their heads and run amok. Like those who panic and stand up in boats when the water gets rough, they need to be told to sit down, be quiet or row or bail.

Government, professions and groups, the churches, and the universities, which we will examine individually in later chapters, are full of examples. They are also full of examples of people who contribute greatly to their own and others' relevance and happiness every time they participate. So are all segments of society. The difference is one of responsibility and contribution. Some are able and willing to back their participation with work and with an understanding of what they are doing; others are not. For the latter society needs, not association with serious matters, but diversions to keep them busy and make them feel relevant and happy. No one can judge initially who these people are. Diversions permit them to save face by getting themselves out of the way of others, either on their own initiative or on the manoeuvring of others, when they are not prepared to assume all that the more significant forms of participation involve. Then those who are so prepared will be able to do more without them.

These arrangements are effective only if the *opportunity* for effective participation has a minimum and no maximum. Freedom demands no less. And tyranny thrives on attempts to keep everyone at the same pace. Effective participation in a society takes two forms. One is what society collectively permits and enables individuals to do, and includes the effects of necessary laws, rights, obligations, and social services. This form of participation everyone should be free to take advantage of, if he will. The second effective form is what individuals do for society, groups, and themselves by their own initiative, over and above, and in harmony with, the basic effort encouraged of everyone. A society can only be healthy if it encourages both forms, and one form cannot exist for long without the other. The first is essential if everyone is to share basic assets and opportunities. The second is essential to encourage individuals and to increase the basic share for everyone. No one should be without the first; everyone should be permitted full scope and encouragement in the second. In both forms of participation an encouraging attitude makes a happier and more efficient society than a preventing one. From the creation and enjoyment of goods and services to the exercise of the rights of free speech there should be, as Winston Churchill put it, a floor for everyone and no ceiling.

A final qualification is a most important limitation on human action. Every participation displaces other participations. When a society over-estimates the time, energy, and desire people have at their disposal for doing things and getting information, and when people are not selective in becoming involved, what work and pleasure are being displaced? If this question is not asked, new activities may cause old activities to deteriorate, crowd out pleasure, and promote an over-serious society. Another question is equally important: is the new participation worth the effort? If this question is not answered, ardent democrats, careless about their causes, are bound to fail whenever people will not react as they wish. The answer would often be derisive if a busy dentist or machinist were asked after a hard day's work to participate in a dull evening meeting put on by eager community leaders in a highschool gymnasium, or requested to read the literature put out by information services, of which much is badly written, indeed unintelligible. Other questions inevitably follow. Who will coordinate people's participa-tions? Who will distribute information? How big a bureaucracy will be necessary? and who will be in it? Who are the people who seem to have ample time for participation? what else do they do? and how well do they do it? Is the performance of regular work not participation? If these questions are not answered, society may find its leadership transferred from its effective participators to its busybodies. If participation increases to unmanageable proportions, participators may actually have no power at all, and achieve no results from all their time and effort because they are really just listening to, and checking up on, one another, and building, running, and being run by, a huge and voracious bureaucracy.

To avoid such a situation society cannot allow political participation to crowd out other forms. 'Politicization' is useful to the extent that it invites public interest and participation in public affairs and provides appropriate opportunities for them. But political interest is only one of many interests in a society, and the others must have ample scope and recognition in participatory democracy. Indeed many citizens with no actual interest in politics can contribute more to the life and spirit of a people than many politicians, and they can often do it better if their work is not politicized. It is a tragic mistake to overemphasize political interest to the point where it is considered democratic for every endeavour and every citizen to be politi-cized. Too much 'politicization' usually means one of two things: totalitarian-ism or a situation in which people do not trust their public officials or one another.

These qualification on participation might be summed up in a theorem demonstrable in all human endeavours: in a given activity and at a given level of activity the people involved are divisible into three *approximate* categories:

one-third competent, one-third mediocre, and one-third weak. Of the competent about one-third are able. This division is apparent in any legislature, board of directors, cast of performers, team of athletes, faculty of professors, class of students, chapter of clergy, trade union, committee, or other organization of citizens. Diners in hotels and restaurants know this division among waiters and cooks. Those who attend meetings know it among speakers. Readers of Ann Landers know it among citizens. Even in so rigorously selective and august a body as the Supreme Court of the United States, when 96 justices were rated in a poll of 65 legal scholars, 12 were judged 'great,' 15 'near great,' 55 'average,' 6 'below average,' and 8 'failures.'[5] People get into the categories by their own abilities, experience, and efforts and by traits such as honesty, patience, judgment, courage, and dependability. Certainly all people are equal in dignity, rights, and citizenship. But they are not equal in their ability to participate in things, and their ability in one activity does not necessarily carry over into another. These differences are natural and inevitable, and to pretend otherwise in any institution or group is to invite trouble and failure. In some of society's activities, such as music and athletics, we make no pretensions whatever and are ruthless in placing people in categories. In others, such as medicine and aircraft flying, we encourage elaborate screening. Despite such selection the categories exist.

In still other activities, however, such as the talking ones – teaching, theology, and politics – many pretensions are permitted because the categories are harder to define. This practice is also natural and inevitable, because man has not been able to assess accurately kinds of talk and action resulting from talk, either in advance or while they are taking place. So we listen to, or watch, many people, and reserve judgment on them until events or their qualities indicate what it should be. We therefore include equality of opportunity and freedom of speech in the theoretical fabric of democracy. We sometimes forget or refuse to admit, however, that the three categories exist, and, while hoping opportunity and freedom of speech will produce helpful ideas and actions from all citizens in every category, neglect safeguards or diversions for the inadequacies or stupidities of citizens. From field marshal to store clerk, from bishop to labourer, society can get splendid service or base treachery, and, in any system, especially one which features participation on a wide scale, safeguards and diversions are essential if encouragements are to be fruitful.

None of these qualifications are related to ability, age, wealth, sex, occupation, education or station in life, and all the characteristics described vary little among classes and categories of men. Participatory democracy rightly holds that anyone may participate, and effective participators are found everywhere. The qualifications relate only to the ability of people to handle power, which they exercise whenever they participate. As later pages indicate, some people can handle it effectively, while others are incapable of exercising even modest amounts of it when they venture outside their work, and some are unable to exercise it even in their work. People who cannot handle power are almost invariably poor participators, and democracy needs methods of occupying their interests while declining their preferred help, or while enabling them to get the knowledge or experience which will enable them to participate effectively. They undoubtedly have the right to participate, but society collectively and other individuals also have the right to protection from abuse of those rights. It is often too late, however, to protect after someone secures power; prevention is better. There are ways of finding out who may get drunk on power by encouraging some harmless intoxications in special activities. In the words of W.S. Gilbert, 'Let's make him tipsy, gentlemen, and try.'

These characteristics of men and their participation in affairs will be illustrated in the following chapters in major enterprises and in situations where small and large numbers of people participate. The enterprises are government, professions and groups, churches, universities, and cultural affairs. (I have dealt with another enterprise, the public schools, in an earlier book.[6]) While we will examine each area separately, its characteristics are not unique to it. All illustrate phenomena found in most organizations. They are based on splendid principles. They are obviously vital to man. They have all attracted lively controversy throughout the world.

The most spectacular arena in which to observe power, the postures and politics of men, and the need for qualifications on participation is government. The huge cast, elaborate sets, complicated plots, and unending entertainment, both tragic and comic, dominate history and absorb contemporary attention. The enormous activity has given men splendid service and raised them to peaks of glory; it has betrayed their trust and consigned them to despair and slaughter. Government brings out the best and worst in men because it operates on power, a volatile element affecting people in strange and unpredictable ways.

Men treat government in ambitious fashion. They devise splendid political theories as nostrums for universal contentment. They draw up intricate constitutions as foundations for their states. They invent countless public functions and fashion elaborate institutions to perform them. They also recruit in diverse ways all kinds of men from among themselves to put the theories into practice, make the constitutions work, carry out the functions and run the institutions. A vast literature describes and discusses the resulting politics and interprets the intentions and actions of the leading characters.

No great show, including government, is successful without props and promptings because the cast is human. The limitations of the participants, however humble or eminent, require compensations. Their behaviour, for example, is not predictable, whatever their abilities and motivations might be. Nor can their work be assessed with accuracy. Governing is not an exact science, but a largely unpredictable human activity. Two parts hydrogen and one part oxygen always become water under certain conditions. A head of government, some ministers, and a legislature can be combined according to an exact theoretical and constitutional formula with results directly opposite to the most expert prediction. Human nature motivated by power is so uncertain that even suggestions of compensations are accepted with reluctance. Political man is proud, and he will not readily admit his limitations out loud or even to himself. And men collectively are even more reticent about examining frankly their groups unless they are provoked into it by others. They raise theories to sacred levels, glorify groups, and, tending to be exclusive in allocating political virtue to themselves, use theories and groups as excuses for any action, however good or bad, and defend them against others, even to the death.

Experience teaches severe lessons, however, and wise men anticipate practical necessity. Accordingly there creep into government certain compensatory practices, often unheralded and unexplained, which balance or dilute some of the aberrations of men. They are unheralded because the need for them can rarely be admitted; they are unexplained because they often work best when incomprehensible. No political party, for example, will admit publicly that certain doctrines and proposals are designed merely to get elected on and are useless in practice. In power it must devise ways of honouring them without observing them. No prime minister can admit publicly that some of his ministers are incompetent. He must, nevertheless, render them harmless. It is fearfully difficult in turn for ministers in any government to cashier a strong unsatisfactory leader. They must praise him publicly and find in private ways of counteracting his influence or disposing of him. Moreover government always has two relationships with the people. There is the splendid acknowledged one, such as the allegiance of a devoted populace to a glorious leader in a dictatorship, or the close participation of an interested citizenry with a fully responsible administration in a democracy. There are also rarely admitted relationships requiring all sorts of practice to make such theory workable.

It is not only participants that make compensations necessary. The public have exaggerated notions of their own status in relation to their institutions. They emphasize institutions and functions which cater to their pride, theories, and assumed capacity, and often regard as irrelevant to them and to government those others which make compensations for inadequacies. There is, therefore, widespread misunderstanding of the Crown, an upper non-elected chamber in a legislature, an auditor general, parliamentary debate, public corporations, as well as of certain channels of communication, ceremonies, personalities, events, and checks and balances. Things which appear relevant and which everyone admits to be relevant form only a part of government. Ignoring or abolishing the equally relevant other part which compensates for human behaviour leads to great inefficiency, and perhaps even to the destruction of governments, because political man simply cannot do without it.

The public, and political theorists too, may also forget that, in human institutions as in human bodies, actions are both voluntary and involuntary, and there is little they can do directly about the latter. A man uses his arm, leg, and mouth to play the piano, walk, and talk, and he is performing voluntary actions over which he has conscious control. Meanwhile his heart, lungs, and liver perform other actions which are involuntary and over which he has no direct conscious control. He can affect involuntary action somewhat by regulating exercise, sleep, and the intake of cigarette smoke, food, and drink. Even then the amount of control and its effects depend, not on what a man can or should do, but rather on what he chooses to do, and he can be careless and unpredictable about it. Whether imparting information or overloading the liver with alcohol, men often deliberately encourage involuntary action in both types of functions.

Men also perform both controlled and uncontrolled actions in institutions. They have direct responsibilities which they may exercise fully or which they may neglect or slough off on someone else. They also perform other actions which are involuntary, like inspiring someone with music or leadership, giving someone measles or a wrong impression, or causing great benefits or troubles to contemporaries by varied assertions. Indeed many actions take place that both individuals and groups have no control over at all. Every war is an illustration. So is much bureaucracy. It is often themselves that men cannot control. They can be prudent or careless, and even their best intentions can have bizarre effects. Government often operates on good intentions, but in it men need many compensations for their tendency to act involuntarily on those intentions.

This tendency makes people wonder how much to trust government. Now they rely on it so much that it has an overpowering influence; now they suspect it and seek to limit its authority. Often they want to curb the amount of politics in it, but find it difficult to separate the performance of functions from the politics which accompany and perhaps displace it. Even in international affairs where man is struggling to set up inter-governmental organization one notes the plea, 'Get politics out of the Olympics,'[7] and the comment, 'The political path is the path to destruction for any international non-governmental organization ...'[8] On the local scene the idea that because government does something it is therefore democratic is now featured on the assumption that government is really the people, and now condemned because elected authority can readily become authoritarian or stupid. Like that of individuals, governmental participation is not an unmixed blessing because it can be both actively voluntary and carelessly involuntary.

Other spectacular arenas illustrate similar situations. Churches of countless varieties concern themselves with no less a field than connections between this world and the next. Universities as communities of scholars sponsor the search for knowledge and the cultivation of the intellect. Professions direct vital services in all categories of activity with duty fortified by pride. Cultural leaders are guides to the very traditions of man and purveyors of creative and emotional stimuli for his individual mind and his collective spirit. These are important institutions and pretentious responsibilities. In these fields, as in government, participation and relevance defy easy assessment, and the peculiarities of men require ample compensation in the form of special postures and politics which encourage ability and divert stupidity.

Contemporary assessment of institutions is severe and vocal enough. But what is being assessed? is it just the institutions and their responsibilities? or is it also man's handling of them? All of them are impressive enough, and each one can be defended for its excellent intentions. Now, however, assessment of them is so negative that it has become fashionable to undermine the very foundations of institutions and deprecate man himself at a time when the idea of widespread participation is advocated. Social discussion is moody and gloomy. We seem to be participating in negative confusion rather than in harmony, with a peculiar combination of over-seriousness and lack of confidence, and not having much fun in doing it. The judgment which our use of physical resources has earned — man is the most destructive of all species — we seem determined to maintain also in political and social matters. We are taking ourselves as individuals and groups so seriously that we cannot adapt to our environment and are becoming inhuman. Our institutional environment, like our physical one, cannot stand this seriousness.[9]

The remedy for too much seriousness is enjoyment. Man can enjoy his institutions in two ways. The first is appreciating them when they give him reasonable service while understanding and remedying their weaknesses. When he goes to the trouble of setting up institutions it would seem logical for him to get the best out of them in both work and pleasure. He does no such thing. He tends to emphasize running and expanding rather than enjoying them, and then to look around at other people's institutions and meddle in them. Or he gets a reform complex about his own, and becomes so emotional and virtuous about weaknesses, or so mesmerized by some ultimate Utopia and blind to existing blessings, that he attacks entire institutions, ignores their happy features, and even attempts to destroy them. He ascribes well known phrases to this kind of social arson: 'throwing the baby out with the bathwater' and 'using a sledgehammer to kill a fly.' But he does it just the same, even to the point of destroying a nation or a people for the sake of some debatable principle. It is difficult to get reform this way, because all-out attacks encourage all-out reactions, and no one benefits. Opposition to one section of the quarry while enjoying the other gives more assurance to the quarry and takes less of the attacker's energy, especially when there is no guarantee of who is right.

The second way of enjoying institutions is to brighten them up with colour and entertainment. Efficient operation, routine, and especially modern office technology become dull and boring to participate in and watch and do not give the public the impression of service they deserve. Man does not have to be drab to be conscientious, or solemn to be dedicated. Colour and wit are part of his equipment and there is something entertaining about everything he does. When looked at objectively, he is a highly amusing animal to watch, and he therefore needs a well developed sense of humour to understand himself and appreciate others. He is also an entertaining animal, and he needs culture to project his own personality and talents and to understand those of his fellow men of all races and nationalities. Understanding and appreciation are hampered, however, by a puritan streak which is almost always motivated by ego, disguised by pretensions of rectitude, and accompanied by ruthless arrogance; it thrives on solemnity and makes a virtue of drabness. Man is at his most dangerous when he is puritan, and until he recovers from his puritanism he will behave like the usually docile black rhinocerous or waterbuffalo on an inexplicable rampage. Anything that keeps him out of such tantrums is enjoyable to him and relevant to his institutions.

Certain postures and politics guarantee tantrums. These man needs to understand and abandon. Others discourage or prevent tantrums and promote happiness. These man needs to emphasize for the growth, enjoyment, and survival of civilization.

2

Must democracy be drab?

The colour with which nature has so richly endowed the world is as relevant to human activity as it is to other physical and biological phenomena. There is harmony and usefulness in the laughter of man, the hues of his raiment, and the expressions of his culture akin to that of the songs and plumage of birds, the beauty of a landscape, and the customs of animals. We boast of the endowments with which we were created, and certainly God has given us many skills for creating and expressing colour in rich and endless variety. This priceless gift can give us much pleasure, scope for our talents, and outlets for our emotions. It also provides ways of administering our affairs and communicating with one another. But we may allow our puritan tendency to overcome our humanity and become drab, a practice as unnatural to us as a peacock pulling out his tail feathers, a porpoise refusing to play, or a rose blooming grey. One of the reasons for contemporary human skittishness is the burying of too many colourful talents and the hiding of too many lights under bushels.

Government illustrates the problem, yet it is not unique to government. It can be seen in family life, where a lack of colour and culture can help break up a home; in communities of every size, where no economic facilities can make up for a decline of community spirit; in business, where humanity is often subordinated to organization; and in individual experience, where material success or status seeking are not guarantees of happiness without that ethereal but substantial element called 'meaning in life.' Government, however, involves everyone, and the postures and politics associated with it indicate some of the ways in which colour and the lack of it affect emotions and the affairs of men. And the political environment, like the natural one, lends itself to contrasting richness and simplicity, work and play, noise and silence.

Colour has been a normal feature of public affairs in every state in every era. Celebrations, ceremony, honours, costumes, and symbols have pleased the senses, catered to the emotions, and served practical functions in administration. They are natural postures of governing. They can neither be ignored nor mixed with the wrong activities without unnatural consequences.

Our age is exceptional. In North America particularly democracy has lost its colourful traditions. We have cut the efficiency of government by neglecting many of the instincts, senses, and emotions of politicians and administrators on the one hand, and of the public on the other. We have become so puritan as to invite an overdose of nonconformism, latitudinarianism, and iconoclasm. With the best intentions we have wanted to simplify government and avoid snobbery and frivolity. The first we have not done; and, in an inverted way, we are more snobbish than ever, and not frivolous enough to avoid taking ourselves too seriously. We are aggravating the problems posed by the new technology by letting our affairs become inhuman. Democracy neither presupposes nor deserves this condition which is directly attributable to the neglect of postures.

The subjugation of postures and the phenomena which accompany it are illustrated by our clothes. Future generations may well regard us as the worst and most drably dressed people in history. Colourful raiment has been the rule in the governing of men and it met many of their physical and psychological needs. When we are tempted now to think it irrelevant, we should also assess the relevance of unrelieved black, blue, brown, or grey in standard patterns. The political puritan may consider drabness democratic. It is actually undemocratic because it favours the few who are physically well equipped for public scrutiny. It was all very well, for example, for Sir Wilfrid Laurier to say that gold-laced uniforms 'may be suited to Westminster, but in this democratic country the simple black coat unquestionably appears better.'[1] Laurier looked splendid enough to wear anything, but most of his colleagues were not so fortunate. And why should a non-colour symbolic of mourning be considered democratic in a country whose original citizens enjoyed lavish display?

In earlier times capes, ruffles, wigs, and frock coats hid natural deficiencies, and the fat, thin, bald, and ugly could be fairly matched with those better endowed to present an image. Public men of all ranks and all physical endowments were impressive in groups and imposing as individuals. Today, however, they have shed the compensatory camouflage natural in all species and adopted a permanent appearance of moulting at a time when the media picks out every deficiency and audiences are critical about images. Even minor characteristics like receding chins, long faces, and stubbly beards can now affect elections, and most public figures not endowed with the appropriate if irrelevant physical assets, can do little about it. Moreover, when men are all in drab clothes only the leaders tend to be noticed; when they are in costume or uniform the attention is shared more generally. A subtle change takes place, for example, at the first dress rehearsal of a stage production; when the members of the cast don their costumes a new enthusiasm strikes them, particularly the secondary characters. The same phenomenon can be observed on special occasions among the clergy, professors, military officers, members of fraternal or religious orders, and hippies, and the effect is noticeable especially in the junior ranks.[2] Prime Minister Trudeau's famous remark about 'nobodies' outside Parliament and the numerous complaints about dull proceedings inside make one wonder if the political drama is being staged properly. We package many things according to taste and appeal; why not politicians? If this is fanciful, what pray, is the virtue of drab?

The effects of curtailing the use of special clothes have been neglected in other fields. Professors, for example, have considered it sensible to discard gowns for lectures. Yet perhaps some of the negative attitudes of their students may be the result of looking for many hours at the fat ones and the thin ones, especially at those who work often at the blackboard. Such visions suggest that gowns, as well as the Prince Albert coat and the swallow-tail, were not frills, but practical and aesthetic necessities in a world where the Adonis is in the minority. As for society generally, drab clothing alters the behaviour and environment of people and encourages unnatural characteristics. Contemporary man is one of the few living creatures with colour of which the female wears the colour while the male is drab. This phenomenon is abnormal even for man who conformed to nature before the nineteenth century. Robes, ruffles, ornaments, even hair arrangements and scent, were male fashions, and the ladies, whether equally or less decorated, were not considered to be less attractive.

Yet modern men, except perhaps the Asiatics and the Highlanders on parade, delude themselves by 'wearing the pants in the family.' Actually the skirt in various forms is the traditional male attire. The Roman legions wore mini-skirts, and men of many races wore, and still wear, the midis and maxis which have been masculine fashions for centuries. Modern psychiatric and social problems suggest that clipping peacocks and gilding doves spoil the natural beauty and dignity of both. The young males who now wear long hair and colourful clothes and decorations are returning to the accoutrements of their species, and they are joyfully followed by some older males who have rushed to adopt bright shirts and loud ties. If nakedness is the natural state of man and he must, nevertheless, clothe himself, why should he not do it colourfully? Indeed it is not too much to assume that the popularity of nudity in many countries[3] may be a reaction, not to clothes, but to colourless clothes.

Surely, the sartorial puritan may ask, one would not suggest such nonsense as, for example, sky-blue breeches with garters. Perhaps not. But he should consider which is more nonsensical: such breeches, or the standard blue jeans, dipped in acid to discolour them, knees and seats scrubbed to show wear, cuffs ripped off, and topped by a costly suede jacket with the bottom cut in ribbons. Our fashion may be considered by future generations as puritanism and inverted snobbery which provide an undemocratic advantage to the few who look well in drab clothes and are a major cause of declining individuality. Negative effects on public and social life may also be noted, because inevitable popinjays who could once humour their vanity harmlessly by preening in the by-ways of fashion are impelled instead to strut in the corridors of power.

The subjugation of postures and its results are also illustrated by fashions in manners. Biologists have indicated that men have discarded as irrelevant many postures which served special purposes, and have adopted other postures which may be self-defeating because they conflict with human nature. Courtesy, for example, may seem old-fashioned, undemocratic, or irrelevant, but scholars have been finding sound natural reasons for it. It is, wrote one, 'the ritual by which we avoid hurting other people's feelings by satisfying our own egos.'[4] The decline of it in contemporary society has certainly been followed by hurt feelings in abundance. Rights are dependant on courtesy. The mere possession of them is not enough; their effectiveness depends on how they are used and how a conflict of rights is resolved. Courtesy facilitates their use in ways that do not offend other people or belittle their rights.

Homage may appear to be grovelling, the bow demeaning, or flowery language insincere. But man wants recognition whether he be president or clerk, and if he does not get it in harmless ways he will seek it relentlessly. He wants to recognize others too, and the gestures of harmless homage are deterrents to indiscriminate hero worship and preventives for aggression. And his unadorned actions are often antagonistic or misleading to others if there are no postures to cushion reactions. There are even more practical reasons for good manners too. Standing up in the office of a senior, for example, may appear degrading: but we pay for pride; when we sit down we take much longer to do our business and he has less time for his affairs and for other visitors. It may seem pleasingly democratic to say 'Johnny baby' rather than 'Sir' to an official, to refuse to tip one's hat or stand up in the presence of others, or to deem studied casualness or antagonism an asset rather than an affectation. But it is not sensible to complain simultaneously that other people 'over-react.' They are bound to over-react if there are no postures to prevent them doing so. Manners to man are like tail-wagging to dogs; the action may appear irrelevant, but a dog that does not wag his tail seems dull and unfriendly however big or small he may be. Man simply does not have the mental or physical equipment to express himself or impress others without a repertoire of suitable postures.

The way people use or react to manners is everywhere obvious. So are the negative effects of a lack of them. It does not take many manners to turn a cashier from a faceless routineer into a charming acquaintance, a policeman from a law enforcer into a friend of the public, a student from an irritating customer into a deserving scholar, a professor from a boor into a gentleman, or an official from an arrogant bureaucrat into a devoted public servant. Even a letter can be a dull epistle or an interesting communication. It is a mistake for people, individually or collectively, to think that all they have to do is to perform a service or invoke a right regardless of how they do it. The service or right is more acceptable to both parties if it is enjoyed by them, and the desires involved are more likely to be fulfilled if gestures are made to people's pride.

Indeed bad manners may kill service or rights by provoking people into wanting to do the opposite of what was intended. A divorce court hears many such instances, and countless homes are made unhappy by bad manners between adults and children. Even a neighbour with a just complaint about a noisy child or a wandering dog can make an enemy or a friend when complaining, and by his attitude can encourage one to solve the problem or tempt one to compound it. Regardless of merits or rights, the courtly give and invite more service with better results for a given amount of effort than the inconsiderate or the 'sourpusses.' Indeed the latter may turn interesting obligations into dull routine and pleasant tasks into ordeals. Even unpleasant tasks, whether performed by a bill-collector or a government, are often rendered acceptable by the manner of performing them. Some poet caught the spirit of the matter: 'She kicked him downstairs with such a sweet grace that he thought she was leading him up.'

The behavioural puritan may consider manners to be an artificial, perhaps dishonest, means of appearing to be what he is not. He may prefer to 'be himself' and expect other people to accept him as he is. This is an unnatural approach. Manners are needed because many people seek to appear to be what they are not as a matter of course and cannot carry it off, and their services or rights fail. Manners are also needed because, for many people, 'being oneself' fails because other people will simply not accept them as they are, or wish to be. Governmental, church, and educational activities present many examples. The minor official who poses as an important personage and deals condescendingly with the public, the ardent churchman who exudes pretensions of goodness, and the scholar who seeks to impress are neither being themselves nor displaying good manners, and other people will not accept them. Anyone can test this by visiting an automobile licensing bureau, a church social, or a faculty club: one will find there that manners are less pretensions than antidotes to pretensions. For some people and groups this distinction is crucial to them and to the society in which they participate. Their individual and collective weaknesses and pretensions may, without compensating postures, render them offensive, their services ineffective, and their contemporaries hostile. This is a bad combination in any society. It is particularly dangerous in participatory democracy.

Colour in state procedure has long been useful in administration. Show, feast, and fun impress and amuse people. Without them men take themselves too seriously and lose their sense of humour, either of which defect is dangerous in public officials and depressing to the public. Without them major events and achievements pass unnoticed and unappreciated, which neglect weakens the spirit of government and discourages public interest. The administrative value of a good show rests on the fact that government cannot be run only on the business aspects of men's personalities and affairs. Inviting public men to come together on congenial and glittering occasions under non-political auspices helps their association in business matters by giving them a change of pace, a sense of belonging and participating in great events, and a chance to show themselves to both advantage and disadvantage. It also gives the wives of officials something memorable to do – itself a vital factor in administration.

Colourful official entertainment facilitates communication. Tough and wary men who haggle at meetings are more amenable after a delectable luncheon.[5] Strangers are more co-operative after sizing one another up on convivial occasions. Wise men and fools reveal themselves more quickly at a dinner table than at a committee table or on the floor of a legislature. Great occasions are often the only memorable contact with affairs of state for lonely backbenchers, the numerous people who have nothing to do, those who are currently out of favour, and the many hangers-on who inhabit the fringes of any government. But a stereotyped gathering in a hotel salon or a parliamentary cafeteria is inadequate for these purposes. The occasion, the environment, and the food must be sufficiently distinguished to help the participants shine.

Government relies too much on meetings for communication. Although they are important – indeed fashionable in participatory democracy – most men and women do not shine in meetings. Good chairmen are rare. Some members talk too much; some talk too little; many waste time. Most people get a very limited sense of participating at most meetings. Indeed a surfeit of unrelieved meetings makes men overly serious and women overly pretentious. Refreshing alternatives make meetings more effective because people who have only meetings to make them feel relevant are not effective participants.

Unhappily, however, modern government has replaced state occasions with a costly substitute at which few men and women shine – the cocktail party. Neither a splendid occasion nor a relaxing diversion, it is like the herding of too many horses in a small corral; none stands out; none shows his paces. The food is indigestible; the liquor is consumed in a way unwise to the guests and unfair to the liquor; the standing is tiring; the noise is irritating; conversation is unmemorable; and personal relationships are limited to brief encounters. In terms of business and enjoyment the state gets little in return for its countless cocktail parties in comparison with the colourful affairs they replaced.

The political puritan criticizes ceremony and entertainment as frivolous diversions from business, expensive luxuries embarrassing to the under-privileged, and undemocratic barriers to equality. He tends to suppose that they are therefore wrong and that sombre goings-on are more respectable and sensible. In doing so, he asks too much of both officials and the public and forgets that tight halos shut off circulation to the brain.

Those who govern, like everyone else, *are* frivolous from time to time, and if they cannot satisfy their egos and release their emotions in harmless ways they will do it when exercising power. Few can restrict themselves to performing duties; most must also make impressions and gather satisfactions. To this end they will accumulate functions, build empires, and meddle in matters which are not their business, not always because their ministrations are essential, but often because they are dissatisfied with existing duties. Indeed among the major problems of government have always been those who use public business to make reputations for themselves, undertake nothing, however necessary, that will not promote themselves, and become hyperactive in enterprises which have no other advantage than their publicity. Sometimes they are bored, unhappy, or over-ambitious, too old, too young, or less competent than people think they are. At these times the public needs protection from their hyperactivity, and other officials may need to keep them out of important matters by occupying their time and authority with practical diversions. Officials, moreover, tend to be sequestered and secretive if not illuminated, and anything which gets them out of the official cloister to meet and talk with people in non-official ways is more valuable than the exclusive ministrations of an inner circle on the one hand and the equally unrevealing hand-shaking cocktail circuit or whistle-stop trip on the other.

Rank and file politicians and officials need colourful business more than ministers. Few public men in any system lead spectacular lives. The great majority work in the shadows. Some do essential and exciting things in the background and their work is their entertainment and reward. Many, however, do little of interest and have neither official nor public images. The few monopolize attention because the colourful means of obtaining it are limited, even in this age of communications and mass-media images. And for the others, memorable occasions do not highlight their duty as they blend into a drab environment and schedule. This blending-in is neither natural for man, nor desirable or democratic for officials, because it encourages them to adopt the habits of rare colourless male birds that sit in nests, blend with their background, and hatch eggs instead of soaring and hunting like most of their kind.

Non-soaring birds in government pay too much attention to the nests. Colourful activity provides an alternative to an excessively costly expansion of governmental apparatus and to the more deadly characteristics of bureaucracy. Much office work, as Parkinson says, is merely time filling and therefore unnecessary. Many negotiations are simply status seeking and aggression and are accompanied by no real work. Drab administration is nit-picking, over-virtuous, and expansive. Deadly serious duty ultimately becomes irrational and irritating to the public. Colourful activities are a more efficient and less expensive means of filling time and absorbing energy.

Consider, for example, federal-provincial relations in Canada and the vast, costly apparatus devoted to that juggling of powers and responsibilities – incomprehensible and irrelevant to most citizens, but a favourite occupation of officials and spectator sport of professors. This activity is not governing; it is simply a continuous frustrating rearranging of the apparatus.

The people involved are busy and serious and a little of their activity is necessary. But they are like the fanatically tidy wife, engrossed in relentless housecleaning to the point where her husband's and children's happiness is sacrificed to immaculate but joyless household arrangements, and she becomes a slave to the house rather than a mother or a wife. The services of government and the rights of the people depend to a limited extent on apparatus. But no service or rights will be proportionately assured by the fantastic amounts of time, money, controversy, and deadly seriousness devoted to federal-provincial relations. Furthermore, efforts in this area are incredibly dull and expensive, and add little to national feeling and community spirit; unfortunately they are the only activity which many participants have to talk and get emotional about. If government were more colourful and provided other opportunities for working off emotions the participants would have more time and more inclination for real service. And the urge to success would be greater because it is much harder to allow and admit failure after a good show than after a drab meeting. Meanwhile the citizen would enjoy and appreciate his government and country through public celebrations and spectacles more relevant to him than a non-productive and expensive squabble over whether his welfare cheque comes to him from one office or another.

This drab exercise is not the real Canadian tradition in such matters. The colourful business of the original confederation negotiations of 1864 included a continuous, spectacular, and joyful programme of ceremonies and festivities as the fathers met and travelled around the Maritime Provinces and up the St Lawrence. Indeed at the first confederation conference they took up the carpet in the PEI legislative chamber, invited in a group of young ladies, and danced all night. Not to be outdone, the provincial government gave 'a great public "Ball and Supper" ... the proud and the gay, arrayed in fashion's gauds, flock to the scene where revelry presides; the balls glow with gay trappings and gorgeous decorations; the lights are brilliant as the stars of heaven.' A month and many similar events later, Quebec provided what the press called a 'stunning jollification' with which everyone was 'hugely delighted.' The cabinet ministers were 'inveterate dancers.' 'They are cunning fellows; and there's no doubt it is all done for a political purpose: they know that if they can dance themselves into the affections of the wives and daughters of the country, the men will certainly become an easy conquest.'[6] This approach is one reason the fathers were so successful in settling seemingly insurmountable difficulties and making one of the longest-lasting constitutions in the world. They negotiated, not only by means of meetings, but also by personal contact in full and interesting view of the public, rather than by the dull, limited, and much more costly routine of memoranda-writing, task-force bureaucracy with which no one seems 'hugely delighted.' Their business suggests that they did not take themselves too seriously, that they would be bored to distraction at contemporary conferences, that colour is not alien to the Canadian governmental tradition, and that current constitutional matters could be eased and aided by some 'stunning jollification.'

I do not suggest that government should be turned into a grand carnival; postures should not overwhelm action. But some carnival, secondary and complementary to action, is practical. One would not propose specifically, for example, that ministers do a tribal dance around the table prior to cabinet meetings, or that a band play accompaniments and a chorus sing hallelujahs at legislative sessions. Yet these very practices are ancient in the government of men, and it is difficult to claim that contemporary austerity is better. One would not seriously advocate that a company of jesters should dart in and out of civil service offices, waving cap and bells at ministers or making barbed jokes at the expense of deputies. Yet the jester in some form was an effective political institution in many governments because he was often the only one who could both sustain and puncture egos in high places; and it is difficult to claim that such services are not required now.

Nor would one suggest that officials wear state uniform at meetings. Yet perhaps they would enjoy more the sight of one another and, because of the discomfort of the apparel, get their business done in less time.[7] One would not suggest that courtiers and flunkies hover around official potentates. Yet their counterparts flourish in contemporary administration, and there is no evidence that impressively titled men in grey flannel suits are more effective or less mischievous than sticks-in-waiting. Nor would one interpret government as altogether the institutionalization of instincts. Yet men have a Valhalla instinct, for example, and dream of all sorts of social Valhallas on earth and both pleasant and painful ones in the hereafter: they have experimented with them in government, from councils of departed spirits in tribes to second chambers in legislatures and havens of patronage in political parties. These phenomena and others like them are still relevant because the instincts and postures involved are today as powerful as ever.

Reactions between governments and their oppositions are much affected by colour. The opposition secures status and satisfaction from it, especially if it is out of office for a long time. Anything is practical which encourages association between both sides in the common service of the people and keeps them from taking themselves too seriously and not taking their opponents seriously enough. In practice ceremony and celebration are the only type of activity they can share unreservedly. Business by itself drives them apart. If the governmental atmosphere is too dull men take themselves too seriously; they raise their nostrums to sacred levels and glorify their groups beyond their desserts. While tending to be exclusive in allocating political virtue to themselves, they stoutly defend their theories and groups against others even to the death, and the whole populace suffers.

The opposition instinct also suffers if it is taken too seriously. Vital in any government, the opposition needs power and status to be effective and to be considered non-treasonable. It also needs colourful apparatus to dampen, contain, divert, and channel over-sensitive or erratic forces which, like any power, destroy when unleashed. Without such apparatus over-sensitive and erratic people exploit the fact that chronic negativism is itself colourful because it is spectacular, and fascinating because it is morbid. It becomes an unhealthy, but accepted, substitute for real colour. Effective opposition then gives way to organized tantrums. This kind of release of the opposition instinct is like a binge or a bad trip; everything else is subordinated to the indulgence, and reaction always follows. Puritan respectability, as much a cloak for the opposition as for the government, is accompanied by iconoclasm, and any image becomes a target. Opposition then becomes a state of mind; it can be happy with nothing except its own alleged virtue. The atmosphere becomes cheerless and dogmatic as negativism becomes fashionable. It is also contradictory; in this iconoclastic age we are desperately concerned with image and motivated by it.

The ultimate opposition to government comes, of course, from enemies within and without. Enmity may have a legitimate basis; but it may also rest on envy, jealousy, and ambition, even on the part of persons close to authority. It is rarely feasible either to dismiss or to ignore enemies, and colourful apparatus may smooth ruffled feathers without damage to government itself. No elected leaders are free of enemies, and many successful ones follow the tactic explained by Louis XI: 'My father,' he said, 'drove them out by force of arms, whereas I've driven them out by force of venison pies and good wines.'[8]

Colour is also useful in the economics of the state. Economic expansion presents as many problems as political expansion when it is overindulged in because of the vain hope that satisfaction will keep pace. The more people get the more they want; the more they want the more they depend on mass action; the greater the mass action the less they count as individuals and the more they complain. Emphasis on economic satisfaction without compensating colourful activities tends to focus man's neglected postures on material matters. He devotes his status seeking to rank and possessions, his creative instincts to organization building, his emotions to the exercise of power.

A puritanical society forces him in this direction. He needs some healthy distractions to satisfy his wants in ways which make him an individual and not a mere projection of an organization. Some distractions do occupy him as a spectator, but, as television has taught us, that is not enough; he needs to be colourful himself. The average person now does very little directly by himself for himself; his wants are satisfied by a collectivity and the service is largely anonymous. Theoretically this is teamwork, but in practice it can become an excess of togetherness which, when overdone and unaccompanied by postures for the individuals, makes man skittish. Contemporary demands for the right to 'do your own thing' suggest an urgent need for increased personal achievement and satisfaction, and for countless people colourful activities are the only means of obtaining them.

Postures like dressing up, attending ceremonies, following protocol, observing society, dancing in the streets, singing in pubs, watching and marching in parades, and entertaining and being entertained are harmless outlets for the exhibitionist tendencies, combative instincts, jealousies, and rivalries which are always part of public affairs and which, if not diverted, act directly on administration itself. Such actions involve some fantasy and make-believe; but surely no function of man is more susceptible to fantasy and make-believe, indeed reaching to hallucination and insanity, than the exercise of power. Any endeavour is practical, therefore, that separates these from power. Alternative ways of asserting significance or expending energies absorb a common inclination to create difficulties and hinder other people in an effort to be active and important. The capers of some people may be ridiculous, but they must be endured in some form, and it is better to give them harmless outlets than to allow them to depend exclusively on business.

To some the outlets may appear trivial, but, nonetheless, they serve serious purposes. Trivial functions in government occupy the time of persons whose minds go in trivial directions. Without them little minds dabble in great functions with disastrous results. They also occupy part of the time of persons whose minds go in over-serious directions and thereupon bring them back to reality. The outlets are also useful when they are just enjoyed as amusement and entertainment for all officials. Even government itself desperately needs wit and humour to relieve collective pomposity. Society, says Wilde's Mabel Chiltern in *An Ideal Husband*, is composed of 'beautiful idiots and brilliant lunatics.' These people are real characters in any government and its environment, indeed in any large organization, and, when colourful events decline they drift to other activities in which they can exert their egos and bedevil their contemporaries. Many political aberrations and social discontents have sound bases, but many are merely the playthings of nuisances. Despite the right of participation in public affairs which democracy offers to all, some people, including many in office, best serve their country by keeping out of other people's way. For them a schedule of interesting busywork is a useful diversion.

The decline of colour has changed the place of women in public life. Wives of officials and female officials, including many distinguished, beautiful, and witty women, suffer from the prevailing austerity. They receive virtually no public notice compared with their predecessors because they do not have a colourful environment in which to shine. Politics in Canada, for example, boasts no women who are the models of artists and photographers, the subjects of poems or literary praise, or the toasts of a generation. The history books ignore them. Well known women must assume an air of belligerence to secure a grudging and controversial publicity. May not this lack of opportunity for exercising their natural charms be a reason for many discontents about the 'status of women'? May not the dullness of men and their activities have become so unnatural that many women are drifting away from them by means of club service, divorce, and other forms of 'women's liberation'? Meanwhile the public must look elsewhere – to the movies, fashion magazines, beauty contests – for the elements of glamour which statecraft could use to advantage in an age of image.

This glamour is not just show. It can be a vehicle by which women exercise a continuing judgment on public figures and events. How crucial this judgment can be was revealed in a statement ascribed to Nikita Krushchev to the effect that he owed his favour with Stalin, and indeed his very life, to the support of Stalin's wife.[9] In earlier days the drawing room was an important political institution, and men like Tallyrand and Disraeli made effective use of it. From it the power of women radiated in a manner impossible in a modern meeting or cocktail party. Women are often much more observant of the affairs and foibles of men than are men themselves; they have to be. And men are more revealing about themselves to women than to other men, not because they have to be, but because they want to be. Not withstanding women's liberationists to the contrary, this process rarely operates when women act in official capacities because of the powerful yet subtle difference between 'female' and 'feminine.'

Ladies of the drawingrooms were well informed on affairs and their advice and judgment were useful when passed along the gossip circuit or relayed to their admirers. Furthermore the drawing room had a relaxing atmosphere in which men, freed from official restraints, gave unique glimpses of their inner resources. There, for all to note, were the able and the stupid. For any man making his way in politics, social encounters provided the most severe and effective test, and countless careers were affected accordingly. Despite the enfranchisement of women, wrote Duff Cooper, 'neither from the polling booth nor from her seat in Parliament has she as yet succeeded in exercising the same control over the lives of men and the fate of nations as was hers while she remained merely the centre of a select circle in her own drawing-room.'[10]

The decline of colour accentuated the uninteresting and shabby features of public business. Government, like most enterprises, needs taste and style and requires scope for developing them. Efficiency in procedure is dull and sterile by itself. Routine becomes tedious and commonplace. Government needs colourful compensations for these and for the inevitable mistakes, bad speeches, shoddy tactics, periodic scandal, and bitter rivalries which no grand political theories can prevent. People should see their government 'warts and all,' but they like some compensating cosmetics to improve the general *visage*.

It is tempting to regard colour as irrelevant in the new technology, yet colour is essential to it. As government gets bigger, it becomes less human as a matter of course; it becomes rapidly more impersonal with computers. As it gets more technical people understand it less and perhaps suspect it more. The government works hard, but legislative debates and office activity do not usually encourage a public sense of great things happening and are inadequate symbols of national spirit. De Gaulle added something more, *grandeur;* the Kennedys style, glamour, and entertainment; and the Queen and Prince Charles dignity and a sense of history at Carnarvon; while in all three instances the world watched and understood, and the citizens concerned, whether they supported the government or not, knew that something was going on and felt a part of it. Men need to be attracted to government as well as occasionally repelled by it. The service government performs will not itself attract or compensate for repulsion. Men have never appreciated bread without circus, or medicine without sweetening.

The idea that colourful activities are expensive luxuries insulting to the mass of people has proved untrue. Drabness destroys images, and society then spends huge sums trying to resurrect them. It is a frustrating and expensive process and to make it at all fruitful we concentrate on the image of one man, even to the point of blaming party fortunes on him if we are not impressed. There is nothing democratic about concentrated image making, denying images to other competent people, or removing illumination from incompetents whom colour shows up quickly for what they are. There is nothing economical about saving a little on colour and spending lavishly on futile attempts to brighten shadows. There is nothing economical either about destroying the demand for the many useful goods and services associated with colour. And it is not economic or democratic to destroy through disuse the talents of performers, cooks, craftsmen, and countless others which are essential public assets stimulated only by colour.[11]

As for citizens of all classes, they have always expected a show from their state. It is a sensible expectation because people are rightly suspicious of other people and organizations that are too serious, and too concerned with their own virtue and service. They are also rightly suspicious of drabness because it is not stimulating; they sense correctly that a society should be a mosaic, not a plain pattern. It needs some extremes so that, in the words of J.B. Priestly on the Regency, 'a vitalising electric current' may 'pass from pole to pole.'[12] They may also suspect that democracy relies substantially on colourful people who are generally the most independent of men, inclined to guard much of what freedom stands for. People also need self-stimulating occasions which move them to action which they would not ordinarily consider. Just as a family tidies its house before a party, a community repairs and decorates before a centennial or a royal visit and uses the event as an excuse for special facilities and services like arts centres, public gardens, scholarships, and festivals. Many of the finest assets of most communities orginated with commemorations and celebrations rather than need, and provided more pride for citizens and interest for visitors than routine facilities. 'Oh, when I have something to do,' exclaimed the butler in Enid Bagnold's The Chalk Garden, 'something to create, everything is clear again ... if we had guests oftener! The sense of rising to something,' Contemporary terms like 'motivation' and 'being turned on' indicate the same longing for expression and creativity.

The ordinary service of the state will not satisfy this longing. Few citizens of any class in any system understand the business of the state but all want to be moved by its spirit. For those in straitened circumstances their pride in it may be all they have. Citizens are not happy, no matter what material possessions are given them, unless they are proud of their country and loyal to themselves as a people. Pride and loyalty are not stimulated by legal and constitutional matters, welfare, public works, or pronouncements on rights and jurisdictions because, important as these things may be, they are dull and controversial to most people. There must also be a feeling of emotion and community spirit in public affairs if the state is to maintain unity, and its people a mutual understanding.

Democratic participation in public affairs will not alone produce this feeling. It is ineffective or predominantly negative unless it is accompanied by phenomena which cause the occasional lumps in people's throats and the periodic cheer in their hearts. Any Scot on St Andrew's Day or citizen of Singapore on National Day will verify this fact. Do we feel the lumps or cheer during constitutional conferences or while participating in welfare or using public works? As we occupy the welfare state long dreamed of by social reformers, and wonder, in our age of material opulence, at the widespread discontents around us, we should examine the view expressed by W.H. Lewis: 'France,' he wrote, and his words apply to most countries, 'has rarely been grateful to those who have expanded her influence by unspectacular methods, and more rarely still forgives the man ... who shows an open contempt for *la gloire.*'[13]

The lack of communal ceremonies and celebrations is depressing. Few parades bring citizens by the thousands to the street. Civic holidays, the sovereign's birthdays, Thanksgiving, and the rest raise little community interest. There are, therefore, few excuses for enthusiasm on a community scale, for public spectacles, fireworks, decorations, parades, and amusements. Some carnivals and festivals are superb exceptions which illustrate what most communities miss. But where is the state, its functions and traditions, in such festivals? It is simply not logical to convey Santa Claus to a department store in magnificent splendour and a Governor-General to Parliament in quiet progress, certainly not in a democracy where the opening of the people's legislature is worthy of widespread interest. Nor is it wise in an age of passive spectatorship to deprive citizens of enjoying and participating directly in colourful affairs from ceremonials to dancing in the streets.

Without colour it is no wonder apathy is so prevalent in participatory democracy; getting involved is too serious an effort. No wonder the young seek group stimulation on a large scale and the restless complain of alienation and resort to violence as an outlet for emotions and energy in a joyless political system. No wonder loneliness is the lot of many old people with little to participate in and be entertained by. No wonder the cities are tense when their denizens can commune neither with nature nor with one another. No wonder the universities are havens of puritanism – not permissiveness, puritanism – where Joe College has been replaced by Hairshirt Horace and the campus newspaper seems to be issued from the penitent bench. No wonder the children consider society dull when their elders celebrate nothing and when they must even be warned against razor blades in their treats on the one occasion when they can dress up. People without enough of direct, pleasurable significance to do and see are bound to seek the perverse ecstasy of negativism and magnify little annoyances into great wrongs. Collectively they succumb to social misanthropy for which the best cure is colour and good fun. We may be amused when we consider the traditional costumes and customs of earlier days, and think smugly that such frivolities are not for us in this enlightened age. We should think, however, of what the future will say about our customs and about the extent to which we enjoyed our society and its government. It is likely to say that we took ourselves so seriously we forgot we were human.

Contemporary North American politics frowns on honours, but human nature does not. This dilemma causes disillusionment with political performance because three human needs are ignored: the reward of service, the fulfillment of ambition, and the search for heroes. Notwithstanding political theory to the contrary, officials thrive under Pavlovian treatment, just as countless citizens whom they serve like their status, patronage, bonuses, and tips. Serving for the good of the state or society is neither universal nor constant.

Democracy does honour lavishly a few of its servants and showers on them attentions, publicity, awards, degrees, and other distinctions. But it is not the state that does it. Government needs means of encouraging the ablest men, and it must also have ways of easing out the weak ones, even against a popular mandate which often obscures the difference. Otherwise a situation develops which favours the safe man, the man who 'stands pat,' and penalizes severely the person with the courage to 'stick his neck out.' 'You get no thanks for it' is an attitude no government can afford. Nor can government safely afford, in the long run, the common habits of deprecating the services of its political opponents and ignoring the achievements of its predecessors. If it does, it denigrates governing itself by featuring temporary personnel only and encouraging an impersonal anonymity not consistent with any theory of democracy.

The fulfillment of ambition through honours serves practical purposes in administration. Government attracts the ambitious partly because of the service they can perform and partly because of the attractions of power and personal status. But only a small percentage of them wield substantial power or achieve distinction. There is always the problem of fulfilling high hopes with limited means; and numerous people of all ranks and abilities feel they are not sufficiently appreciated. Honours and awards have been used for centuries to meet these problems. They have been inducements to and thanks for service, pacifiers for frustrations, and face-savers for both anonymous competence and entrenched incompetence. They help satisfy the dignity of those whom the musical chairs of politics eliminates lest the game be spoiled by a demand for more chairs. They also humour those powerful people with or without ability who are temperamental, who are too strategically placed to be removed or denied promotion, and who tend to become incompatible or dangerous if they are not humoured.

Honours, particularly offices which bestow honour, help to solve politically insoluble personnel problems in government. Memoirs and biographies of public men indicate how hard it is to deal with the old but not retirable, the brilliant junior not readily promotable, the stupid junior who should not be promoted, the distinguished but not electable, the tired in need of a rest, the incompetent but not disposable, the michief makers not easily sidetracked, those with ambitious and troublesome wives, those who bore the brunt of crises for which they were not individually responsible, and those whose political abilities were not commensurate with their other reputations. The representative principle often aggravates these difficulties. The inclusion of representatives of interest groups is excellent when the sharing of power is combined with the use of ability. Too often, however, the representatives are men of modest or no ability who must be appointed to satisfy the claims of interest groups which will sulk if their men are not sufficiently recognized. In all these instances harmless and inexpensive recognitions can enhance status either to increase available talent or to diminish power by saving face. If, according to the Peter Principle, 'creative incompetence' is a feature of modern administration, that last undesirable promotion may properly be avoided by 'creative status' which is cheaper and less troublesome.

The abhorrence of vacuums operates in such a situation. Lack of harmless and inexpensive means of recognition invites the use of patronage, junkets, unwise appointments and promotions, the proliferation of well paid jobs, and the retention of outmoded offices, all of which are inefficient and expensive. The Canadian Senate and the United States diplomatic service, for example, together with many important boards and commissions, have suffered because of the lack of alternatives to unwise appointments. The reasons for such mistakes cannot be avoided; it is better that they be met with honours than with patronage, with dignities instead of power. Dismissal is not in practice always a reliable alternative, especially in a democracy. If, like Franklin Roosevelt, a president deals with questionable officials by ignoring them and adding others to do the work, he might find honours help him grasp the nettles more readily. If, as Gladstone said, a prime minister must be a good butcher, some honorific anaesthetics can make it easier for the victims and their supporters and therefore more practicable for him.

Government must command service at the highest level of competence, and it cannot afford indifference, anonymity, and shabby treatment which can be compared with the opportunities of other employments, especially when the political drama can be described as 'the distemper of our times.' Obstacles to service become more formidable as public life becomes duller and as opportunities for recognition become fewer and, therefore, public life less attractive to the abler and less impressive to the observer. Society itself, no less than its governments, cannot afford indifference and anonymity. Its recognitions of service in all the activities of life are evidence of appreciation, encouragement of further service, and a tribute to the value of the service itself. Honours are the cheapest and most effective means of giving these recognitions. An OBE or knighthood costs nothing save a ribbon or medal. But a profusion of administrative titles, such as 'vice-president finance' or 'director of supplies and services,' which always arises when honours are abolished, requires extra salary, premises, and staff to go with the dignities. In public honour the beneficiary is not just the recipient but also the state and the society to which the recognized service is rendered. It is not hard to find evidence of these problems in contemporary administration – in universities, to cite only one example, where it is becoming increasingly difficult to get both student and academic leaders to assume the colourless and often thankless posts, however impressively labelled, which a belligerent society offers them.

It is always difficult to separate the deserving and undeserving whether in honours or in anything else. Actually everyone knows how much merit is involved in honours, including the recipient. The deserving is happy to be recognized, and the undeserving and his friends are relieved he came out with his dignity intact. Just as Melbourne noted no 'damned nonsense' about merit in the Garter, and the Académie Française worries little about deserving omissions from its ranks, being passed over is not insulting if appointments are whimsical. Irrational as such a procedure may seem to those with an excess of confidence in human nature, public service is itself whimsical and a government is naive to depend on merit alone.

Snobbery, which many associate with honours, is actually a feature of government requiring compensation because it cannot be removed. If depressed in one place it pops up somewhere else. Democracy has done nothing to abolish it. The expanding celebrity cult and studies of pyramid climbing and status seeking indicate that snobbery is increasing in all levels of society. More dangerous to democracy, however, is inverted snobbery which discourages character, ability, and individuality in a quest for sameness disguised as equality. It is especially dangerous when inverted snobbery becomes viciousness and parades under grand slogans in the style of Robespierre under liberty, equality, and fraternity, to the point where a man could be condemned without fair trial and addressed as 'Citizen' as he knelt at the guillotine in view of thousands of other 'Citizens.' Such a picture is not overdrawn at a time when democratic people cannot go out at night in cities in the 'land of the free,' and when a murderer can call himself a political prisoner in the 'true North strong and free.'

Many problems cause inverted snobbery, but a major one is drabness reinforced by puritanism, which people cannot tolerate for long. As individuals we cut loose, as groups we seek escape, from conformity to over-standardized behaviour, excessive togetherness, and hobbled individuality which are variants of inverted snobbery. When people look out on society and see everyone the same they do not feel democratic, they feel bored and indifferent. They often imagine themselves in other people's lives, no matter how interesting their own lives may be, and their interest and hero worship is not just admiration but also a fanciful projection of their own personalities. The removal of so many colourful individuals from public life has not increased equality, but it has deprived people of natural characters who ornamented, inspired, entertained, or perhaps amused them and forced society to create other kinds of characters to provide contrasts in the human mosaic.

This deprivation has permitted excessive scope for morbidity. There are times when sadness and dejection are natural, but, in the absence of contrasting experience, they become habitual. They may ultimately become respectable, and even be considered democratic. At this stage happiness may be regarded as indecent. This stage is inverted snobbery in its worst form. How general it is can be noted by a reading of student newspapers in the universities during the 1960s. But life is not all tragedy and tears. There are comedy and laughter everywhere, and he who neglects them misses life. The effect of this neglect on society is like the effect on literature. 'His outlook on life was too narrow,' wrote one Australian writer about another. 'He saw – not the things that really matter, but the mean and petty-things, and he used his talent to give these mean and petty-things a mischievous prominence. There is little of uplift in his writings, they contain no inspiration for Australian youth. The fact is that it wasn't in Lawson to write a truly optimistic thing – and without optimism there can be no success either for a man or a nation ... He had the hell-given habit of seeing the worst side of everything ... and the God-given gift to write ...'[14] The dismal personal life of the writer was not surprising. Nor should unhappiness be surprising in a society which devotes an insufficient portion of its God-given gifts to the happy features of life. Serious social problems are never solved by lamentations alone. And people who take themselves too seriously rarely take problems seriously enough to solve them; indeed they create more than they solve.

It is a mistake to associate colourful events and honours with aristocracy and cliques. Colour matches all governments and has little to do with their weaknesses which are attributable, not to forms, but to the peculiarities of human nature and power. Aristocracy and cliques exist, in various forms, in any system and no less in drab than in colourful ones. Colour in democracy is not incongruous, therefore, and no more signifies a class society than puritanism. Changes to responsible government, universal suffrage, constitutional monarchy, lifetime honours, and mobility between classes removed a few notorious concentrations of power. Some colour disappeared with these changes, but the bulk of it was displaced, not by reform, but by political puritanism. Fashionable melancholy then set in as political introspection displaced the outgoing habits which colour encourages. But neither the government nor the people became any happier, and, not wishing to appear flighty in the prevailing gloom, they looked elsewhere to satisfy their inner needs.

The airs of the more pretentious members of any class, aristocratic or otherwise, contributed to their downfall in major revolutions. And in many localities unworthy children of 'old families' often destroyed their family effectiveness in society by flaunting status with no personal merits to justify it. An incompetent but status-conscious member of a trade union may do similar harm to his organization. Indeed the 'we came over on the Mayflower' syndrome is a strong protective device in all walks of life because practically everybody can claim something like it. But it becomes ridiculous when the user is not deserving. The trouble in such instances is not the postures of colour, which have many advantages when used effectively, but the fact that a few people do not back them up with action or know when to turn them off and use other postures. A cavorting animal of any kind that did nothing but cavort would soon create or attract enemies, and would not last long either. Nature will ultimately react to excessive posturing with no action behind it, and many of our contemporaries are inviting this very retribution. Is there any difference between a rich, idle, and profligate dandy of the eighteenth century and a state-supported, indolent, and 'rapping' 'flower person' of the twentieth? But social reaction that swings to puritan extremes is as inefficient as it is joyless, and puritans are the most dangerously pretentious because they are so often destructive. Reaction therefore encourages a natural and inevitable search for new sources of colour which in many instances are no more justifiable by the puritans or explainable by the rest of us than the old. In short, actions without postures and postures without actions are equally unnatural to man.

Abundant evidence indicates that *all* citizens are attracted by colour and recognition and that if they do not find them in one place they will try another. A celebrity always draws a crowd. Women will touch a 'personality,' while screaming girls thrust forward their autograph books. Consumers of goods and services are attracted by testimonies of celebrities who get large fees for their backing. Millions of avid citizens make best sellers and wealthy people of butlers, nannies, and ladies of easy virtue who can raise a gust of gossip. They pay huge sums for the spicy revelations of a racketeer in difficulties with the law, the participants in a celebrity divorce, or the principals in a scandal. A titled person is an attraction at any gathering, whether distinguished by a peerage or knighthood at one extreme, or by a prison record or a place on a most-wanted list at the other. A 'big name' who cannot speak will draw a greater attendance at a function than the most polished orator. The patronage of an eminent or notorious woman secures a full house for a charity tea. The professions are most susceptible to colour and honours. An archbishop outshines and upstages a moderator at any event. Judges and lawyers turn out in greater numbers for a lord chancellor than for a chief justice. Professors, notoriously allergic to visiting speakers, will stampede to hear and meet a celebrity.[15] A glittering ball attracts crowds to watch the guests arrive and the press devotes space next day to what the ladies wore. An Oscar night attracts nationwide audiences. Radicals and protestors are no exception; publicity-conscious leaders make every effort to become local Che Gueveras; they imitate celebrities and, if colourful enough, are treated like celebrities or are offended if they are not.

Is all this healthy? It is if colour and honour are openly associated with the postures to which they belong. They should not be suppressed in government and then attached to other, less significant activities. It is healthy too for people who are trapped within the confines of a limited environment and need release from social claustrophobia. Pericles gave full scope to colour in an earlier democracy. He 'let loose the reins to the people,' wrote Plutarch, 'and made his policy subservient to their pleasure, contriving continually to have some great public show or solemnity, some banquet, or some procession or other in the town to please them, coaxing his countrymen like children, with such delights and pleasures as were not, however, unedifying.'[16] Napoleon emphasized one reason for this colour. 'It is with baubles that men are led,' he said. 'Sacrifices must be made to vanity and the joy of possession ... I do not believe the French people love liberty and equality ... They are what the Gauls were, proud and frivolous. They believe in one thing: Honour! This feeling must be nourished and channeled.'[17]

One may quarrel with this appraisal, but one must consider with it contemporary phenomena such as the morbid scandals and inflated trivia of countless movie and personal-experience magazines which for millions of citizens are the only alternative to honour. One may quarrel, too, with the delights-and-baubles theory of earlier times, but one must also consider the view expressed by a contemporary political public relations expert: 'Most every American loves contest,' he said. 'He likes a good hot battle, with no punches pulled ... *so you can interest him if you put on a fight!* ... Then, too, most every American likes to be entertained ... So if you can't fight, PUT ON A SHOW'[18] Perhaps the reverse is true – without a show fighting is an alternative. The second reason for associating colourful postures with government is also practical. Government is too important and interesting to be colourless; and democratic government is too fine a concept to be puritanical. Public men and the service they perform and others who distinguish themselves in the service of the people and their deeds should be more colourful and more honoured than any other characters in society. If big government is here to stay we may well enjoy it.

The contemporary danger to democracy is the likelihood that big government as we know it may disappear because we are not enjoying it. The people's attention is a prerequisite to the people's support, and if the service of government is drab and unrecognized the people may be convinced there is no service. The prevailing lack of colour may cause a public reaction inviting a change to a more exciting, if less democratic, system which will provide colour in large measure. A puritanical Cromwellian government with all its efficiencies will be followed by the lively displays of a Charles II; and a revolution dedicated to even the highest-sounding aims will be followed after a bloodbath by Napoleonic spectacles. Today's democracy with all its advantages is colourless compared with violent revolution, dictatorship, and military administration; to people starved for show these are alluring alternatives. Indeed democracy can now be upset easily by the first demagogue that offers the government and the people a good show, and since any kind of show will mesmerize us because we are not accustomed to it, we will likely put up no defense. Totalitarianism is always colourful, which is one of its attractions, and if democracy ignores men's natural need for colour, they will look for it in some kind of totalitarian society where, in contrast to democracy, it is difficult to control. Contemporary complaints that some people are unable to 'relate' to their system may foreshadow the change.

They cannot relate when there are no colourful or emotional things to relate to. And are not 'love and joy' among the words they use most frequently? Thus democracy may face the alternative of brightening up or disappearing.

It is, therefore, time the state celebrated its occasions and painted individuals and their achievements in bold and healthy colours against lively backgrounds. Contemporary citizens, like all men throughout history, need not only to be served by the state, but to be inspired, entertained, rewarded, and amused by it as well. The necessary colourful elements are all traditionally governmental. It is, therefore, logical to suggest for democracy, for its own protection, a moderate injection into the body politic in periodic doses of Roman spectacle, French *gloire,* and British ceremony, with occasional applications of oriental mysticism and tribal folklore – that is, with the natural postures of man long and everywhere relevant to public affairs.

3

Preventive politics

Many postures and politics in government are palliatives for the political counterparts of three well-known ailments of man: the bends, faulty accommodation, and neurosis. Their existence in turn causes a natural phenomenon, refraction, which requires correction in all political systems.

These ailments are always found in any system of government, in any group of men who administer affairs, and in any section of the citizenry that participates in community enterprise. They are not organic; they are psychological. Because of them preventive measures become necessary to make participation in public affairs healthier and more dependable. This is particularly true in governmental institutions, parliamentary or administrative, where about one-third of the personnel are competent, one-third mediocre, and one-third weak. The difference among people is not just one of ability; a host of other attributes are involved. Some such as sagacity, courage, loyalty, and, above all, patience, are obvious in political history and in contemporary institutions, and they require nurturing and a featuring of persons with appropriate combinations of them and with at least some immunity to political ailments. Those who suffer negative attributes such as stupidity, cowardice, and treachery, like dandelions, can never be got rid of; they pop up inevitably. For them a political counterpart of DDT is required – stimuli that will force them into sudden growth and bright light so that, for the protection of society, they will destroy themselves as authorities or stand out without impeding others around them.

Men suffer the bends during rapid changes from one level of atmosphere and pressure to another. It is a common ailment in three media: water, air, and politics. In the first two nitrogen acts in the blood; in the last power affects thought. In all three the results are serious, perhaps fatal, and the symptoms are the same. History clearly illustrates the political bends. Even a small rise in position and power from private citizen to mayor may bring on giddiness, while major ascents from back-bencher to minister or from minister to head of government can cause acute distress of the equilibrium. The effect varies with individuals. Some can absorb power and adjust to new levels of authority more readily than others; some know when unaccustomed atmospheres are disturbing them; others become intoxicated. Constitutions have provided various remedies. A sure cure has not yet been devised, however, and the bends remain a major occupational hazard of authorities which some overcome for varying periods and to which others fall quick and tragic victims.

Accommodation is a process by which the eye adjusts itself to the intensity of light. Faulty accommodation makes people near-sighted or far-sighted, and spectacles are prescribed accordingly. Political phenomena differ in intensity like rays of light, and people see them with varying abilities, however well or ill informed they may be. A few have magnificent political vision and can accommodate it to variations in time, distance, and intensity. Many, on the other hand, are exceptionally short-sighted in government, incapable of taking the long view and inclined to assess the significance of things only within their restricted range. Still others can see far but are unable to bring into focus matters directly before them. There are places for all three in government, but, since there is no political counterpart to spectacles, other arrangements must be made to counteract the deficiencies.

Neuroses of various kinds are well known. One of them is a nervous disorder characterized by abnormal sensitivity. It is endemic in government, and it affects many officials soon after attaining even the humblest public office. They may suffer from it even earlier, because of over-serious exposure to it in other places, in which case the weakness is doubly disturbing in government. The manifestations are common. Some people react violently, for instance, to the most obviously justifiable criticism of their particular political belief or method of administration, or defend or assail a public figure or policy with an intensity bordering on madness, even when no such reaction disturbs them in other activities of life. Certain special hallucinations, such as delusions of grandeur, can provoke fearful destruction and death because of over-reaction to a fancied slight or insult, to the fear of defeat, or to a feeling of being indispensable or divinely chosen. Unfortunately such political attitudes are highly contagious and can reach epidemic proportions.

Refraction is the deflection of light when it enters obliquely one medium from another of different density. Anyone looking at objects through water is aware of it. Political refraction is the deflection of ideas and actions as they pass from one institution or process to another. What comes out rarely travels in the direction of entry, and some constitutionally prismatic compensation is necessary to turn it back on course. This alteration does not refer to change in substance, which is usually obvious, but to change in direction, which often goes undetected. Institutions vary in their deflecting characteristics, and the direction of political action depends greatly on what kind of medium it must go through, that is the kind of people who make up the institutions, and the extent to which they suffer the political ailments.

Each of these phenomena brings to mind many examples in government, regardless of its form or the theory which lies behind it. A combination of any or all of them, without adequate compensation, has wrecked even the most logical, sensible, and morally justifiable systems. Consider, for example, an over-sensitive, short-sighted neurotic, dizzy with power and miscalculating the direction of his actions (and there have been many in authority), and determine what political system can best accommodate him. The chances are that it will not be the theories of government, but the compensations for the theories, that will provide the answer. But men like theories and are impatient with compensations. Consequently the latter ususally have to be implemented behind the scenes while the theories are lauded out front, because once men assume actual authority and responsibility they find it is not theories which govern, but men. Democracy, socialism, communism, and totalitarianism are all logical in theory, but they break down as the ailments attack them and refraction frustrates them. The best of them is not the most logical or sensible in principle but the most human in operation.

Prevention of the bends is the same in politics as in water and air. Complicated procedures select those who are to make the political climb; ascent by stages is sometimes provided, perhaps by planned pauses in the back benches or the opposition; checks and balances may provide weights to regulate progress. Control of those in high places is arranged through established contact with those below. Most difficult of all, some arrangement must end the stay in political orbit of those who have been there long enough and cannot or will not come back by themselves.

In selecting those who make the climb we invoke splendid concepts such as the judgment of the people. Actually we employ an old method by which certain tribes put would-be braves to the test – running the gauntlet. The endurance races of party leaders and candidates over many months through back rooms, primaries, conventions, and elections under the merciless scrutiny, ecstatic support, and ruthless criticism of the citizenry and the media are no less rigorous than a run over hot coals between switch-wielding tribesmen. This is, however, still just an endurance race which tests availability and the desire and ability to run, but not the capacity to govern, and which, unlike the gauntlet, eliminates many who run the course without becoming braves. Systems may make the mistake of over-emphasizing this stage and, while appreciating its undoubted value and necessity, ascribing more significance to it than it actually merits. Electoral success is like Darwin's survival of the fittest, that is of the most adaptable. The determination of fitness in the sense of competence is yet to come. Election is also dependent to a large extent on party appeal rather than the appeal of a candidate. Personal qualifications to govern are yet to be demonstrated.

Ascent by stages is the necessary means of further determining abilities and deficiencies. When these stages are planned properly, the candidates for power themselves reveal their attributes. Certainly the theory of parliaments is based on the idea of representatives of the people coming together to express opinions and make laws. But the practice also provides means by which the wise are noted, the stupid label themselves, and all are kept out of mischief. Observers of parliamentary procedures grant the first, but are impatient with the other two. There must be, however, ample means by which members display their qualities, such as special debates, ceremonies and duties to test their ability, and social events to test their talk, loyalty, gregariousness, and inhibitions.

The debate on the address in reply to the speech from the throne, for instance, does much to separate the men from the boys in a new parliament, and, should there be any doubts, a social function or two may clear them up. Parliamentary committees perform such useful functions as their number and size permit. 'There are one thousand rooms in the Palace of Westminster,' Prime Minister Harold Macmillan is reported as having advised newly elected members in 1959, 'but only two are worth entering – the Chamber and the Smoking Room. Don't waste too much time on the party committees. They were invented by the Whips after the 1931 election to keep our majority out of mischief.'[1] Fact-finding tours abroad, especially if there are numerous entertainments, not only add interest and experience to the lives of back-benchers, but provide splendid means of noting those who keep or lose their heads when they get recognition and the extent to which they can profit from it.

Without such means it becomes easy for the wrong people to attain high levels simply on the assumption that election has given them special virtue, and for able people to be ignored because of lack of opportunity to show their ability. Incompetents will get past these barriers in any event because governments are unworkable when composed of able people alone. But it should first be determined which incompetents are harmless and thus safely promotable, and which are dangerous and necessarily disposable. Systems can make the further mistake of neglecting this testing apparatus in the interest of an institutional 'efficiency' which is not possible without appraisals of human efficiency. Nor is it possible without means of discovering and tolerating human inefficiency.

There must be, for example, busywork and innocent rewards at this stage to keep happy and flattered those destined to receive no real responsibility or advancement, as well as a few glittering blind alleys for the influential but undeserving who must be given some recognition to placate them and the interests they represent. Many governments have disintegrated because of the presence in them of fools or misfits whom their colleagues could do nothing about. There is an alternative of course: governments without parliaments, tests, and distractions may resort to purges, banishments, imprisonment, executions, and other effective but disagreeable methods of disposal. This alternative is habit-forming, unfortunately, and is also readily used against able people. This is one reason totalitarian regimes render impotent or destroy their legislatures, and why so many unwise men rise to the top and able men are eliminated to ensure the ultimate destruction of such regimes.

Another reason for these stages is well known but rarely admitted. The kind of work men are able to do at high levels varies among men. The splendid colonel does not necessarily become an excellent general or the latter a good army commander, not because of differing quantities of ability, but because conditions of work differ according to the atmosphere in which it is done and men adapt to these conditions in different ways. Increased responsibility, decreased direction and guidance from above, the brighter glare of publicity, the exhileration of command, even a sense of a rendezvous with history do strange things to ability and to a man's relations with other men.

It is remarkable how the 'coming man' of great ability reveals in the way-stations of government how that ability will stand the rarified levels of power, and how high his ceiling of activity actually is. Furthermore different times require different types of leadership, and tests indicate for all to see the categories of men from which a system may make its choice. Election alone rarely reveals these distinctions; neither does a formal selection procedure by itself. The distinctions are so subtle that men must have ample opportunity to make the revelation themselves, not just by assiduous polishing of their own image but also by showing their character without knowing they are doing it. It was in such manner that the House of Commons judged George Curzon: 'It found,' wrote Churchill, 'something lacking in Mr. Curzon. It was certainly not information or application, nor power of speech nor attractiveness of manner and appearance. Everything was in his equipment. You could unpack his knapsack and take an inventory item by item. Nothing on the list was missing, yet somehow or other the total was incomplete.'[2] The same kind of testing put Churchill himself in a distinctive category – rejected for leadership in peacetime but summoned to command in war.

The general desirable tests at various stages are well known: public appraisal at election time and on the media, performance in various offices, and popularity among colleagues. But essential as these are, they are not enough because they assess an image, a figure, a personality which may be quite different from the reality. *Both* potential for higher office and the lack of it may go unrecognized if the only effective judgment is that of those who know images but not reality. And the assets of one level may be the liabilities of the next. Moreover it is not difficult to conceal deficiencies, especially the bends, by camouflage, excitements, and splendid protestations, as the history of demagogues only too clearly illustrates. Other tests are the unconsciously self-revealing situations which the lesser known processes of government may provide for estimating glittering personalities. They also illuminate the sombre-hued personalities, the Attlees and Homes as distinct from the Curzons and Churchills.

What are these tests? Performance in formal but unimportant jobs; in ceremonies where ability, behaviour, and character are obvious; in places where women can exercise their perspicacity; in situations where the effects of anger, frustration, and jealousy can be noted; at functions where reactions to liquor tell much about inner drives, and where propensities to gossip show the quality of loyalties; in short, in all places where character and sensibilities can be observed, where personal guards can be lowered, and where the postures of men give other men opportunities to appraise them. For the man at the very top these situations also provide signs of erratic behaviour or declining powers long before they become obvious in official routine or in relations with the public.

Lord Moran started this last line of thought by reflecting on the health of Churchill, and it applies to other attributes too. The physical condition of leaders and prospective leaders is often unknown to the public and rarely admitted by close friends and supporters. Even if the public does know, as in the case of Roosevelt and Eisenhower, it rarely worries.[3] The man himself will not admit his infirmities. During certain periods of their political careers men who held high authority were in uncertain health – from Woodrow Wilson to Adolph Hitler, from Gladstone and MacKenzie King to Stalin and Abdul Nasser – and in every case the condition was kept secret. The toll of ill health can never be avoided; temporary ailments are weak excuses for ending careers, and great men can occupy frail bodies and overcome physical handicaps. The stages in ascent to power cannot forecast coming health crises. Nevertheless they are useful in revealing the ability to compensate for existing handicaps and are excellent in showing weaknesses of mind and character which foretell inadequacy.

Stupidity is, however, a much more dangerous weakness than ill health. Some people recognize it in themselves and compensate for it, for instance, by learning how to take advice and from whom to get it. Others are incapable of recognizing their own deficiencies, and, for many of them, the electoral process does nothing to reveal them. Indeed part of image-making is the hiding of deficiencies. But stupidity is quickly and easily determined when special postures and politics are devised to enable the stupid to be stupid in harmless ways before they are entrusted with power.

The stages, like election, are insufficient by themselves for this assessing process. The two together, although not infallible, greatly reduce the risk.

Special activities that reveal character are useful for the assessment and training of rapid risers. A few people can rise quickly to the summit of power without losing equipoise. Like Pitt the younger, they may have unusual training and opportunity to show their fitness for responsibility. Or they may indicate their potential in other fields and, when their abilities fit the demands of politics, justify rapid promotion. But such men are not numerous. Rapid risers more often get the bends or fail to apply to politics the experience of other careers. They may burn themselves out by overdoing responsibility before they are ready for it or learn the hidden traps of politics. Or they use an early post or an immediate crisis as a stepping stone to higher office and either ascend prematurely or fail, destroying their effectiveness in the earlier office as well. Indeed many problems of government are caused directly by the use of office for purposes of promotion. It is better to reveal limitations before, than after, the assumption of high office, and to temper the impatience of the ambitious by less harmful and more revealing means.

In earlier days these means took the form of tribal rites, feats of endurance, skill in battle, and conquests in the drawing room. These tests, except for the last, are hardly appropriate now, but little except election campaigns replaces them. It is often superficial achievements that provoke decisions to promote, especially when a high percentage of voters know little or nothing about candidates. Big electoral tests reveal what money, availability, showmanship, and popularity permit. They can also aggravate the bends by propelling public men into the heights of power by spectacular means. Other tests, if there are enough of them, provide appropriate political decompression and facilitate the early assessment of ability to climb.

There is no sure cure for either short- or long-sightedness in government. Some practices do minimize the dangers, such as organizing men in group executives and combining lay ministers and expert advisors. Freedom of speech and the right to overthrow the government by constitutional means force official sightings both in the immediate vicinity and along political horizons. Nevertheless defects in political vision are common, and still other arrangements are essential.

Planning, a popular activity in government amounting often to an obsession, is plagued by long-sightedness. Over-enthusiastic professional planners may look so far they see mirages in the distant haze, and as they proceed the mirages recede. Meanwhile they miss immediate obstacles to their plans or ruthlessly turn them aside in the scramble for distant goals, in which case the practical obstacle either blocks the theoretical plan or deprives the plan of some essential support or necessary institution. Then the plan needs another plan to keep it going and remedy mistakes, as well as accompanying increases in personnel and cost. And each time the government changes, indeed each time the planners themselves are changed, a new set of conditions arise, the mirage recedes still further, and a huge bureaucracy is the result of much frenzied but groping effort.

Elections may provoke weaknesses of the opposite type by limiting the vision of many participants to the next contest. It is easy to confine policy and action to what attracts votes and shows immediate results. With a series of immediate objectives the range of political vision becomes too short, and direction is obscured, perhaps to the point where the participants are ultimately back where they started.

Mere movement in public affairs, therefore, is not necessarily progress despite assurances to the contrary by both the long- and the short-sighted. There is too much evidence in an age of hyperactive government of officials stumbling over immediate problems while chasing mirages or losing direction by neglecting distant objectives. The ideal solution would be the elevation of men of perfect political vision, but they are scarce and there is disagreement over who they are and what constitutes such vision. Few people in power will admit faulty vision anyway. The more practical solution, though not a completely dependable one, is to make ample provision in government for offsetting one type of faulty vision with the other.

This offsetting requires, first of all, the imposition of many qualifications on political theories. Theories should be guides, not dogmas; negotiable principles, not non-negotiable ones. Most people do not understand them, however devoted they are to them, and few can explain fascism, communism, socialism, democracy, and the rest. Actually they all hold out a set of exclusive panaceas leading to a distant mirage of perfection. According to the lessons of history theories deserve careful attention, but not the fanatical devotion which always causes acute long-sightedness and contemporary tragedy excused in the interest of distant goals.

The offsetting of the long- and short-sighted also requires the difficult task of minding one's own business as well as that of others. Cooperation, help, charity, and public administration are vital in a society, but beyond a certain point people who are always minding other people's business do not devote enough attention to their own, and the total effort of their society is thereby diminished. They may become politically short-sighted because they accompany their activities, not with glances ahead to see where they are going, but with concentration on the activities of others. People then fall over one another and over the obstacles they did not see. A society of busybodies and official peeping toms spends more time watching than doing and becomes overly concerned with short-range activities of limited significance. It is especially sad when much of the watching is devoted, not to the service of others, but to the exercise of personal or group power and to the prevention of others from doing what the watchers themselves are unwilling or unable to do.

Political long-sightedness is developed in part by rear vision or a sense of history. Those who have practised the art of viewing the affairs of men over long periods of time are better able to assess the significance of contemporary events than those whose only concern is for the immediate. They appreciate, not just actions, but also the consequences of actions. Mistakes are easily repeated through ignorance of the past, and the future is too easily mortgaged by people who do not understand that their time is both the past's future and the future's past. People flatter themselves unduly if they think the future is based on only the contemporary. This has been said often enough by devotees of history, but the lesson is still unheeded. On the other hand, some people look behind so much that they live in the past and ignore present realities and future challenges. This nostalgia causes a reverse-image vision which reveals ahead only a reflection of the past, with its unpleasant realities faded and glories magnified out of proportion to their real significance. It is an advantage for a society both to feature an appreciation of history and to prevent an obsession with it by bringing it into contemporary political and social affairs in order to benefit from accumulated experience and to emphasize the transitional status of the present.

One instrument for developing historical perspective is culture, which will be discussed in detail in chapters 14–16. It is the strongest ingredient holding a society together and the highest common denominator of the human race. It can never be enjoyed on a purely contemporary basis because it caters to both a form of ancestor worship and an urge to live on after death which are natural human feelings. Indeed of all a society's phenomena culture stimulates the most far-reaching wide vision. (Religion is thought to stimulate a long vision – from the creation into both heaven and hell; but the range of vision is extremely narrow because of the sects, and both ends are veiled in the mists of conjecture and conflict). Moreover culture is the one human force which is readily visible from one society to another: music, literature, the dance, art, and architecture are universal languages through both time and space. Culture should, therefore, not just be developed as a social force by itself; it should also be mixed with politics and economics both to strengthen them and to give their participants a clearer perspective.

Another means of combatting long- and short-sightedness is the accumulation of usable and disposable experiences in government. It is a weakness of many systems that much experience gained by men in public life is wasted by assassination, electoral defeat, banishment, fall from favour, and abrupt retirement from office. Undoubtedly a country can put forward many reasons why Stalin needed purges of high officials, why Robespierre required the guillotine, why there was no place for a Truman when an Eisenhower took over, or why any kind of 'has-been' should be consigned to limbo. But surely the wastage of talent in politics is abnormally high, even allowing for all the necessities of the struggles for power, and government itself suffers from both the wastage and the temporary nature of political leadership. Surely also the wastage promotes much short-sightedness because it discards experience and features short-range objectives. Administration then proceeds through a spasmodic series of hectic encounters with power instead of a continuity of knowledge and experience over a steadily changing sequence of events.

A political Valhalla, described in chapter 4, is a useful institution for remedying defects of political vision. It does not cure them, but it provides perspective and retains experience in the process. Unfortunately men like to confine entry into a Valhalla to their own group, and a political party will as quickly name its own members as a church will confine sainthoods to its own deceased devotees. Nevertheless the Valhalla is a means of providing both the long view and the short view when other institutions neglect them, because knowledgeable non-elected officials have a different, but still relevant, view of public affairs which they can express with less fear than their elected counterparts. This combination of two opinions is as old as government, but it has deteriorated in status with the emphasis on election. Its value has never disappeared, however, especially where the non-elected have rightly given up power and confined themselves to giving advice and help which elected officials can accept or ignore at their will, and where there is ample provision in other institutions of government for frequent changes of personnel.

It must be emphasized, however, that experience, perspective, and the like, so often expected from the retired or defeated, even from those who simply change jobs, vary greatly with people. Some are of invaluable assistance; some are nuisances. This is why such a person should only be available, and never be in a position of power in the organization he has left. He can be invaluable if he is in a position to be called upon. He can be dangerous if he views action through limited or outmoded ideas; he may be hard to advise; he may even resent how well things have gone on without him and cause difficulties in, perhaps even destroy, the organization. A Valhalla should therefore be designed on the basis of availability, not power, and with enough dignity to satisfy the so-called indispensable man.

The Valhalla instinct in another form is actually a potent weapon of the long- and short-sighted. The distant reward is their stock-in-trade. The planner and the theorist who look to Utopias and the politicians who deal in promises say in effect that all will be well if this plan or theory is followed or if that promise is ensured by electing the right people. They also cause disillusionment when their enticements are not fulfilled. Colour is useful in these situations. The people have a long wait, and it would seem sensible to give them colourful things to enjoy in the meantime, and some compensation for the ideological and political rewards which, in the great majority of instances, they are not destined to receive. Of the rewards which they do ultimately receive they should be more appreciative when their patience is not strained by over-serious expectations unrelieved by fun.

Neurosis in the form of abnormal sensitivity is well illustrated in the history of government and in our contemporary touchy society. Many men who assume society's burdens on their shoulders ruin their work by carrying chips on their shoulders too and, in effect, inviting others to knock them off. They are not content with the basic role of government – to do collectively what citizens cannot do individually. They must raise their method of doing things to the status of a great truth, a unique philosophy, or *the* best system. Then they feel obliged to tell the world of their enlightenment, thereby denigrating other systems and inviting hostility. Proselytizing follows, then dreams of worldwide application of their method, then war. Within a system governments at various levels are sensitive about the encroachments of other governments on their prerogatives, and much activity is necessary to prevent and remedy injured feelings. At humbler levels officials expected to do particular jobs may make routine out of them which they defend vigorously and expand by empire building. Indeed a large proportion of all government activity is dedicated to the fact that people bruise easily, and to catering to the sensitivity that makes perilous the vast network of channels of communication in public affairs.

People sometimes confuse over-sensitivity with temperament. Temperament is useful as a mechanism for defence or as an initiative for people with talent, and it can be admirable, for example, in a Toscanini. But it is a dangerous affectation for people who use it simply because they are too sensitive or because they wish to hide lack of talent and get undeserved attention; ultimately they convince themselves that temperament is a sign of talent. Society needs means of testing temperament to see which kind it is.

Normal sensitivity is to be hoped for. Insensitive officials and institutions tend to be blind to the realities of the world and of human nature. On the other hand, over-developed sensitivity can be exploited or distorted when people over-react and become temperamental, skittish, nervous, belligerent.

Little can be done to eradicate this political ailment, but it is essential to recognize fully that it exists, indeed that it is endemic in public life where there is so much scope for the ego. Once admitted, it can be contained by two kinds of apparatus in government. One, the opposition apparatus, flushes officials and policies into the open where sensitivities must be defended, reactions assessed and criticized, and judgments tested. This test includes the right to present alternatives. It does not prevent over-sensitivity; it discourages it or at the very least makes it harder to tolerate.

The second kind of apparatus caters to over-sensitivity by giving it scope in harmless ways and thereby diluting its impact in government. This apparatus is the colour, described earlier, which is associated with entertainment, ceremony, and rewards which have long been part of public affairs, but which our particular society has neglected and for which it has devised odd and unnatural substitutes. Contemporary problems indicate that both insensitivity and over-sensitivity have reached almost epidemic proportions, and that there is a close relationship between them because opposites attract one another, in politics as in physics. Both politicians and those they serve may display the same neurosis a house dog does if he is not given the occasional tickle under the chin or ball to chase – especially if he lacks in a city apartment adequate means of staking out his territory.

The opposition apparatus, although one of the most ingenious devices in government and a precious and practical possession of both politicians and public, has a fundamental weakness – it can go too far. The problem can be seen in some families. Spouses and parents who give advice and criticize may, if they are not careful, get into the habit of doing it to the point where they nag and manage. Perhaps they do it with the best of intentions; perhaps they are simply relieving tensions or indulging a taste for control. Example, trust, tolerance, a sense of humour, and other intangibles are well known antidotes, as any study of divorce or runaway children clearly indicates. In public affairs the citizens' right to disagree with the government and with one another sounds as splendid in theory as marital bliss, parental leadership, and family unity, but in practice it has similar defects when it becomes, not a right or duty, but a habit. Then discussion, which theory declares to be constructive support and criticism, or perhaps even constructive destruction, becomes mere nattering and nagging based on chronic negativism kept festering by the tut-tutting of habitual grouchers.

The penalties of grouchiness are severe. The more negative affairs become, the more time is spent in preventing than in acting, with a resulting slowing down of the business of society. When grouchiness becomes so common that it becomes 'legitimized,' and slow-downs are accepted as inevitable, happiness goes out of fashion and a society may disintegrate. For these reasons the opposition apparatus is not good enough by itself; it must be accompanied by something to dampen *chronic* negativism of a neurotic kind. Tough administration and force only aggravate it. Colourful and cultural activities are by far the most practical means because they tend to soften, not constructive criticism or opposition, but what is mere grouchiness based on aggressive instincts. Social reformers too often think that they can solve the problem by suppressing or giving in to the aggressive neurotic; they cannot. 'The idea that we can get rid of aggression,' says one authority, 'seems to me to be nonsense. Surely everything we know of behaviour of men in groups contradicts this conception ... Man's aggression is more than a response to frustration – it is an attempt to assert himself as an individual, to separate himself from the herd, to find his own identity ... My observation of individuals leads me to suppose that aggression only becomes really dangerous when it is suppressed or disowned. The man who is able to assert himself is seldom vicious; it is the weak who are most likely to stab one in the back.'[4] We require a supply of flourishes to provide satisfactions for the assertive and to stay hands that hold daggers.

Refraction is as natural in government as in physics. It cannot be prevented because of the volatile human element. It is always increased by the ailments we have just described. Some politicians are fully aware of it and compensate for it with great skill. Many ignore it and devise wonderful institutions through which their plans proceed in unintended directions. They assume that their ideas and legislation will proceed directly to and through an institution in a straight line. But such directness is rare because it requires a unanimity of unimpeachable abilities and a complete absence of mistakes, which happy combination cannot reasonably be expected in most political processes. Obliqueness is almost inevitable in the operation of any system, and refraction always follows it.

Two features of refraction must be clearly understood. One is the fact that, where the angle of refraction cannot be measured beforehand, a condition occasional in physics and almost inevitable in politics, compensation for it is only possible afterwards, in physics after a ray of light enters and passes through a medium, and in politics after a theory, policy, or action enters and passes through a political process or institution. In the one case a prism will send the ray back to its original course; in the other something with a similar function is necessary. The other feature of refraction is that it varies with the nature of the medium. Air deflects at a different angle from water, and the presence of other material in either changes still further the variation. Similarly legislatures, party executives, cabinets, royal commissions, and other institutions deflect at different angles, and the presence in them of certain people affect the variation.

These two features of refraction are often neglected in both the theory and practice of government. People tend to forget compensations or set them up before instead of during and after a political process. They miscalculate the direction of the process by ignoring the different natures of institutions and the human elements in them. Political history tells of countless institutions conceived in splendid theory and logic and destroyed after a brief, turbulent existence amid wonder about what had happened to so splendid a structure or what had given rise to so futile a phenomenon. Looked upon objectively, there was nothing wrong with the intentions of those setting up the foredoomed institutions or movements. They were just naive in expecting their intentions to proceed in straight lines, and negligent in failing to compensate for the nature of the political medium which comes between the conception and the fulfillment of political ideas.

Refraction is one reason for the existence of two chambers in a legislature. By the time a public policy is directed through a party caucus and through a house dominated by a cabinet and a party majority it gets deflected according to the viewpoint and membership of the government. The weaknesses or strengths of the government leaders affect the deflection because, although they may profess the exalted status of representatives of the people, their ability and character are principal mediums for fulfilling the popular will and for carrying out necessary policies which are not popular. An effective opposition also changes the angle of deflection. A numerically weak opposition or any opposition with weak leaders will, however, have little effect. And an abnormally large opposition may cause the sharpest deflections. The results of such a system are not necessarily the will of the people, because what is to a system's advantage is not necessarily to the public benefit, or what is expedient is not necessarily right. We suspect this and often joke about the inadequacies of politicians. Yet we call irrelevant or undemocratic certain political prisms which may prevent abnormal deflection of public intent or welfare, and emphasize only the elected apparatus.

The second chamber and the Crown in the Commonwealth countries, presidential vetoes in France and the United States, and judicial review everywhere are not *democratic* in the popular sense. They are constitutional prisms compensating for deflection. They do it in two ways: they may make changes on their own initiative; or they may simply promote change by their presence or by their advice, and be the more effective because they are not backed by political power. The mere fact that there is another medium has a significant and practical effect on the work of the first, which knows that another interested and knowledgeable body, especially experienced individuals in it, will examine its action. Indeed governments have been glad at times to shift to other bodies responsibility for reducing deflection by review and delay when they knew the legislature's work was not well done, yet could do little about it. As chapter 4 will indicate in detail, the prisms are not designed to diminish the power of the popular chamber but to correct the direction of policy and legislation.

This kind of correction is evident within a government. If a policy were put through a cabinet only, the chances are it would be unworkable. If it went through a civil service alone, it probably would by unbearable. It must go through both so that each will correct the other. A personal catalyst also is common. Experienced administrators often deliberately appoint someone to counteract or stimulate someone else. Indeed, as in marriage and team sports, this relationship is often the secret of achievement, because it is based, not just on action, but also on balancing of skills and attitudes which makes the action effective. The same correction can be so deliberate that officials will set certain colleagues against one another so as to provoke inner conflict which will settle or avoid an issue. Or 'divide and rule' may be used to prevent a union of opposing forces which can prevent action or destroy authority.

The need for correction is also noted in an administrative hierarchy that is too tight and tidy. The desire for an *efficient* organization often provokes a logical sequence of levels of authority which looks splendid on a chart but fails because it has no counter-balancing or stimulating apparatus to redirect the consequences of human energy. There is no excuse for sloppy confused administration, but how often the best work is done by the most illogical organizations in which the illogical features can only be explained as prismatic action. At one end of the political scale the voting apparatus seems silly in a democracy because all kinds of correction are necessary to meet the trickery and cupidity of both voters and candidates. At the other end the cabinets in both the British and American systems are chaotic by pure administrative principles, and can only be justified by the varied ways in which politicians work together. In between, however, organizers seeking efficiency are apt to overdo their devotion to theory and logic – in the school system, for example, which suffers from over organization at a high cost in money, work, and frustration and widely deflected results.

The correction which public officials provide within their own offices is at once the most difficult to get and the most successful in operation. Individuals, like institutions, cause refraction requiring prismatic compensation. The nature of government makes it exceptionally hard, however, for officials to admit shortcomings. Most men who will plead inability to manage without experience a bank, a farm, or a hotel will accept with alacrity the headship of a governmental organization or advise with confidence on how it should be run. A totally unfit politician will take over any portfolio with a feeling that he deserves it because he has been elected. Most political theories avoid the consequences of this fact. But the practice of government must include compensation for it; when it does not the theories fail, however splendid they may be.

The best place for this compensation at the highest level is in the offices of the officials themselves. The most successful statesmen are often those who, while possessing a massive ego and a forceful drive, admit at least to themselves that they are not skilled in all branches of administration and either delegate authority responsibly or have close to them men who can make up for their deficiencies. The visionary with no sense of money matters, for example, needs a financial potentate near him, and the financial wizard needs the constant attendance of an imaginative genius with no practical inhibitions. Civil servants rarely perform this function well; they are advisers whose advice is official, and most of them are not in a position to speak frankly on a personal basis or are unable to do so. It is often difficult, indeed dangerous, to play the role of the strong confidant, and the pliant yes-man is too often preferred. Nevertheless the lack of strong back-up ability is a cause of the downfall of able politicians at all levels. It is also the main reason for failure of the even more tragic weak, inexperienced, or ignorant official who will not admit, even to himself, that he is unfit for the job. The presence of men with strong back-up ability is also the reason why less qualified men are often successful in government; if they learn how and from whom to ask and take advice, they can compensate for many other deficiencies.

Man's turbulent history illustrates the three political ailments we have discussed and recounts numerous prescriptions for their treatment. Many have suggested cures, from skilled political physicians of experience to researchers in theory, and even to social witch doctors muttering anathemas and incantations. Deliberate killing of the body politic, amputation of structures, and transplants of ideas and institutions have had varied results but often put the body politic in shock. There are numerous milder treatments: injections of ideas, vaccination in the form of artificially provoked disagreements, the use of social pills to deaden pain, the provision through electoral defeat of enforced rest for feverish officials, and the use of a political prosthesis to remedy deficiencies or improve appearances. People vary in their wish for the cures. Some are social hypochondriacs who always feel or fancy the onslaught of a political ailment and search frantically for relief from expert or quack. At the other extreme are those who see trouble as the lot of others and give no thought to deficiencies in their system. Most people fall somewhere between, but the two extremes cause most of the trouble in both theoretical and practical politics.

To eradicate political disease is difficult, expensive, and often fatal, as wars and revolutions vividly indicate. To recognize symptoms and to use preventives in advance, on the other hand, are as wise in politics as medicine has comparatively recently found them to be. Many preventives have been in use for a long time, but men make the same mistake over and over again, saying in effect that 'our theory and system is perfect,' 'others are sick and need our cures.' Or, like people who are careless or fearful of check-ups and visits to the dentist, they shrug off the need for political examination, and decay proceeds unhindered and often undetected. Consequently the communist is fanatical about his observations of other systems, his desire to replace them, and his cheerful dismissal of his own troubles. The democrat will swear by his interpretation of political formulas and minimize the obvious fact that pure democracy ensures its own destruction. A socialist sees the state as bringing blessings to all and ignores the direction he may take toward totalitarianism. The fascist says his system is best, but ignores the fatal qualitifation, that it only works if leaders are perfect and remain that way. And so with other *ats* and *isms*. They are non-negotiable theories advocated pure and unalloyed. And because they are unalloyed they are brittle. We rarely hear favourable reports of qualified communism, socialism, democracy, and totalitarianism. We are suspicious about such departures from pure theory as capitalist thoughts, non-elected institutions, reactionaries, or betrayals of the glorious leaders. In this age when political ailments have reached epidemic proportions we still neglect much preventive political medicine in the form of qualifications of theory and compensations in practice.

Let us now examine in chapter 4 such qualifications and compensations as operate in practical ways in two very old institutions, and in chapters 5 and 6 in contemporary forms of administration.

4

Crown and Valhalla

Two ancient institutions adapted to contemporary politics illustrate how human nature in government is handled with subtle treatment. The Crown and a parliamentary second chamber have numerous constitutional functions which have been described often and which need not be included here. Their compensatory functions are rarely mentioned, however, because public men are reluctant to admit shortcomings or resist status and power, and democratic theory, like most political theory, is largely based on what men should be rather than on what they are. These institutions are often the only ones that permit correction of the political ills described in the previous chapter. They also permit certain postures which are inevitable in government and which must be catered to so that they will do the most good and the least harm. And they contribute substantially to meeting one of the most difficult of all problems in government – organizing leaders into workable and responsible teams. The fact that neither institution is elected prompts some people to regard them as *undemocratic.* Actually they have long since been adjusted to democracy, and some of their special features help make it work.

A constitutional monarch protects democracy from the results of the bends at the heights of political power.[1] Some human being must be at the summit of government and much depends on his stability. Unfortunately great talent, public acclaim and hero worship, and even assumptions of divine right have not been reliable stabilizers when the head of state wields power. We therefore place two persons at the top: one is at the very summit and he stays there permanently and is accustomed to living at that level; the other is temporary and he is made to understand that his position there is sponsored and may be ended at any time.

The constitutional monarch holds the governmental power of the state on behalf of the people and is the personal symbol of authority which man finds necessary in every system. Heredity makes his tenure unquestioned and ensures a rigid training for the job. Pomp and ceremony attract respect and provide the show which people always expect from heads of state. But the monarch is not allowed to wield the power of a head of state by himself; the pomp and ceremony are all that he can manage safely at his level and normally he wields power only on the advice of others.

These others are the sovereign's ministers, especially the prime minister who is the head of government. He is almost at the summit, but not quite, and that difference is crucial to democracy. He is given no power of his own; he advises the Crown on the exercise of the Crown's power; that difference is also crucial to democracy. He has no special pomp of his own either, so that he knows that he is not an indispensable symbol. He is a trustee into whose hands is placed the exercise of power but not the power itself.

This separation of pomp and power at the top took centuries to develop and is the result of the mistakes of many sovereigns and ministers. It is also the result of the oft-proven inability of the people to prevent politicians from becoming dictators. The people either can do little about it or actually encourage it and repent later.

Arrangements for such separation in other systems do not go as far as in the British system which makes the monarch so colourful and the prime minister so powerful and responsible an adviser that each, regardless of the personalities concerned, knows his place. The German chancellorship under Hindenberg, by contrast, was not detached and colourful enough, and Hitler could combine it with his own presidency and outdo monarchs in power and pretensions with disastrous results. Later the aged Chancellor Adenauer dominated both the presidency and parliament. Napoleon became dissatisfied with republican status for himself, assumed an imperial crown, and even raised several relatives to thrones. Later De Gaulle took the headship of government with him when he became head of state.

The constitutional monarchy therefore serves democracy by keeping ministers in second place as servants of the state – electable, responsible, accountable, criticizable, and defeatable – a position necessary to the operation of parliamentary government. The people and their parliament can control the head of government because he cannot identify himself with the state or confuse loyalty to himself with allegiance to the state and criticism with treason. He is discouraged from the common tendency of officials, whether elected or not, to regard themselves as, and make themselves, indispensable, to entrench themselves in expanding power structures, to resent accountability and criticism, and to scoff at the effects of prolonged tenure of office or advancing years. Moreover such control avoids the charges of treason, executions, assassinations, revolutions, and miscellaneous other expensive upheavals which so often accompany attempts to control and change governments which take themselves too seriously.

The democratic sensibilities of some people are disturbed by the idea of an elite, a symbol, an official who is neither elected nor chosen by someone who is elected. They err if they think the removal of a monarch also removes such elements from government. These elements are characteristic of government itself, whatever its form, and are simply transferred to other institutions when a monarch disappears. Men will have elites and symbols whatever their system. Heads of government, elected or not, will take to themselves, if they can, the prestige and power of monarchs, disguised perhaps, but with the same basic elements; they find them a natural and necessary feature of governmental authority.

De Gaulle, for example, overshadowed republican France and its government and called to mind the old monarchist slogan 'l'état, c'est moi.' The Kennedys took on many of the colourings of a royal family. The collecting and revering of Mao's sayings and the displays of his photographs on the walls of stores and the coat lapels of store clerks seem in fact no less monarchal than the adulation of the ancient Chinese emperors. One can compare Red Square ceremonies with Czarist ceremonial, and Stalinist purges with the persecutions of Ivan the Terrible. And the idea that the people will not let their leaders become undemocratic is not as a rule true; they have permitted many elected heads of government to become in effect absolute monarchs with absolute power. François Duvalier of Haiti became president for life and named his son to succeed him. It took a revolution to elevate Castro and it will take another to remove him. Opportunities for criticizing or removing Franco in republican Spain are nearly negligible. Meanwhile the existence of a constitutional monarchy can protect the head of state from such temptations. Britain can defeat a Churchill after making him a national hero; and Canada can withdraw her mandate from a Diefenbaker after giving him an unprecedented majority in Parliament. In Britain and Canada such men are not at the very top and the change can therefore be made with relative ease.

Monarchal phenomena are common in other activities of society. The cult of the celebrity is as dominant in our day as it ever was in history. How often is 'I touched him' heard in a screaming crowd! The elite in athletics have always been admired and well paid. The universities feature academic ceremonial. There are many resemblances between churches and royal courts — the raiment and titles, the powers of the clergy, even the throne, tiara, and crown. And in the smallest communities the dignities and regalia of fraternal and religious lodges are reminiscent of the potentates and knights of old. These are such natural and acceptable phenomena that it is not difficult to understand governmental officials taking advantage of them. Man has found, however, that in government it is hard to advise, criticize, or, if necessary, remove, a dignitary in robes or uniform who also wields power and has a retinue. A constitutional monarchy discourages these things as much as possible for working politicians and, recognizing that they will arise inevitably, bestows them on the Crown, partly to provide a good show, mainly to strengthen the democratic state.

Every system, including democracy, contains the means for its own destruction. It is in times of crisis, when some serious and unexpected dislocation takes place for which there is no normal remedy, that a system breaks down. This century has had a surfeit of disintegrations. In many instances the head of the government was the prime target of the destruction, and his fall often carried away other institutions and the constitution as well.

Parliamentary government presupposes change as required; but such change means orderly alteration of power, not conditions of general panic and destruction. When an electoral system is stalemated, when a parliament breaks down, when a prime minister dies in office and there is no obvious successor, when a leader becomes very ill or insane and neither he nor the public knows it — these are among the times when political paralysis is brought on by shock and uncertainty. In such circumstances a constitutional monarch provides a symbol of continuity and authority. He cannot, of course, step in and take over; he can only encourage others and sponsor the search for an orderly solution of the difficulties. He is above suspicion and can command confidence because of his prestige, because he is above politics and ambition for personal aggrandizement, and because he does not exercise power on his own initiative. Even in a period of such modest upheaval as an election he represents the state as a whole while the parties involved, including the government, can oppose each other to even the most vituperative extremes, a process which should never be taken for granted. No elected political leader can be a symbol of the whole state either in a crisis or at an election; nor should he be in a parliamentary democracy. This is the monarch's job. On the other hand, how often opposition parties and elections have disappeared in republics throughout the world.

There are other purposes of the Crown: the encouragement of dignity and respect for government, the example of a royal family, the colour of pageantry, the sponsorship of good works and the inevitable governmental social activities, the source of honours and awards, a continuing focus of loyalty and emotion, a unifying force among the people, and headship for a family of nations. Each of these functions has its own merits and weaknesses. Whether or not one approves of any or all of them, one must remember that none is irrelevant or disposable; each one crops up in some form in every system of government. When a monarchy disappears other institutions soon take its functions on. Then trouble begins because of the transfer of such functions to the power structure. Officials and political parties from right to left have found many ways of using such functions to protect themselves and their powers and prestige from the legitimate operation of democracy in their own country, and to give them excuses for meddling in the affairs of other countries. They are in safer hands, and are more effective, with the Crown.

Indeed the disposal of these functions affects the whole image of government. Being governed in a constitutional monarchy is like being part of a cooperating family composed of benevolent parents and responsible children. Being governed by a dictator, whatever his title, is like enduring the dominance of an over-bearing parent. Being governed by a republic is like being brought up in an orphanage: there are functionaires and care, but only limited identity.

An elected non-political president is often used as an alternative to a monarch. His main problem, aside from the temporary and relatively colourless character of his office, is the ease with which he can be overshadowed by the prime minister and, worse, the ease with which he can compete with the prime minister. However, everyone concerned knows exactly where the monarch and his advisers stand in relation to one another and to the people.

An elected political president wielding power directly is a completely different institution at the head of a different system of government. He could not function in the parliamentary system as we know it. As many American presidents have testified, this kind of official also finds burdensome the combination of head of government and head of state.

Which is the *best* system? No one knows; some people tend to think their own is best whatever it is; others tend to admire any system but their own; some are more concerned with the kind of system they have than with how it works. Two things are clear however: that systems are not automatically transferrable from one place to another – too much depends on the environment; and that any system must allow, not just for logical forms and cherished principles, but also for peculiarities of human nature in government, particularly the hierarchical bends.

Canada amply illustrates the process because, at federal and provincial levels, she has no less than twenty-three people sharing power at the summit of government – a sovereign, a governor-general, ten lieutenant-governors, a prime minister and ten premiers. On the whole Canada's constitution is one of the stablest in the world and the relations between the Crown and the ministers have worked extremely well. The sovereign and eleven representatives together cost two or three cents per citizen per year. Indeed the net cost is less because their duties would cost more if governments handled them. By no stretch of the imagination can they be considered to have played any significant role in actual government in our time, or to have obstructed or overshadowed their premiers. Their job has been to occupy the top levels in their respective jurisdictions and to handle the decorative and emergency functions, while leaving the prime ministers and premiers to handle the powers of government without actually possessing them, and to be electable, responsible, accountable, criticizable, and removable. The governor-general and the lieutenant-governors are something more than constitutional presidents; they have the sovereign's auspices to signify authority, to enhance their prestige, and to clearly mark the line between pomp and power.

The democratic process has given Canada a mixed lot of heads of government over the years. Some have been everything democratic theory describes, real leaders of a parliamentary system. Some have been virtual dictators; some could control their legislatures personally with an iron hand; some had delusions of grandeur; some would do with their constitutions exactly what they could get away with. Some, on the other hand, have been weak, indecisive, ineffective – inadequate to the demands of high office. The offices of prime minister and premier, like all offices, are only partially what the constitution says they are; they are in large measure what the talents and personalities of the incumbents make them. In all cases the fact that the officers were elected gave them a mandate; it did not ensure good government, but it did make them initially responsible and disposable. The existence of the Crown made sure they stayed that way.

Without a monarch the functions of the Crown would remain and pass to the heads of the federal and the provincial governments and their officials. Nothing in Canada indicates that it could escape the resulting processes so obvious elsewhere. The control by a Maurice Duplessis of government and politics, particularly of the legislature, invites thoughts of what he would have done if he had possessed as well as wielded power. A William Aberhart and a Joseph E. Smallwood with supreme power that was their own provide tantalizing speculation. Similarly a dominant party in unassailable control with a leader who is a symbol as well as a master is not difficult to imagine at either the federal or the provincial levels. The fact is that in Canada such men and their parties cannot now attempt such things, even if they dream of them. They are not allowed to; the powers they wield they wield in trust.

Those who worry about the monarchy sometimes doubt the relevance in Canada of the sovereign herself because she is queen of several countries. Yet such a situation is common in Canada: many citizens owe allegiance to outside heads of their businesses, churches, unions, international political parties, and other groups. Nevertheless a shared head of state is controversial. Perhaps Canada may ultimately have a sovereign of her own. In any event we need to remember that under the constitution the sovereign is a part of parliament and is the formal ultimate source of political power, and the law sets out the facts of power with clarity for all to see and recognize as authentic. Governments in Canada may have quarrelled over which may do what, but power to govern has itself been unassailable and unquestioned from colonial times to the present. This stability of law is by no means universal around the world in an age when constitutions have been unusually short-lived and unreliable and when human rights have enjoyed only modest protection. Governments and their supporters come and go, but the Canadian people know that the powers of their state enjoy a solid, recognized base and the validations of centuries of usage. The Crown is the legal expression and the sovereign the permanent non-partisan personalized symbol of that fact. Human nature, particularly in relation to its ability to handle power, is far less stable than law, and the Crown is a practical bulwark against some of its most dangerous and undemocratic tendencies.

Parliamentary second chambers are always targets for suggested reform. Anyone professing pure democracy and emphasizing the virtues of representative government can make a case against a nominated upper house with tenure safe from the verdict of ballots. This case is invariably concerned with powers and rarely includes consideration of the adjustments necessary for the operation of human nature in government.

One adjustment takes the form of manoeuvering personnel. It is impossible to guarantee that there will be round holes for all round pegs or that round pegs will not find their way into square holes. Manoeuvering is required because the challenges of offices do surprising things to incumbents; some people meet them with perhaps unpredictable success, while others fail miserably. The usual challenges of any job face public men, but, in addition, the demands of power and ambition are strong in governmental office, and the ability of officials to meet them varies widely. No political system can make adequate provision for this variation, but it is a weakness of the electoral system that too many people overlook in their emphasis on popular mandates.

Government leaders may wish to move elected officials to make room for able people for whom no places are available, to shunt aside incompetents or the intolerable but not disposable prima donnas who cannot work in a team, to retain talents that should not be wasted, to recognize distinguished service, to avoid having to reward incompetence with positions of power, and to be able to provide promise of entry to a Valhalla to ensure work and good behaviour from those whose ambitions are so directed. No government, however splendid the theory behind it, is without people in these categories. They are often impossible to secure, dismiss or move if they are all elected; and if they are not so manoeuvered the teamwork of government may suffer.

A nominated parliamentary second chamber permits such moves. Although it also performs many valuable constitutional functions, it is its services as an antichamber to the elected and administrative institutions permitting leeway for organizing personnel that makes possible much efficiency in government. It is not difficult to pick out many men who went to the British House of Lords or the Canadian Senate to make room in the lower house or the cabinet for able newcomers. Others went whom the government wished to retain within parliament because of obvious talent or experience: the House of Lords is a reservoir of scientists, military leaders, educationalists, labour executives, lawyers, business men, and others whose services and advice are available at little cost. Others went because they were incompetent or intolerable and could not be dismissed, for no prime minister can ask a constituency to retire one of his own supporters. Men who deserve recognition after years of service, particularly those with enthusiastic wives and supporters, can be given a place in the limelight with minimum dislocation; only those who have faced the problem know how difficult this process can be. Party potentates, public heroes, and the favourites of interest groups invariably expect prestige and power, and, if it is not in the public interest to so reward them, a place in a second chamber may prevent much trouble – perhaps provide them with something useful to do, perhaps keep them out of other institutions while pacifying their friends and supporters. Furthermore it is astonishing how much work and loyalty a government can exact from many followers if it has a few peerages or senatorships to use as carrots in front of donkeys. This is one reason why a prime minister rarely fills vacancies one by one as they occur; he lets them accumulate for the maximum strategic use. Like a pope, who does the same thing when appointing cardinals, he is not just filling vacancies; he is also manoeuvering personnel and organizing a team.

All these translations are more essential to democratic government than to other kinds. A totalitarian regime can change or remove personnel by means of direct orders, banishment, or liquidation, and it rarely gives explanations. Many thousands of public officials of all shades of ability have been disposed of in this manner in contemporary governments around the world, including governments that call themselves democratic peoples' republics. Where there are free elections and responsible administrations, on the other hand, prime ministers and presidents must support their teams publicly while securing all the talent they can get and rendering harmless both incompetence and intransigence. In turn politicians are physically safe from prime ministerial whims. Democracy also requires such translations because candidates or elected representatives must build up support among electorates and interest groups, and the latter, often unable to accept the fact their representatives are able but unelectable or incompetent though popular, must be kept happy by carefully managed rather than abrupt change.

As far as good government is concerned, there is no indication that nominated second chambers contain more or fewer able or incompetent members than elected lower houses, or that they are less efficient or less responsible to public opinion. 'In 25 years of active public life,' testified Prime Minister Sir Robert Borden, 'I found the Senate a more efficient legislative body than the Commons, and far more thorough in the work of its committees.'[2] The virtues of able men in a House of Commons, indeed of all members, are always extolled and are well known because these men must be elected, their parties need their seats, and the light of publicity shines on the House. The virtues of peers and senators are not as well known – they do not have to be extolled for electoral purposes – but they are there nevertheless. On the other hand an idle peer or incompetent senator is easily made a figure of fun; he is seen as a beneficiary of patronage or an 'old political war horse put out to pasture,' and it may be hard to see why he was appointed or what he does. Actually the same types are in a House of Commons too, both in the front and the back benches, and in no lesser numbers than in an upper house. But no political party that wants to win elections can admit it includes among its candidates incompetents or idlers. The virtues of all the members must be extolled on political platforms, and many attributes of members must be tolerated because of constituency support. It is ironic and all too common, for example, to hear a leader ask for the voters' support for a candidate whose presence in the House he would just as soon be without. Indeed holding down seats for their parties is all some members do. Moreover, when the plight of the back-benchers or the reform of a parliament are discussed, it is only behind closed doors that a basic fact of these problems is mentioned – the inevitable presence of men whose contribution is very small because of their own limitations.

The arguments in favor of a representative house are well known and sound; they form a cornerstone of democracy. All kinds of people secure election to a lower house, however it may be constituted or elected, and they carry with them mandates, theoretical or actual, to perform or help perform the business of the state. What is not generally understood, however, is the fact that members of upper houses are only one step away from this electoral process; they are appointed by elected representatives of the people. Indeed, if one analyzes the difference between, on the one hand, the procedure by which many members of lower houses are nominated, perhaps by back-room manoeuverings or even by default or acclamation, and then how they are elected, perhaps by a minority of an electorate or perhaps because they were the lesser evil of two weak contestants; and if one then considers on the other hand the procedure by which an executive with a popular mandate nominates or is required to nominate a peer or senator, it is hard to decide in many instances which was in fact the more democratically selected. With the exception of hereditary peers, whose position is becoming less supported with the passage of years, all members of upper chambers in parliaments are, therefore, dependent on the electoral process for their initial appointment. Any dissatisfaction with the membership of an upper house is largely the fault of the government, not of the house.

One notes here a major difference in form and practice in the British Commonwealth and the United States. Members of the cabinet are not elected to Congress in the United States and both houses are elected. Thus American cabinet ministers are selected by the head of government in the same manner as members of nominated second chambers are selected in the countries of the Commonwealth — without preliminary mandates from the voters; and members of an American cabinet sit in neither house. There is, on the other hand, no place within the Congress for the kind of personnel mentioned earlier, or for retaining within the government the reservoir of recognized talent and experience which can be used or not used as required. A Truman, a General Marshall, a John L. Lewis, a J.P. Morgan, or a Harvey Cushing can never be retained or brought in like a Clement Attlee, a Herbert Morrison, a Sir Alan Aylesworth, or a J.A. Crerar. It appears a waste to let usefulness which can be had at little cost disappear when abilities of many kinds may be needed, especially frank and experienced advice which every political leader finds in short supply. American and British political biographies illustrate the difference. The former almost always end, often with pathos or disillusionment, with the termination of office; the latter usually continue beyond this point for several chapters, discussing the subject's participation and interest in public affairs, and the note on which the story ends is much more cheerful. 'In England,' wrote Edward R. Murrow, '[Adlai] Stevenson would be in Parliament lighting the hearts of the people of the free world, but here he sits around waiting for a few tired old friends to come in and have a drink with him.'[3]

The reasons for the initial appointments, together with freedom from further selection, gives nominated upper chambers other functions of a psychological nature useful to government. The Valhalla instinct, which is as old as politics itself, is substantially satisfied; it can never be disposed of in any government, and it is better located in an upper house than in a diplomatic corps, a judiciary, a civil service, or, in the case of some governments, the next world. Patronage is also an inevitable and expensive alternative. Many politicians do not look to a second chamber for fulfillment, but many do; and even more wives of politicians do. And in all governments many look for rewards for real or imaginary service. Whether political figures make it or not, the fact that a Valhalla exists is a comfort, a hope, an enticement for service, and an indication of permanence in the shifting world of politics, especially during personal emergencies which often beset politicians. Many of these emergencies involve face-saving which is another ancient factor in government. For example, the defeat of an outstanding person who has had to assume responsibility for an unsuccessful action for which he was not personally to blame may require a face-saver which permits him to accept his fate with dignity and equanimity, and to remain within the precincts of the parliament and contribute to its work. What happened to Anthony Eden and R.A. Butler in Britain and J.L. Ralston and Guy Favreau in Canada illustrates that it is the system that suffers when men of this stature face special problems requiring their departure.

A second, and perhaps paradoxical, psychological factor is the desire to get certain work done with the minimum of politics. 'Keep politics out of it' is a familiar admonition which can often be obeyed by entrusting certain duties to members of an upper house who, while loyal to a party, can afford more independence from it than a member of a lower house. This degree of independence is a real and useful asset in a parliament whose work often requires freedom to speak out without fear of punishment in polling booths or party councils, ability to 'fix' nasty issues, availability to devote long periods of time to special investigations or public or party chores, and the readiness to undertake necessary tasks for which there will be no public kudos and perhaps a great deal of criticism. Elected members can do those things in theory, but in practice they are reluctant to do so, and often it is unfair to expect them to remain long away from their political work or to do things for which the sure reward is defeat. Certainly democratic theory would hold that any MP should be able to chair an investigation of sexual matters in England or problems of the press in Canada, but democratic politics would punish him for it.

There are in every form of government certain *inner* or *shadow* institutions or officials who have the confidence of political leaders and who work behind the scenes quietly and unobtrusively. The inner cabinet, the shadow opposition, and the *éminences gris* are well known. Cronies are recognized and usually suspect. Responsible government in countries of the Commonwealth has rested on the principle that the advisers of the head of the government must have a mandate so that there can be no 'family compacts' or 'chateau cliques,' and, therefore, ministers are elected first and selected after. This process, however, goes only part of the way toward providing prime ministers with the kind of backing, advice giving, and trouble shooting they need. There evolves in any administration a special group of people of wisdom, ability, or experience upon whom a chief relies, especially on difficult occasions. This group is very small and its members change with administrations. But its presence is vital, because, as any chief executive will testify, an organization may include much talent, but the people who can be relied on for difficult tasks or in times of crises are very, very few. Simply getting frank, unbiased, and sound advice is hard for the occupant of a high office who is surrounded by dependents, favour seekers, ambition, and gossip.[4] Even in a cabinet all are colleagues but few are friends of the head. A cabinet, a House of Commons, and the civil service provide some such special people, but a second chamber increases the supply and does so within the confines of the parliament and under appropriate oaths of office. If the people are not there a governemnt can put them there. Cronyism and compacts may still exist, but the need for them drops sharply where there is an obvious reservoir of experienced talent in an official position.

The unique and perhaps most practical aspect of this arrangement is that governments have such people available to be used or not used as they see fit. If they are in an elected house they have to be used, whether or not the government or their own fellow members want to use them, or else otherwise be kept happy and out of mischief. For these same reasons opposition members in an upper chamber perform the same services for their leaders and colleagues in the lower. In an upper house there is an atmosphere of dignity and some colour which keeps available those who can perform useful service and keeps those for whose service there is no demand in harmless honour unaffected by power, itself a useful concession to reality; it keeps others who are not in office in a state of distinguished suspension while they aid the opposition or until their time for renewed service comes, itself a practical tactic in the orderly alteration of power.

A second chamber is a prism for political refraction. The theory of representative government is that the people speak through a lower house. Practice must modify the theory, however, because it is no more possible for a lower house to produce legislation without management and manipulation than it is for a choir to sing without arrangement and direction. Within a house itself a large book of rules and forms testifies to the need for abundant practice which often must fly in the face of theory by limiting speech, preventing conflict, and forcing action. The control of the executive over legislation and how it is presented and passed is well recognized.

The second chamber in modern legislatures has another role. It provides a review, a 'sober second thought,' a 'cooling,' a suggestive and improving process, all of which have long been regarded as useful, whether provided by the chamber as a whole or by experienced individuals in it. It does not exercise a frustrating control, because the will of the lower house prevails. It provides something still more useful – a compensation for the deflection of the popular will, however that may be defined, as it is exercised in the lower house, as well as for the deflection of judgment which is inevitable in an elected house. Bad legislation is common. So is legislation designed purely to get votes. Legislation passed with a bare and forced majority is to be expected. And legislation may even emerge which was opposed by a majority but passed because of the pressure of party discipline. Indeed much legislation is passed, particularly on technical matters, which few members understand at all. The will of the people is therefore rather intangible in many such instances, while the people themselves can and do pay little attention to either the process or the results in most routine legislation.

This situation is inevitable in any system of government. What parliamentary theory does is to provide that the situation is open, and that it and the people involved in it can be got at, criticized, and changed if necessary. The second chamber adds another correction – the passing of the parliamentary will and judgment through a second and different medium to clear distortions caused by personal and political deficiencies in the first medium. The fact that the second chamber is a different medium from the first in that it includes the kinds of representative citizens mentioned earlier brings to legislation judgments which were quite impossible in civil service departments where much of the legislation originated, and in the cabinet and the legislature where it may well have gone through in a hurry. The popular stamp of approval may be given in the lower house; but much of the review in the upper house itself, or among experienced members of it, indeed the very fact that there is review, contributes greatly to the quality of the legislation, which, after all, must work. In the end it appears to be more democratic in fact to have this second political review than to leave the lower house dependent only on the official initiation and review by the civil service.

Indeed the need for this review is increasing as the ability of a House of Commons to express the popular will, inform the public, and cope with legislation is being assessed. Governmental functions are now so numerous and complicated, and the presence of bureaucrats and technocrats is so overwhelming, that all sorts of people, including politicians, have devised schemes to control the House and even by-pass it. The House needs all the support and participation it can get from the kinds of citizens an upper house can accommodate in a parliamentary setting if a parliament is to remain democratic and efficient in a hyper-administrative age.

The Crown and the second chamber are not checks and balances; they do not supervise, or pit one group of officials against another. Rather by their mere existence and the functions they perform they serve purposes which, if they did not exist, would have to be handled in some other ways. In effect they are concerned with the human and practical needs of democracy. In practice they fill a need in government for institutions and individuals that do things which other bodies will not, cannot, or should not do. This is why the Crown and the second chamber have lasted for centuries as political institutions. It is also the reason why absolute monarchy and dictatorship, which are really the same thing, usually die. It is complicated, and sometimes impossible, to find alternative ways of getting the functions of the Crown and the second chamber performed while keeping the government democratic. Certainly many republics have had enormous trouble keeping their leaders responsible and their legislatures powerful, to the point where many republican heads of government have become, in fact, absolute monarchs. The instability of numerous legislatures has been obvious around the world; they appear and disappear, change their structures, or become rubber stamps. And several republican electoral systems deny any freedom of choice. Indeed a dozen contemporary counterparts of Hampden and Pym, who did so much three centuries ago to strengthen the structure of parliamentary government, could find much work dear to their hearts in the republics of the world as democratic principles run up against the unavoidable fact that humans can get sick on power, that their political ailments require preventives and remedies of the most subtle yet practical kind.

5

Conflicting postures in administration

Men are rarely able simply to work at a political job because they like to run things and other men, and, however modest the job, many use it to secure status. Their institutions therefore increase steadily in number and complexity to get work done and to accommodate the postures of control. Most men are prone to talk while controlling, and numerous devices cater to exchanges of opinions, complaints, wishes, advice, and decisions. This mixture of work, control, and talk includes incessant political activity among varied personalities and complicated navigation along channels of authority and communication. There emerges a category of behaviour called bureaucracy, as well as a sphere of influence popularly known as 'the establishment.' There also arise many expeditors and information officers to explain what is going on. Ultimately some of the original work gets done, but with accompanying flourishes comparable with the mating dance of the lyre bird.

Men like to consider themselves rational, and regard as quaint the postures which accompany the actions of other creatures. Actually men are prone to the wildest and most irrational accompaniments to action and surround many of their interests with a host of diversions. Indeed the interest of some people in political and social action in all systems is motivated more by the need to perform diversions than the desire to do work. These diversions are themselves natural, but they are often attached to the wrong actions with devastating effect. The lyre bird would be foolish to indulge in the flourishes of the mating dance when hunting food or engaging in combat. Man has no such inhibition; he disperses his antics with abandon among his pursuits. Or he may be careless, eager, vain, or egoistic and use no postures at all. Lyre birds impress with postures so that their ladies and their enemies will have a chance to appraise them and their intentions and to react appropriately. Man, on the other hand, often seems to expect others to react without a chance to look him over and consider whether he is worth reacting to. Both these failings are unnatural, and they could lead to man's extinction.

The reason is not difficult to note in practice. Postures are too often replaced by theories and dogmas in a vain effort to make men more acceptable to other men. A man may declare that he is a liberal, a Marxist, a Presbyterian, a trade unionist, and say in effect that he carries all the attributes of such credentials and must be accepted accordingly by others. Such labelling is most unreliable; it is his character and the behaviour that results from it that indicate what he really is and believes. Ideological labels have little relationship to character, and privileges based on them are often undeserved. It is postures men need in order to reveal themselves to others, that is, means by which they can show themselves and explain their actions for others to appraise. Any indication that a man wishes others to accept him just as he is or as his ideology advertises and without appraisal of him is little short of vanity.

Theories and dogmas thus become in countless instances little more than instruments of personal labelling and advertising. Meanwhile the postures do not disappear; they are adopted by the institutions which promulgate theories and dogmas. In the Nazi movement, in the New Left, in churches and schools of philosophy all the physical and intellectual displays associated with postures became prominent, indeed blatant. But, because these are misplaced postures, that is, postures associated with institutions and ideologies and not people, they tend to displace the actions and beliefs they were called upon to explain and are mistaken for them. Meanwhile men who give up personal postures by which other men can know them seek explanation of themselves by means of institutional postures which explain nothing but institutions. But we cannot understand institutions without understanding the people in them. In the absence of opportunities to appraise men fight and destroy themselves. This they do, not because they dislike one another, but because they hate the institutions which cause them to misunderstand other men. If men assumed their own postures they might understand one another more and therefore fight less.

One action which attracts many postures and mixes them up is power wielding. Some postures are suitable for power; many, however, are linked to power in the absence of suitable alternatives. This is why man's administrative arrangements are enormously complicated and, in many instances, grossly inefficient.

The situation can be seen in any large organization, especially government. Three categories of effort can be noted in its administration. One is what is necessary to get work done. A second is what controls the cupidity and temperament of those who are served. This category is needed because all the members of the public do not react favourably to what is done in their name. The third category comprises a great variety of actions which meet the emotional needs and personal characteristics of those who administer. This last is the effort that causes most of the unnecessary expansion in administration – indeed it is the basis of Parkinson's Law – and it is the most active category for the accumulation, use, and misuse of power. We shall note many examples of how these categories operate in the institutions discussed in later chapters. We should first consider, however, some general observations on the wielding of personal and collective power, because people who wield power tend to place more emphasis on handling the peculiarities of those they serve than on coping with their own.

Administration at higher levels combines power wielding and slavery, each of which makes the other possible. Power and the accompanying prestige, or the hope of these, attract people to certain tasks and make them bearable. Slavery in the forms of responsibility, hard work, and the whip lash of criticism provides opportunities for service and makes the power productive. This combination is both natural and sensible. Society must ask certain people to leave their regular work and normal lives to perform duties of leadership. Because society thereby delegates much control over itself it exercises the right to criticize, obstruct, punish, and perhaps even assassinate these people. It gives a few of them great glory as encouragement to all and as compensation for making many of them miserable. It provides exciting moments to lighten months of routine. It inflates the ego with status to offset drudgery and command respect.

From children to prime ministers men like to be set apart from others, to be given a special role to play or duty to perform, and they will often endure any work or hardship to preserve the distinction. A member of a legislature listens to speeches he would not tolerate as a student or churchgoer. A president must please a multitude of people, master massive amounts of paper, attend numerous meetings, and listen to many complaints which no non-administrator would put up with. Most branch heads or committee chairmen receive a distinction and remuneration which bear little relation to the extra time and trouble they take. These people and thousands like them pay handsomely for being selected, but they do essential things which others will not or cannot do in return for whatever distinction they may enjoy.

Power accompanies administration. Without it work could not be done and men with a taste for it would not become involved. Thus power wielding may be directed toward getting work done or toward building personal status and ego. A person may mix the two or concentrate on one, and how he places the emphasis often determines his success. Power is not a clear element in administration however. Like a gas, it is elusive, often invisible; it concentrates, disperses, and evaporates unpredictably; it is volatile and often inflammable. Like a mirage, it can be apparent rather than real. Whether power is directed toward work or toward building status and ego it is difficult to appraise. Historians therefore take years to determine the effectiveness of statesmen, and at less lofty levels it is hard to distinguish real work from 'empire building.'

One reason for the instability of power is the unpredictable and varied effects it has on human beings. As with alcohol or drugs, men behave differently under its influence and are susceptible according to the kinds and the dosages. Some can assume large amounts of power and remain sober and stable; some lose their heads with just a little bit. After individual points of tolerance are reached, men may get childish, reckless, surly, or stupid. Power makes some so uninhibited that they cast off all their principles, scruples, and morals. Afterwards, when the spree is over, the celebrant may find the results of power less pleasant than the anticipation and suffer a hangover in the form of disillusionment. Not only is it impossible for others to tell in advance how a person will react to power, but the individual himself rarely understands his own behaviour under its influence. History records the power sprees of rulers, but anyone can observe similar phenomena in office clerks, parents, teachers, and chairmen of club committees. This problem is different from the bends, which we discussed in chapter 3: the bends are caused by unaccustomed heights of power; intoxication, however, can occur in any situation involving control by one person over another or over some function.

'Bottoms up!' is as common an urge in the consumption of power as it is in drinking. A sip, a swallow, half a measure are rarely enough, and comrades are always eager to pour more. Indeed the public often cheers the drinker on, later to repent when he becomes intoxicated. It is a characteristic of power that those who would wield it successfully must be able to say 'no.' They must learn not only how and when to use it, but also when not to use it, because certain powers are most effective when used in moderation. Not only is the wielder safer from his own excesses, but other people have a chance to participate. Indeed some power is most effective when it simply exists and is not used at all. Much of the power of a constitutional head of state, for example, is like that of a fire extinguisher: it exists for emergency only, everyone hopes it never will be used, and, as many systems have shown, tinkering with it in normal political circumstances makes a mess. The parallel in family life is obvious: parents who exercise power to excess usually destroy either their own authority or the initiative of their children.

The thirst for power is caused by another human habit, that of collecting. Even clerks may exhibit the same tendencies as coin or antique collectors in their search for the minutiae of power, and they will often treasure little variations, as stamp enthusiasts do exact shades and watermarks, and protect their powers by vociferous empire building, memo rattling, and rule making.

The grander collectors of power behave like great art collectors and indulge with similar enthusiasm. Consider this perceptive explanation of the collecting instinct, substituting 'power' for 'art': 'For each of them,' wrote Aline B. Saarinen, 'the collecting of art was a primary means of expression. Interesting human beings, actively engaged in life on many levels, their involvement with art collecting was passionate and urgent. None of them bought just what he needed or could use. They were all zealots in whose lives this passionate pursuit had deep meaning. They were not only possessors: they were also possessed.'[1] Unfortunately for the wise use of power, there are few ways in which the possessed can be confined to what they need and can use. If they are not so confined the obsession becomes selfish. The more power is given to a dictator or to a state, to a church or to any other large organization, the more inclined he or it is to resent others exercising any independent power in the same field.

The amount of power is no indication of its effectiveness. Much depends on how it is used. The mistakes of people who have accumulated large amounts of it are well known. Less appreciated is the extent to which the uses of power cancel one another out when there is too much of it. In any large organization or society so much power may be devoted to opposing other power, even to the point where frantic activity shows no practical results, that it is useless and wasteful. It may also be dangerous. The thrust of power may be too much for the size of the organization and the amount of work it does. Like a Model T Ford with a Cadillac engine or an 8-foot boat with an 18-horsepower motor, the organization can shake itself to bits or overturn. Or, like an engine that has to run at full capacity for too long, it can get over-heated and burn itself out. Furthermore the effectiveness of power depends on the postures which accompany its use. Its possessors cannot simply wield it for long: they must also make it acceptable.

These peculiarities of power and of the people who wield it complicate administration, and they are among the weaknesses of participatory democracy where many seek power. A simple apparatus and predictable people are too much to expect in any organization. Chains of command, committees, coordinators, checks and balances, compensations for errors, and methods of encouraging ability and rendering inadequate people harmless multiply as an organization grows. Officials like to dignify all this effort with the status of administrator. Actually the bulk of it in large organizations is glorified clerical work. This work is not real power. It is illusory. It also diminishes in effectiveness as it grows. The reason is human. In any activity there is a limited supply of able people, and an expanding organization must rely more and more on the mediocre and incompetent. The latter, in turn, rearrange their powers and productivity to the level of their competence, and the efficiency of the organization and the effectiveness of its power inevitably fall. A host of compensatory political activities are also made necessary by the inevitable temperamental official, talkative member, busybody, waffler, or person with less knowledge or experience than he thinks – all of which types wield power and often with misdirected seriousness. Similar political activities are necessary for relationships among people: A doing one job and B another may entail complicated arrangements to enable them to work together, and these arrangements increase in geometric proportion to the number of people. They increase still more when whole bureaucracies work together, and a slow, complicated group ritual is added to the personal relationships. Politics is also required to enable people with talent, judgment, and the ability to work to get on with the job with which the organization is concerned.

When the administration thus gets too complicated much of the skill available is directed to running the organization rather than doing the work, and promotion may be based accordingly. Then the amount of administration is increased further, not because it is necessary, but because administrators want to make their reputations and secure status. Were it understood that reputations and status could only be secured by most people through the work the organization was set up to do, there would be far less administration, and most of it would be recognized as what it is – glorified clerical work.

Clerical work is necessary, respectable, and satisfying, but not when it is inflated. It means nothing when it becomes an end in itself, an illusion of power, and people become irked by it. Indeed one may wonder how much of the demand for participatory democracy is a reaction against inflated bureaucracy. This situation is often overlooked by over-enthusiastic people – from the reckless dictator to the assiduous clerk to the irresponsible activist – who are concerned with wielding power rather than doing work. They like power, see themselves as capable wielders of it, and react strongly to it. But they forget that the consequences of their exertions are often just bigger organizations, more complicated manoeuvres, and illusions of power, rather than real service. This short-sightedness is not confined to the panjandrums of institutions alone; it is applicable to men at every rank, something which totalitarianism always neglects, and which democracy, in its efforts to be participatory, has not yet had a chance to correct.

It may be asked whether expanded administration is not desirable, in that it provides many people with jobs and income. Here is one of the great fallacies of our time. Mere make-work is neither satisfying nor productive. People know how significant their work really is. If it is significant they can be happy in it, whether it involves running a bank or cleaning the streets. If it is not significant they are rarely content, even if it brings them great wealth and prestige, although they will not usually admit it but bolster their status to maintain their pride. If an administration is inflated so that its personnel are frittering away their lives on inconsequential errands, it will become a breeding ground for discontent. The remedy is not still more work of the same kind, but, as we shall note later, emphasis on significant and creative alternatives.

Excessive emphasis on what Lord Acton called a tendency of power to corrupt is perhaps like a prohibitionist's attitude to alcohol. The corruption and the evil undoubtedly arise and the tendency to them is strong. But other tendencies are also present. Power brings out splendid qualities in some people which they themselves may not have known they had. 'A place,' said Bacon, 'showeth the man and it showeth some to the better and some to the worse.' Administration, therefore, is not simply directing work and people; it is also fitting men into places which suit them and controlling both their intake of power and the direction it tends to send them.

Who does this fitting and controlling is another complicated aspect of administration. There are many views on leadership, from those favouring authoritarianism to those stressing the judgment of the masses. It is clear from the history of administration that no one view is dependable, for leaders have risen from every kind of experience by every kind of theory with varying results. The most extraordinarily competent and incompetent people turn up at every level. Consequently administration needs flexibility as far as the wielding of power is concerned because leadership, being elusive, rises through unpredictable forms of osmosis. If an organization is not loose enough leadership may evaporate, as many tottering organizations testify. Looseness is also essential to a kind of administrative drainage that allows incompetents to run out at various levels. Otherwise an organization may stagnate or become inflated because too much incompetence accumulates.

The vast literature on administration presents many formulas and observations on leadership and how to exercise it. These are useful and important, but they explain only half the matter because the other half is inexplicable. Personality, charisma, performance under stress and in crisis, health, the times (varying times call for different forms of leadership), the ability to seek and reject advice, home life, types of wives, the abilities of colleagues, and countless other things like honesty and patience bring out the best or worst in people and contribute to their success or failure. These are the attributes for which postures provide opportunities for appraisal. We know these attributes exist. But what we do not realize sufficiently is that much organization and politics result from them. Every time we set up a body to perform a function we include in it features which compensate for the peculiarities of the people who run it, and much cost and time is devoted to this compensation. The bigger the organization, the more of it is necessary. Indeed in many growing organizations, from governments, churches, and educational institutions to local societies, the work done may progress arithmetically while the compensatory politics progresses geometrically. The weakness of much contemporary administration is not that this problem exists – because it is unavoidable; it is that we do not recognize and control it enough because we are too theoretical and optimistic about human nature, especially at the totalitarian and permissive extremes. Participatory democracy, especially, cannot afford this theoretical optimism.

The committee is a good illustration of the problem. It is a valuable instrument in any administration and its virtues are well known. Its limitations, however, are numerous. In participatory democracy committees have multiplied in some places so vigorously that their limitations have overtaken and destroyed their virtues. Even a small society may have literally millions of them, and thereby present the appearance of untramelled democracy without the substance. The more committees there are, the fewer good committee members are available, especially chairmen. Only one in ten persons may make a good chairman who can lead a committee without dominating it and get decisions and action. And good available members are not plentiful. Their contributions depend on those who will not talk and those who talk too much, those determined to get their way and those who cannot take a stand on anything, those who are respected and those who are not, those who do their homework and those who are unprepared and uninformed, those who attend meetings regularly and those who do not, those who will assume responsibility and those who avoid it, as well as on the ability of the members to get along with one another.

In actual fact much of the work of many committees has to be done outside the meetings, and by perhaps a third or fewer of the members, in order to overcome these variations. The effect on people is obvious: many officials spend half or more of their working lives on committees and have little time left for regular duties; the attendance rate drops as the number of committees increases; many committees slough off work on subcommittees; many of the silent contribute nothing and waste their own time and their employer's or sponsor's money; some talkers contribute a great deal, but others are nuisances who waste other people's time and patience, force undesirable compromises, or gossip about confidential matters outside the committees. The effect of a surfeit of committees is also evident in increased work and cost in the form of secretarial help, memoranda, distribution of information and decisions, liaison with officials and other committees, and the need for providing alternative ways of getting the members' own work done. The effect of the proliferation of committees on democracy itself is the ultimate paradox. The more committees there are, the more difficult it is to locate authority, to get decisions made, and to ensure responsibility. People must deal with a huge faceless mass, and the authority they gave to the countless participants is hard to find, let alone contact and get satisfaction from. Administrators in the most obvious positions can be appealed to, criticized, and removed, but even they are limited in what they can do without consulting the participatory structure. Consequently work becomes harder to do. If enough people and enough groups are consulted enough times any initiative or policy can be destroyed however good it may be.

This observation, it must be emphasized, is not a criticism of committees or of the democratic principles which lie behind them. Rather it is an opinion that in committee work, as in most things, too much of a good thing breeds its opposite. The number of committees is now so great that it seems that people no longer trust other people. Participatory democracy therefore shows signs of ineffectiveness which, by default, may lead to an authoritarian reaction if the huge committee system fails to work. The consequences are human. Give a child a few toys and he will enjoy them; give him a room full of them and he will not appreciate them and prefer to play with an old cardboard box. Give men and, even more particularly, women a few committees and they will attend to them and enjoy the responsibility; turn them into habitual committee members and they will take the work less and less seriously and neglect their other responsibilities.

The effects of administrative expansion and politics make increasing impacts on society as a whole. The mechanization of leadership, the difficulties of planning consistently, and the vagueness of goals are well known results of putting responsibility into the hands of too big an organization and too many people. Administration and participation are excellent up to a point, but beyond it they become inhuman and tend to cancel one another out. Then the total effort of a society declines and people become as unhappy as they are anonymous. The result is a highly organized society which is restless and which wonders what it stands for and where it is going.

One would expect this restlessness to be assuaged by the security of organized state charity. But even charity becomes inhuman. 'As the wheels of philanthropy began to turn,' writes an observer, 'pulling its heavy load of impoverished humanity behind it, any spirit of benevolence that might have existed at the outset grew less. Philanthropy became something very close to patronage.' Meanwhile those 'on the receiving end of this charity, had no trouble sensing the spirit in which it was given.'[2] The tendency of service to become patronizing is a major problem in all large forms of administration, and suspicion and ingratitude, the inevitable consequences of patronage, require special compensations, not just to please people, but also to protect the administration by keeping it human.

More specific individual effects of administrative expansion are also becoming apparent. For example, when there are too many committees busy members have little time for home life. It is splendid, for instance, for energetic parents to lend time and talent to good causes. If, however, they overdo it, and public affairs may encourage them to overdo it, what of the spouse and children? The latter are often proud of this work when they know it to be essential and effective. But if they sense, as they often do, that it is escapism or ineffective busywork they may regard themselves as the victims. Mother's meetings and father's interests can be major contributing factors in countless juvenile problems where one form of leadership has been permitted to weaken another. In almost every case much of the mother's or father's excessive busywork has been irrelevant and non-productive in relation to the neglect of home responsibilities. Young people may succumb to the same kind of temptation. Many campus politicians fail in both their academic and extra-curricular work because they do not know when to stop joining. Individuals, like organizations, can find committee work a progressive obsession and an escape from real work and responsibility. Often the participation itself is inefficient. It declines in value and does mischief when participators do not have the time, the energy, the knowledge, and the talent for all they attempt. A few fortunate people have the rare combination of talents necessary for large-scale social participation which produces useful results without neglecting other responsibilities. But, for the majority, too much participation means an unproductive life in 'the thick of thin things.'

These observations may seem contrary to certain concepts of democratic administration. Actually they are concerned with the neglect of some aspects of that basic element of democracy, the people. One aspect is the protection of men's humanity: people are far less human in the mass than they are as individuals, a point on which much has been said and too little done. More neglected, however, is the extent to which the politics of excess participation kills democracy by encouraging the weaknesses of the mass rather than the strengths of individuals. On a national scale administration thrives on the economics of mass expansion in the vain hope that individual satisfaction will keep pace. The result, always obvious in international aggrandizement, which leads to war from which few individuals benefit, is also increasingly evident in local affairs from traffic facilities to education. Expectations rise, and the more people get as a mass the more they want and the less they count as individuals. An additional factor is that a large bureaucracy and participatory apparatus are not always set up for the democratic purposes of doing or saying things. They can also be used merely to keep tabs on people, and they often illustrate that democratic people will not or cannot trust one another to the extent which they like to think they do. Trust declines as bureaucracy grows, and democracy withers away. It is bound to because, given an impersonal bureaucracy in a colourless society, men lack opportunities for looking one another over and determining how to trust.

Power illustrates the same problem at all levels. Power wielded with lasting impact and achieving results is usually exercised in moderation within a manageable range by individuals who can handle it for the benefit of the people as individuals. The more the power expands, the wider it is dispersed, and the less its wielders as individuals are able to control it or keep up with it; the more it is dissipated, the fewer are its results to the people as individuals. Whether it is in the hands of a Napoleon or of a local citizens' committee, the amount of power means less than the use of it, and benefits to the mass are illusory if benefits to the members of that mass are unappreciated. Our society now has so much administration that it creates and hands out enormous quantities of power which people cannot handle and which therefore does not serve them. When the mass overshadows the individual in this way democracy does not command in practice what it professes in theory. One of the great fallacies of twentieth-century democratic thought is not the idea that collective control is democratic, but the naive assurance that the more control there is the more democratic the state becomes. It neglects people and their initiative without which there can be no democracy. Protest is a natural result.

The dispersal of power, and the over-serious nature of it, may lead to authoritarianism because excesses always encourage their opposites. Concentrating power excessively is just as bad as scattering it too widely: both ignore human nature. The remedy lies between these extremes at a point where power is taken with medium seriousness. Good administration has always been accompanied by an important but widely neglected scepticism of human nature. From successful rulers to particularly distinguished leaders everywhere, the able administrators are, almost without exception, those who made allowances for their own and other people's peculiarities and weaknesses, did not take themselves too seriously, and kept power in its place. The same is true of collectivities of people which can be puritanical or sophisticated, democratic or authoritarian. Like P.T. Barnum people may love people but nevertheless not take an over-confident view of them.

It may seem heartless to say with Barnum that 'there's a sucker born every minute'; but there is. It may seem unfriendly to say that some teachers, clergymen, revolutionaries, social workers, or politicians are frauds dealing in humbug; but some are. It may seem undemocratic to say that the people sometimes want humbug; but they do. Enthusiastic democrats, communists, fascists, and others who take an over-confident and over-serious view of human nature, that is of themselves, and plan their social apparatus and power wielding accordingly deal in theory, not in facts. This is not to say that the dignity and worth of individuals must be anything less than vital considerations in any enterprise. But like gold, they are accompanied by dross; like wisdom, they are ineffective without a sense of humour, and are unsupportable without puncturing much ego. The fortunes of any race of men illustrate the strength of scepticism combined with a sense of humour as well as the weakness of a surfeit of seriousness. Much contemporary protest is caused by the fact that participatory democracy, like authoritarianism, is too puritan in its outlook.

Contemporary political systems and many major human organizations place too much prideful emphasis on the strengths of man while ignoring his weaknesses. In turn people become obsessed with their theoretical virtue and over-confident of their practical capacities. An electioneering politician will tell everybody what splendid people they all are. Churches will not hesitate to state who are the chosen of God. Mere practitioners and casual participants readily consider themselves experts. The individual cannot be told that his demands are stupid when they are, because in a democracy everybody's demand must be regarded publicly as 'legitimate.' Popular opinion enjoys ample status, as is right, but the individual cannot be told publicly that his opinion is wrong, which is not right. The responsibilities of man are not given the emphasis that his rights enjoy.

All this leads to frustrated expectations and negative reactions. Administration in particular is so serious or is taken so seriously that it is becoming increasingly unpopular. Abuse is the daily lot of rulers who no longer can go about without bodyguards. If we consider that Louis XIV was able to invite hundreds of people off the street to watch his daily activities, while today's heads of state must live and work in guarded solitude, leaving their private lives to gossip magazines, we may wonder which is the more democratic in fact. Church leaders face rising discontent with their jurisdictions. University presidents are wailing walls for dissenters. The heads of most large organizations run the gauntlet during their now short terms of office. And the administration of law and order, always difficult, is now the butt of uncontrolled vituperative abuse, despite the fact that its policy is benign compared to that of its predecessors which invoked much tougher laws and punitive methods.

Democracy has paradoxically taken much of the fun out of public service as anticipation and participation have increased. Other forms of government have also found ways of instilling a deadly seriousness into administration. But a surfeit of obstacles, criticism, and perhaps danger leads to negative reactions or excess caution which weaken administration by making it unpopular and perhaps unattractive. Even administration by public opinion is so affected. Participatory democracy suffers when people forget there is no such thing as public opinion; there are public opinions. Those who shout 'power to the people' loudest are inclined to identify public opinion with their own views; they become the most over-serious, and therefore the most negative, of all citizens.

Men who dislike one form of administration generally seek to change the form rather than deal with the human factors in administrative politics which cause the trouble. This mistake is a feature of history. It is also a feature of successive individual administrations which cannot resist reorganizing when they take office. Actually one reasonable form is as good as another in a given sphere of administration, and little may be gained by changing it unless human factors are allowed for. 'Plus ça change, plus c'est la même chose,' is a much neglected administrative fact. It is better to have institutions which are flexible enough to accommodate the various personalities that comprise them and which therefore do not need to be overturned to be reformed, than to have institutions constructed to the rigid, yet fragile, specifications of some dogmatic theory. The constitutional cabinet, for example, is one of the most illogical and flexible bodies known to administration; yet it works because it accommodates all varieties of people. Systems and structures may be impressive in their theories and logic. But their theoretical affiliation, whether democratic, socialist, communist, or whatever, matters less than the extent to which they can accommodate the brilliance and the stupidity of men.

This accommodation is not sufficiently provided for in much contemporary administration. Even a casual reading of the constitutions, manifestos, dogmas, platforms, and prospectuses on which institutions are based reveals that they have an exaggerated notion of their importance and ability. High-sounding generalities and principles impossible to live up to prevail, and often there is not a single reference to responsibility or allowance for limitations. The theories are too good to be true because they have subordinated people to institutional embellishment and postures. Man has therefore found it increasingly difficult to admit weaknesses in himself and in his institutions. Himself he defends on the basis of his dignity and his rights, whatever he may do with them, and his institutions he bolsters with principles. Trouble is then inevitable when men and institutions clash.

It is impossible to make administration accommodate all the characteristics of human nature. Nor is it desirable to turn man into an administrative robot. But it is possible to make special provisions to accommodate or remove some of the more inefficient characteristics so that man can handle his administration with more benefit to society and more pleasure to himself.

6

Eccentricity in administration

The characteristics of men which need to be brought into the open and contained in administration are egoism, excess delegation of responsibility, more commonly known as 'buck passing,' and irrationality or imbalance. These characteristics occur in all systems and in all organizations from governments to local schools. They may be used when they are openly admitted and challenged but they are dangerous when hidden.

The treatment for egoism at all levels of a society is the provision of puncturable dignity and a sense of humour. This is the great virtue of satire, of cartoons and comedy, of court jesters and their equivalents. The effect is seen quickly when a person who is a 'stuffed shirt' marries someone with a sense of humour. Egoism, which provides splendid motivation for hard work, is readily over-inflated, and it becomes perverted when it functions with deadly seriousness. The uncontrolled egoist becomes obsessed with his virtues and the importance of his own untested ideas, jealous of other people whom he is too quick to challenge, and vulnerable to overthrow which his intransigence invites. The egoistic organization behaves in similar ways. Men need to be able to say 'come off it!' to such people and organizations to spur them into either defending their positions or facing reality. Constitutional criticism, including the right of free speech, provides a substantial amount of this interreaction. But something more is needed, because such criticism exercised as a right can itself be too serious or so routine that it is taken too much for granted. Rebellion and violence are the ultimate interactions; but, the most over-serious of all remedies, they are inefficient and destructive.

Inflated ego and taking oneself too seriously may with any person or group disguise the real man. There is usually a big difference between a man in his private and public capacities. Whatever his attributes, once he becomes official, organizational, or ideological, he is a different, and often less likable, person. Remedies which strip away the veneer are useful to both institutions and men.

Egoism needs colour and culture as antidotes. Chapter 2 has dealt with these in more detail. In this context we should note again that men who administer and have their affairs administered are unable either to perform or to appreciate services for their own sake. Colourful activities provide diversions which encourage both dignity and a sense of humour. Culture provides a many-hued background against which men can understand the significance or relevance of their actions. If these are denied them, other less healthy diversions arise. Both provide ample means of diverting excessive, and encouraging latent, egoism and testing virtues and pretensions.

How do colour and culture affect the administration of organizations? In the first place over-serious men with over-concentrated interests do their posturing and relieve their emotions in their business, and, in the absence of broader cultural experiences, fail to appreciate the real significance of the business. Indeed much bureaucracy is an alternate ceremony designed to fill the emotional needs of bureaucrats who have nothing else. They need places outside their business where they can be amused, inspired, and opposed and where they can exercise abilities, engage in controversy, and seek recognition and advancement. The more personal pressures they can work off in this way the less they need to rely on administration to satisfy them and the less subject administration will be to their peculiarities. They also need constant reminders of how insignificant their efforts are in the vast panorama of human experience, and the more they know of culture the better will be the perspective with which they view their administration.

When Otto Kahn was invited to join the board of the Metropolitan Opera he wondered if such participation would interfere with his business. 'You just go ahead and do your art job,' advised his friend E.H. Harriman, 'but don't dabble at it. Make it one of your serious occupations. As long as you do not let it interfere with your other work ... it will do you no harm. On the contrary, it will exercise your imagination and diversify your activities. It ought to make a better businessman out of you.'[1] Prime Minister Heath testified to the effects of such activity in government: 'I have seen too many politicians dying too early,' he said. 'I have seen too many governments grind themselves into the ground because they were preoccupied with politics and government to the exclusion of everything else. That is why I insist on maintaining other interests ... That is why I have music. That is why I like going to the theatre. That is why I sail, and try to organize so that these things aren't interfered with except in extreme circumstances.'[2]

In the second place the great majority of the people at large neither understand the complexities of administration nor appreciate services performed without a flourish. Leadership is not often romantic, but it appears to be, and people rarely believe there is leadership unless they see romance of some kind. Administration is not dull, but it appears dull, and the most difficult forms seem easy when watched from afar. It is hard to assess when the public does not understand the means of assessing it. When people become over-dependent on an organization for satisfying their egos and their emotions an unnaturally puritan loyalty may result, or, if the satisfaction is lacking, disillusionment and rebellion may set in. This pattern is evident in every war, in all ecclesiastical conflicts, and in most social upheavals. The pattern, moreover, is enhanced by passive means of colour and culture. People who watch too much television, for example, forego direct experience and their energies must either atrophy or seek further release in their regular affairs. Furthermore an overdose of colourless participatory democracy can lead to constant nitpicking by people who are hard to please; with other outlets their demands are more sensibly and easily satisfied and their organization can get on with its job. Men who run organizations and men who are served by them do understand, and often state, that there is more to their lives than the operation of their organizations. Without colour and culture, however, the organizations are all they have for the satisfactions they seek – a situation leading to organizational inefficiency and personal irrelevance.

Colour and culture also provide a dilution of power to meet human tolerance for it. Power is too strong for men to wield or accept straight, especially when they tend to accumulate and use more of it than is necessary for their needs. It must be diluted in an accommodating mixture so that its benefits can be enjoyed and its lethal qualities dissipated. But the mixture must be right. Power and church politics make social gelignite; power and economics cause business tumours; power and politics result in volatility; power and social work form a coagulant. Colour and culture, on the other hand, are universal, human and fundamental agents which produce their own direct effects and which, when mixed with other social elements and combinations thereof, make the latter stronger, offset many peculiarities, and above all encourage humanity in its mass enterprises. Throughout history men have indulged in and competed for colour and culture, even to the most revolutionary extremes, without tragedy or the depletion of natural resources. And they have brought more happiness and dignity to man than any other social element.

Colour and culture are also antidotes for overdoses of administration. Man can take only so much politics, so much routine and talk, so much consultation and bureaucracy, in his business. He gets tired of too much participation. There must be just enough of it to make the business worthwhile. If there is too much he will lose patience and interest, and the business will slow down or fail. It is therefore sensible and practical to give him scope for much of his organizational and communicating tendencies outside his business so he can handle the latter with a minimum of fuss and a maximum of interest and initiative.

The second characteristic of men to be admitted and contained in administration is excess delegation of responsibility. Delegation is essential in the exchange of ideas, goods, and services. But excess delegation can lead to dilution and diminution of responsibility to the point where there is no effective responsibility at all. It leads to something else too. The mere passing of responsibility from one location to another and the return of reactions may require, if there is too much movement, more apparatus and politics than the responsibility requires or justifies. Indeed responsibility can go round and round an institution or a society with everyone paying homage to it and adding to it without anyone actually picking it up and discharging it. There are two things wrong with 'buck passing': the buck can be passed too far; or it may not have been necessary to pass it at all.

Delegation of power is normally a process by which large groups select individuals or smaller groups to do things on their behalf, or by which people with overall functions pass on responsibility for details to others. This delegation must be accompanied by sufficient trust and authority to get the job done and enough accountability to ensure performance. Excess delegation of power, on the other hand, normally results from accumulations of unwielded power, that is power which people either cannot or will not exercise by themselves.

People tend to accumulate more power than they can actually use – it gives them a sense of importance and of ability to control. Rather than give some of it up they will delegate it. When the amount of power is moderate, the delegated power is exercised with an appropriate amount of authority and accountability because those who delegate and those to whom it is delegated are few enough and close enough to know what is going on. Where there is too much accumulated power it is either neglected, or if delegated, accompanied by insufficient authority and accountability to get work done efficiently. Power is always delegated more easily and more quickly than responsibility and accountability, yet people are reluctant to give any of it up. The postures that accompany power are too attractive, and people use them to give themselves appearance of power and the status that goes with it, while passing on the actual work to someone else who proceeds to do the same. Each time this happens the postures mean less, both the authority and the accountability are diluted, mistakes are harder to trace, and the politics which always accompany power increase.

The best example of a frequently delegated power is the duty to say 'no.' Many administrators at all levels find it disagreeable to take negative stands with other people face to face, whether being frank with superiors or truthful with those they serve. Courage is important in administration, but it is not common. Cowardice, on the other hand, is common, and it causes much delegation of the authority to say 'no.' As it passes along the line this authority loses impact. This characteristic, perhaps coupled with a need for votes, thereupon discourages negative responses, and services multiply and the apparatus increases. Yet the negative responses must appear ultimately when the price of over-indulgence or over-organization is to be paid. Meanwhile the power to say 'yes,' which is much more agreeable, tends to be retained by its primary holders who may often exploit it; at the other end of the process those asking for decisions may have to go through many middlemen to get a 'yes.' In a given structure of power 'yes' decisions tend to rest at one end while 'no' decisions reside near the other.

The phenomenon is not confined to public administration. It is a cause of trouble in the universities; professors must have academic freedom and much direct responsibility, but many of them shirk saying 'no' to colleagues and students, passing that duty along to committees, deans, and presidents while retaining the pleasure of saying 'yes.' Many politicians, especially near election time, are addicted to this tactic, and it is a problem of political leadership everywhere that pleasant duties, and the credit for them, are accepted with alacrity in the lower ranks, while unpleasant tasks, and the blame for them, are passed along to the top. Numerous parents are so inept at saying 'no' that their children do not learn the meaning of the word. The situation is complicated further in all these instances by a loss of credibility and confidence because those who cannot say 'no' usually have no more success with 'yes,' and those who must say 'no' too much become targets for frustration.

Men may delegate power without considering whether or not it can really be exercised, or whether the amount of apparatus, the cost, and the effort will make the delegation worthwhile. Indeed they sometimes delegate it in the hope it will not be exercised at all. The biography of any dictator reveals the limitations of delegating too much power to individuals. A study of any committee and a comparison between any organization and the work it exists to do show how often the power to talk and act is dissipated in a collectivity. Neither the power nor its delegation are themselves problems, but the practical ability of people to handle them is limited, especially when the accumulation of power is too large. Lack of qualifications is one limitation. But the most fundamental one is the fact that people tend to trust others less in practice than in theory. Accordingly they provide all kinds of checks and balances, compensatory processes, and participatory arrangements which are sensible and necessary when accumulations of power are normal and when those who exercise it assume responsibility for results. These remedies tend, however, to cause expansions and reactions when used to excess.

Another remedy is followed much less frequently — that of not creating or delegating a power in the first instance. The best location for a function is generally in the hands of those whose interests are served by it. Since many functions cannot be exercised in this way either because communal effort is more efficient, as in the provision of utilities, or because people cannot be trusted, for example to obey the law or pay their taxes, they are passed on to others who are given authority to exercise them on behalf of everybody. The logic of this delegation is obvious. What is not so obvious, however, is that the delegation becomes a habit. The more people delegate the more they want to delegate and the less they will do for themselves what is of direct concern to themselves. And those who accumulate power may encourage the shift, partly to provide service and partly to satisfy an urge to control. The habit is useful up to a point, but beyond that it causes the accumulation of excess power, an elaborate administrative structure, and decreasing personal initiative and relevance. The anonymous 'they' become the holders of power and responsibility, and even 'they' are unaware of how much they have. This problem has been debated often enough among free enterprisers and centralists. But almost always the argument is based on principles and concepts of rights and communal obligations. The real question is: What does excess delegation do to the behaviour of people and to the administrators who handle their affairs?

The tendency to delegate is easy enough. A parent who picks up his children's belongings will find the children quite willing to let him go on doing it. A teacher or school that concentrates on handing out information rather than requiring the pupils to get it themselves neglects the old Oriental proverb: 'Give a man a fish and you feed him for a day: teach him to fish and you feed him for life.' Half the divorces are caused by one or both parties being spoilt and not getting the service which he or she considers appropriate. Many other social upheavals are the result of unjustifiable expectations on the part of people who expect other people to do too much for them. In all these instances certain functions should never have been delegated in the first place because, once they were placed in hands that should not have dealt with them, the point beyond which delegation is inefficient was quickly reached. A host of society's activities illustrate the problem, and two results of it are the unrest which man finds inexplicable in the midst of plenty and the depletion of natural resources which he explains with every excuse except the fact that he is spoilt. The great weakness of excessive collectivism is that man wants more and more when he is not responsible for getting it himself, and that he appreciates it less and less as his own direct involvement declines.

The decline of direct involvement is reflected in society's growing administrative structure which seems dedicated to the process of 'taking in one another's washing.' The average person now does very little directly by himself for himself. His wants are satisfied by others and his work is done for others, and both the service he receives and the service he gives are so anonymous and indirect that the sense of achievement, of help, and even of charity is diminished. 'Do it yourself' is the obvious answer to much delegation, but even it has become the slogan for the completion of projects on which the real creative work has already been done by others. Theoretically this is teamwork providing service to the state and society. Practically, however, it becomes inefficient and uncomfortable when over-done because man behaves well in group efforts of modest proportions and becomes skittish when there is too much togetherness. What anthropologists have found about animal behaviour in cages has suggested parallels with human behaviour in cities. It also suggests parallels in large administrative organizations. Certainly history and science have shown repeatedly that group identity breaks down when individual identity and responsibility disappear.

There are many reasons for this phenomenon. The most important seems to be the fact that people who cannot perform primary functions become discontented. For contemporary man even eating may be governed by dietary restrictions, sleep by drugs, and sex by taboos. He loses his sense of relevance if he has no direct experience with creating and producing. Furthermore he may try to remedy the deficiency by creating and producing in administration, which is a frustrating activity because then he is attempting to perform primary functions in what are really secondary duties, and providing yet another reason for the expansion of administrative apparatus. As for collective effort, a society in which everything is done through intermediaries becomes impersonal and inefficient.

One remedy for the excessive delegation of power is to discourage the accumulation of it beyond the point where too much of it must be delegated. Since people may accumulate too much power in an effort to satisfy their egos and their instincts, establishing the colourful and cultural alternatives mentioned earlier may also be helpful in absorbing enough of their time and attention to provide these satisfactions. These alternatives almost always involve creative primary functions. Since people need to perform primary functions, the alternatives may satisfy the instinct in more natural ways.

The third human element requiring compensation in administration is a tendency toward some kinds of eccentricity. Everyone has eccentricity in one form or other; some have it in extreme forms. Extreme forms of eccentricity fall into two categories: in one are those often described as the 'lunatic fringe'; in the other those described as visionaries, 'odd balls,' or just 'characters.' The first tend to be vicious because the ego is generally a weapon for self-indulgence as well as attention getting. The second tend to be benign because the ego is usually an instrument of social influence in addition to attention getting. Attention getting can be harmful or harmless depending on which of the other two it is mixed with. There is a big difference between self-indulgence and social influence; the impact of each on administration can be chaotic, but that of the first is almost always bad, while that of the second can be good or bad.

Categories among eccentrics have no clear limits. It is hard to divide genius from insanity, strength from arrogance, stubbornness from conviction, reform from social arson, self-indulgence from service, and vision from delusion. And what is eccentric at one time and in one place may be commonplace in another. Indeed the commonplace may itself be an eccentricity. No society, therefore, can afford to restrain its eccentrics because it can rarely assess them. They are so often right, and practically every great reform or innovation was originally thought an eccentricity. Nevertheless there are among eccentrics people who are catalysts of trouble, provoking social insanity in any activity in which they participate. Some become rabid in social action. When their egos run wild they may induce excitements and discontents for self-stimulation, and even enjoy morbidly the crumbling of a system or the degradation or death of people they helped to destroy. The women knitting at the guillotine and the clerical observers at the rack have their counterparts at any contemporary accident or disturbance. They may reveal themselves at a ladies' bridge club or in the throes of a revolution. While everyone loses his reason upon occasion, their's is usually balanced on a thin edge, ready to be knocked off with every disturbance, and if there is no disturbance they will look for one.

Society cannot shunt these people aside – they will not be shunted. Indeed they should not be, because the benign ones have much to contribute and the vicious ones are at their worst in the background where people cannot see what they are doing. A collective society based on respect for the dignity and rights of the individual must give them their privileges. But it cannot afford to permit them untrammeled use of privileges when they abuse them. The herd instinct makes men too sensitive, too ready to stampede, to permit vicious people to assume control over others. The very rights that enable them to act, such as that of free speech, may be jeopardized every time they act, and everyone suffers. They may also ruin group action because they are not usually good at team work. 'When you're going to work that close for a year,' said the director of the televized *Forsyte Saga*, 'you don't get anyone who is going to be a bloody nuisance. Well, of course, that eliminated a few people.'[3] This kind of elimination is more likely to help than to hinder activity which eccentrics like to promote. Both reformers and conservatives in a social upheaval can be frustrated in their efforts by extremists more interested in themselves than the cause; they will destroy the credibility of the cause and, when obstacles appear, be the first to desert and complain about the consequences.

Extreme people thrive under extreme systems. A totalitarian system is a fertile breeding ground for them because it stifles discussion and criticism, a good combination, unpalatable to people at the extremes. Both are essential, because such people thrive on one without the other: discussion alone gives them scope for their egos; criticism alone makes martyrs of them. Any study of the Terror in France, of the Nazi regime, or of the Stalinist era indicates how readily unbalanced people misuse responsibility at all levels of administration, even in the family, where a child may be used to betray his parents to the executioner. At the other extreme a society without enough controls also encourages the unbalanced because, in giving them freedom fortified by rights and in withholding criticism in a vain effort to placate them, it gives them free scope for mischief. If democratic institutions protect their lunatic fringes without limiting them they furnish auspices for aberrations as great as in the opposite system. It really makes little difference to the unbalanced whether they live in a totalitarian or in a completely permissive society. Many spoilt children reared in permissiveness, for example, become hopelessly domineering adults; and many of the most extreme protestors against authority are the first to substitute authoritarian attitudes for the permissiveness which enabled them to thrive.

Excessive administration in a society also favours the unbalanced. Totalitarian and permissive societies require more administration than those with comparatively modest controls. Dictators at one extreme require a huge establishment, and 'the people' at the other extreme form one. Managing both functions and people therefore becomes a major occupation for officials and a hobby for participators as increasing numbers of people become involved. The theories supporting both extremes break down not only when there is too much management in relation to production and individual relevance, but also when, as more people are needed, the society finds it does not have enough interested, able people available for administration. At this point the unbalanced, who otherwise can be ignored, find ample opportunity. They tend to wield more than their share of authority because effective discussion and criticism diminish in a growing administration. They also tend to seek power by setting other people against one another. They like this arrangement: it gives them a chance to shine under the aegis of the state, the people, and their own privileges, and provides exciting opportunities to participate in turmoil. And they like power. Society then suffers in two ways:

The unbalanced causes trouble directly in every sphere from the committee room to demonstrations in the streets. And every time he joins any branch of authority, that branch automatically compensates for him by increasing its inner politics and expanding in size. We have already indicated that much administration is made necessary by personal characteristics. Nothing will make it increase more quickly than participation by the lunatic fringe.

The compulsive actions of the unbalanced can be diverted from administration by colour and culture. The lunatic fringe has always been associated with pomp and circumstance, with celebration, with 'high society' and 'local colour.' The arts attract a large number of them. While colourful activities have many intrinsic merits of direct benefit to society, one of their indirect services to society is their provision of scope for the unbalanced who can be steered away from other fields in which they do greater mischief.

It seems that simple direct administration is impossible for man unless his natural tendency to posturing is accommodated in other activities. A society needs, therefore, to provide this accommodation in ways that will associate postures with appropriate activities. Creative and competitive instincts should be satisfied by primary functions at home and in school so that they do not become frustrated and interfere in public business. Such instincts can be satisfied and directed by participation in sports, debating, music, dramatics, and other colourful and cultural activities – anything that absorbs energy, creates lifelong interests and memories, and relates and compares people's skills and peculiarities with those of others. It is possible, however, for countless youngsters to go through school and college, for adults to go through life, without a single, satisfying primary experience, creative or competitive, of this kind, and this situation leaves too many abilities untested, interests unsatisfied, and personal characteristics unknown in an age of automation and spectatorship. And this deficiency is not related in any way to either the sections of society or categories of income from which people come; it applies equally to all. With the decline in opportunity for direct primary action and problem solving in the contemporary world too many people are not sufficiently aware of what is involved when they participate; they cannot understand the politics of a problem or the other people with whom they deal. Watching others do things is not enough; nor is talking about it. Direct primary experience teaches the strongest lessons.[4]

The natural tendency to wishful thinking and make-believe also needs early satisfaction to avoid later disillusionment. The reason is obvious: wishful thinking and make-believe are common in administration and politics when there are no other outlets for them. They are the greatest obstacles to the effective use of power. They are more useful as contrasting experiences than mere escapes, as exercises of the imagination than dreams, and personal stimuli than administrative tactics. Participatory democracy with all its apparatus can be simpler and more effective if it does not have to provide the only release for these instincts and tendencies in activities for which they are the wrong motivation. It is of course impossible, as well as undesirable, to prevent the working off of all urges from entering into participatory democracy and administration; indeed healthy urges are good for them. Misplaced urges, however, are unhealthy and their satisfaction is neither productive for society nor fun for the individual. If man is to live in a highly organized society he may as well make its administration as efficient and his life as comfortable and enjoyable as possible.

7

Collectivized postures

Government is not the only field in which we find postures and politics — society's many other organizations are each a little world of them and together a vast network. These organizations provide numerous benefits for their members; they contribute substantially to the countries' welfare; they give satisfaction to those who enjoy running their business and making professional and social contacts. The amount of organizational work is immense, and a large share of society's total energy is devoted to it. A part of this effort is positive achievement. A part is administration. Still another part is inter-group conflict in which many organizations cancel out one another's influence. As for individuals, they gain much fulfilment in groups. Yet with each involvement they give up some individuality. This loss, not evident or significant at first, ultimately makes the groups impersonal as their numbers increase until one group becomes pretty much like another. The result is a cellular society.

If Shaw was right in calling professions conspiracies against the laity, most people are conspiring against everyone else. Professions are legion. There were once distinctions among trade unions, branches of learning, and societies of devotees. These largely disappeared as all callings became highly organized and certain rituals became common. Many professions are amoebic, dividing and subdividing into new ones; and even auxiliary professions are numerous. Indeed professionalism has become an industry supporting an immense business and political structure. Professions are divided and subdivided into as many categories as there are divisions of the trade and regions of the country. Categories of employment may turn themselves into professions with all the accompanying privileges and ritual. The universities, for example, have associations for every subject on the curriculum, for all branches of administration, and for university teachers and students. Most professions have conferences, publications, executives and office staff to serve each association, and special jargons, powers, and practices to foster uniqueness and give the members a sense of unity. Whether it is delivering babies, watching birds, or playing bridge, solemn conclaves and communications are deemed necessary to give special status to the members and their activity. The large number of activities encourages certain members to become what amounts to professional committeemen, devoting much of their lives to running organizations.

A popular hotel is a splendid vantage point for observing the phenomenon. Indeed the hotel business has been revolutionized by it. Every day and night the salons display stereotyped gatherings which look and act the same whether it is a meeting of a woodworkers union or a society of philatelists. Delegates are labelled. The cocktail parties are standardized, and, after the first drink, so is the conversation. Dinners follow, and the seating arrangements and the menus are common to all events. Chairmen have a standard procedure; the head tables all look alike; the guest speakers exercise the usual functions of entertaining the members and keeping them awake. The proceedings close with predictable parties in hotel rooms as the hotel staff resets the salons below for the same performance next day. Convention hotels are so similar that a convention in Melbourne looks just like one in Copenhagen.

It seems paradoxical, perhaps also inevitable, that a society which professes to deprecate social class replaces it with such an enormous occupational and administrative class system.

The advantages of professionalism are well known. Some of its characteristics become disadvantages, however, if they are not checked or compensated for. It is obvious, for example, that some professions must be monopolistic and powerful to maintain their standards and protect both their members and society. But they can become self-centred and predatory, and lose sight of the interests of both their calling and the public. From the oldest guilds to contemporary labour unions and medical associations, relating the welfare of the professions to the needs of those they serve has been a delicate and controversial task. The interest of the parties may conflict; the profession may be backward in adjusting to change, or it may force change prematurely; other groups may prey on the profession in the pursuit of power; and the profession may contain too many members whose incompetence, greed, or authority are so unjustly protected that they jeopardize its interests. All the advantages of all professions are limited by one weakness more than any other: people are far more inclined to organize than to provide the necessary leadership and control of members. Then others are tempted to intervene to remedy the deficiency. Much contemporary administration and politics are taken up with such interventions.

Another characteristic of professionalism is a tendency to fence raising. Every time a group is organized a certain amount of unity among people with a common interest is developed in the name of cooperation and coordination. But a fence is raised against other groups, and relationships among coordinate interests often break down. And behind each fence participants may discuss minutiae to fill up their time, talk only to one another, write only for one another, and lose touch with affairs of general and perhaps greater importance. They may destroy altogether their communication with others by devising unintelligible jargon, and even confuse themselves by busily interpreting one another. This has happened to the learned societies, and an examination of their programmes and journals indicates how professionalism causes hiving in learning, and how far away it can get from practical affairs and other people. 'Interdisciplinary activity' in universities was forced after too many scholars organized their subjects as 'disciplines.' Some academic fields had become so esoteric that they were isolated from one another, and strange 'programmes,' 'institutes,' and 'centres' had to be developed to renew by administrative means earlier natural associations between fields which were unhampered by 'professional' fences. Nor was this phenomenon confined to scholarship. Doctors became so divided that society feared the disappearance of the general practitioner and, characteristically, new 'colleges' of general practice sprang up. Labour unions have numerous highly organized divisions and subdivisions. Most interests have followed the same trend.

Participatory democracy is partly responsible for this trend. As more people seek to share in the business, societies divide to accommodate them. Bringing people together in this way is useful, but attendance at the sessions, the sharp decline in the quality of and interest in the papers and speeches, the increase in administration and politics of doubtful value, and the enormous cost indicate that there is a point beyond which the benefits of mass participation by narrow categorization drop sharply. Indeed beyond this point togetherness is destroyed by cliquishness and participation becomes hobbled and confined by narrow and standardized routine.

Still another characteristic is the tendency of an organization to displace professional duty by political activity. Any organization, whether profession, labour union, church, or benevolent society, can be used for political purposes. The latter can displace the real purposes by infringing on the time and effort of the leaders and the members and by requiring a large organization. The organization soon demands so much attention that it, rather than the work done, commands prestige, and those who run it make reputations as politicians rather than as workers in their fields.

These characteristics may be illustrated by a fanciful example. A group of devotees of the art of tying trout flies may organize a Fly Tyers Society, complete with constitution and executive. After exhausting one another's ideas every second Tuesday for a year or so, they will join other groups in a National Association of Fly Tyers, or NAFT, with local chapters, an executive director, a central office, and an annual convention. A bulletin, called something like *Lure Lore,* soon becomes obligatory; members will support it with articles and news from the branches, and tackle firms with advertising, the cost of which will be passed on to the fishermen. At this stage would-be politicians will use the society for self-promotion, and members will pass resolutions on social questions.

Meanwhile fly tying becomes respectable, as distinct from enjoyable, and a scholar or two conduct research on it. They will form a learned society and publish a journal, and the art will become a 'discipline.' Theses will appear on 'The Effect of *Machiavelli's Discourses* on the Development of the Parmachene Belle' or 'The Silver Doctor in Eighteenth Century Ecology.' Professors will lecture on 'socialism and the barbed hook' and conduct surveys on 'perceptions of hackles in an urban society.' Jargon will appear. 'Fishing,' a term too mundane, will become 'piscatorial enticement' or 'acqua-conceptionalized encounters.' There is bound to be a degree, BA (hons flyty); and a department, perhaps even a faculty, will be sought by devotees in a university. Eventually students of the Dark Montreal and the Black Gnat will become sufficiently numerous to split off from the main body and form new organizations. This entire process takes ten or fifteen years. But it takes half the time if a government becomes as interested in fly tying as in education, which subject led this trend in academic life. Should the Minister of Education favour a Red Ibis, a division will pop up in his department to promote it, and officials will suggest it as a matriculation requirement. Meanwhile no skill is added or change takes place in the basic task – catching trout.

The most important of all the characteristics of professionalism seems a paradox. Every professional activity suffers from unmixed professionalism and thrives on a generous infusion of lay thought and effort. The worship of the expert is a frustrating rite because those who set themselves up as experts are always limited, however much they know, and many professionals from carpenters to clergymen are not experts at all. Indeed the most incompetent person is often the most conscious of his professional status, while the real master is humble. Nor is expertise reliable even in the ablest people because knowledge of a calling does not always involve skill in making judgments and participating in political matters. It is therefore unwise to rely solely on the collective or individual wisdom of professionals for advancing the welfare of either the professions or society. Whether engineers or singers, teachers or cooks, they work better with lay participation in their affairs.

Many leaders and scholars have testified to this phenomenon. 'If you believe the doctors,' said one prime minister, 'nothing is wholesome; if you believe the theologians, nothing is innocent; if you believe the soldiers, nothing is safe. They all require to have their strong wine diluted by a very large admixture of common sense.'[1] In turn, many have said the same thing about politicians and civil servants.

Lay participation does not mean meddling, censoring, or regulating by an outside authority. This is the mistake of political collectivizers, themselves professional, who often proceed on the idea that others cannot be trusted. It means direct responsibility in the performing of a professional function by able and interested laymen who are part of that function. Nor does this participation mean that laymen must make professional decisions; it means that they ask questions and offer suggestions, query standards in professional matters and make judgments in financial and political ones. The principle that 'war is too important to be left to the generals' has operated well in hospitals, universities, business, the arts, and government, where laymen participate directly, share responsibility, and contribute their special talents. It should be noted, however, that laymen inside the professional processes do not participate well when other laymen intervene from outside, and that the outside layman's contribution is not nearly as effective because his direct interest, his knowledge, and his responsibility cannot be adequate. This fact is a major reason for contemporary troubles in many organizations.

Every profession illustrates the advantages of lay-professional combinations. Architecture can furnish examples which are common to most groups. Architects are rarely experts in *architecture:* they usually know, and are competent in, only one or two branches of it. The good technician may be deficient in aesthetics; the excellent planner may misunderstand practical matters; financial and social results can be forgotten in the excitements of design; and historical appreciation is an attribute which few architects possess. These limitations are of no significance if the architect himself recognizes them and consults others, inviting their criticism and following their good advice. If he is not so skilled a layman should remedy the deficiency.

The layman is the customer in most cases – perhaps the ultimate owner, perhaps officials or a committee directing a project on behalf of some authority or organization. *Caveat emptor* is the obvious warning. The layman must state what he wants and how much he will spend and question every proposal for practicality and appeal, because the architect who is not so questioned may indulge in impractical fancy or unimaginative utilitarianism with slight regard for cost. The architect in turn must question the customer's judgment because many people tend to expect too much for their money, have little acquaintance with technical realities or taste in design, and are lazy about asking advice of people with knowledge and experience. A combination of outlooks is essential for architects and customers in most projects. Indeed the best results are often promoted by regular disagreements among the parties; among good architects and sensible customers disagreements are usually a sign that they are compensating for each other's deficiencies. This combination is not just one of professional versus layman: professionals disagree among themselves, and so do laymen. What matters is the combination of different talents and outlooks which are rarely effective by themselves.

There are many examples of the lack of such a combination. It is simply not safe to entrust an architect, especially a public works architect who is protected by bureaucracy, with the design of a university residence. He will not know the many features which should distinguish it from a hospital, a nurses' residence, a barracks, or a home for the aged, as many universities have learned to their sorrow, and he will invariably raise long-run costs by cutting short-run ones. Professors and students who know residence life have more practical ideas about the building, but are less realistic about technical details, and too impatient about costs. The best residences are generally the result of rugged encounters between the two groups, especially when they are told they have so much money to spend and no more.

For the liveliest experience with the virtues of combined talents one should get involved with the construction of a major cultural centre. The architect will revive all the dreams, and hallucinations, of a lifetime for such a project, and he will produce both atrocities and strokes of genius, usually the atrocities by himself and the strokes of genius at the urging of others. A great project like this takes much living up to, and the architect usually needs discipline and encouragement during the inevitable periods of excitement and depression. He will not get them from other architects; they will hang back and criticize unless they are hired too. A layman with faith in him and an awareness of his weaknesses is his strongest support. The construction of a cultural centre also illustrates the application of the principle of layman-professional cooperation to other professionals. Musicians must be consulted but they can rarely make decisions. Theatre and art personnel will want every facility available but will not know how to combine them and will have little regard for costs; few of them will consider the customers of the centre and the economics of management to the same extent that they think of production or display. They will disagree among themselves to the point where, to satisfy everybody, they will please nobody. It takes a tough group of interested laymen to consult all this talent and combat all the idiosyncracies. The exercise is good for the laymen too, for they will make many unnecessary mistakes if they do not have a lively education in the professional facts of the project.

It takes little effort to note parallel situations in every other profession. The reason is not merely the existence of evil or weakness in the members of the professions – those can be found everywhere. It is the existence of a dual state of mind in most people, a professional aspect for their own work and a lay aspect for their reactions to other people's work. These aspects often conflict. A plumber will be furious with a doctor for doing exactly what he does by way of professional duty; a politician will condone in his own ranks the same weaknesses he criticizes in others. A certain amount of this conflict is inevitable in any society. But when professionalism is overdone, when the professions become so numerous and compartmentalized that there is no room for laymen any more, both the individual and the collective states of mind become unbalanced in favour of narrow professional ones. Specialization is often wrongly blamed for many professional faults; the real trouble is our habit of communicating with one another as professionals far more than as laymen.

The results are the barriers between doctors and patients, between professors and students, between clergy and laity, and between government officials and citizens. There is much evidence that, whereas we may like one another as people, we dislike one another's 'establishments.' Man as a species is said by some authorities to be naturally inclined to cooperate in groups for the main purpose of contesting with other groups. The more professionalized the groups and the less direct the lay participation in them, the more inevitable it is that expert-lay confrontation, which is beneficial within a group, will be aggravated among groups.

We may try to solve the problem by relying upon the government to act as a referee or an interpreter, that is by creating and calling upon still another set of groups with the same characteristics. This tactic, when overdone, usually exacerbates the confrontations by diminishing the already limited contacts among groups, by substituting lay interference and direction from outside the groups for lay activity within, and by adding complicated bureaucracy to the already large group apparatus. Furthermore work does not get done as well if there is too much government interference because so much time is spent in confrontations, because indirect lay participation is less effective than direct, because the professions themselves are usually weakened, and because the procedure to be followed in doing work is lengthened and complicated by the bureaucracy. It thereupon becomes increasingly difficult for a society to handle all its services, and frustrations and breakdowns become inevitable.

Countless non-professional groups entertain, educate, and serve the citizenry of every state. People gain many benefits from these activities by accepting them and being involved. Everything from the relaxation of hobbies to the dispensing of charity adds zest and meaning to the lives of everyone. The activities fostered by groups give interest and variety to a society. These advantages of groups, well understood and widely promoted, are features of the welfare and happiness of man.

Like most things, however, group actions have severe limitations. The problems already attributed to professions also appear in other groups when they become too numerous or too cliquish and when they take their activities too seriously. A bridge club or a charitable organization, for example, can provide splendid relaxation and service, but, overdone, it can also detract from the work and family life of individual participants. A reform group can give much leadership to a community, but, overstimulated, it can become an instrument of aggression and destruction. A sports club can be the centre of recreation and friendship, but it can also be the headquarters of addicts whose lives involve little more. All groups are valuable to a point; beyond it they are distractions offering diluted benefits and diminished credibility and influence. People then get bored with the routine or become slaves to it, especially when they see too much of others like themselves; they either leave the groups or look around for some excitements to justify their existence. Saddest of all are the joiners who become clubby and aggressive rather than friendly and useful, and spend their lives as social butterflies flitting from one organized existence to another without making a real contribution to any one of them.

The most severe limitation of groups is that they can foster loss of individuality and over-identification among their more serious and dependent members. A person can become so collectivized that he ceases to be an individual, and thereupon becomes incapable of thinking and acting as a person. Or his life can become meaningless to himself and others except as it relates to his identity with a group. At this stage people base their lives, not on what they are, but on what they belong to; not on their actions, but on their status. Special privileges or recognitions so based are the same in parties, denominations, clubs, and any social class, whether it be the 'aristocracy' or the 'common man.' They are always inadequate for both individuals and society, unless they are accompanied by personal achievements and identities separate and distinct from mere affiliations.

People belong to groups for one of two reasons, or for both: to participate in the activity concerned and to advance their own status in the community. The first reason is a dual one: the member both performs a service and shares in an activity and also thereby fulfils some of his personal and social needs. The second reason is political: it may be helpful if it is made secondary to the first; if it is primary it is generally harmful to society.

Status seeking is inseparable from group activities, and in the search for status members may perform splendid service for the groups as well as promote themselves. The political and social careers of countless able men rest on prestige gained from community work and holding office in groups. There is, however, a disadvantage: incompetent men with gregarious natures and ample time to spend can gain similar prestige by becoming professional club members and office holders; they can make their reputations through the politics of an organization without doing much of its work. Good office holders are often difficult to secure, especially when they suspect that there will be too much time-consuming activity, and able men are not always available. Groups must often make do with those they can get, and it is common to see offices snapped up by the status seeker. It is also common to see groups thrive under able officers and decline under mediocre or weak ones. The status seeker may do outstanding work for the group and the community; the chances are equally good, however, that he will use the group to promote himself in community affairs or to serve as a springboard to politics, while he neglects or performs inadequately his own occupational work. Many people in this category cause trouble in public life because their basic incompetence has been sponsored by group activity which gave them prestige they did not deserve and could not obtain in their own work.

These troubles arise first in the groups themselves. The status seeker is rarely content with the ordinary work of the group which often involves routine and anonymity. He wants power and publicity for himself, increased prestige for the group, and new projects and functions by which he will be remembered. He likes membership drives and publicity stunts. He is attracted by community improvements and reforms, pontificates often on them and serves on many committees. In able hands these activities can be productive when carried out effectively and without jeopardizing the real work of the group. In less able hands they can weaken the group by diluting its work with frenzied activity. They can weaken the community too by multiplying hyperactivity, encouraging meddling and 'do gooding,' and promoting an overlapping of functions and controversy among groups. There are many tottering organizations barely able to keep going, as well as others whose real value is not commensurate with their activity and cost. Usually these have overextended themselves and departed from their basic purposes in favour of community politics, and it is usually the status seekers interested in prestige and politics rather than the work who have lead them into ineffectiveness or oblivion.

These troubles arise in public life when the incompetent status seekers reach their goal. Such men, now well known on home ground, become nonentities in councils and legislatures. They can be seen in any major elective institution. While able nonentities move up the political ladder to power and fame, they remain at the bottom. If they are content to do so quietly they do little harm, ultimately disappearing into the mists of political backwaters. If they are not content, however, they become nuisances. Accustomed to prestige at home and perhaps supported by their groups, they demand recognition from political leaders or, if ignored, seek it in erratic behaviour. If they secure office because the leaders cannot avoid them, they may recognize their own limitations and do little, becoming useful foils and providing compensation for able prima donnas in government. If, however, they are inclined to do things, or themselves become prima donnas, they become dangerous and either bedevil public affairs or entangle others in endless frustrating efforts to render their activities harmless.

We are inclined in a democracy to blame the leaders for the failures of their government or parties. Too often, however, a leader has had to bear the yoke of incompetent colleagues who were forced on him and whose mistakes were his undoing. We are also inclined to seek remedies for faults in political institutions by tinkering with their structures or reshuffling their powers without noting the weaknesses of their personnel. The blame and the remedies can often be found in the political structures associated with service clubs, societies, churches, charities, educational and cultural groups, and fraternal organizations.[2] Too often they will support for public office any member because he is one of them, regardless of his ability and the way he does his own work, and regardless of whether his community service has been a collection of offices or a catalogue of real achievements. The feeling that anyone is necessarily a good man because he is 'one of us' encourages much incompetence, particularly when an incompetent 'our man' is considered better than a competent 'other fellow,' and cancels out many of the advantages of the principle of representation in public affairs. For this outlook government pays a frightful price.

Groups therefore contribute positively to the personnel of public life by acting as springboards for the able and weaken it by sponsoring incompetents. Which they do depends on how many of them there are in a society, because the supply of able citizens who do their own work and still have time for group politics is limited. Too many participators may ultimately mean not enough doers.

The service of a group depends greatly on how seriously it takes its work in society as distinct from its own status. A bishop made this distinction clearly when he suggested that a church can become a private club in which members interpret the text 'God so loved the world' as meaning 'God so loved the church.'[3] Any group from service club to home and school unit and any profession from labour union to law society can slide into this practice of regarding its good as the general good. It is a common form of collective egoism. It can be controlled, however, or at least compensated for, when the group, however large, remains simple in structure and purpose and limited in social action. It is aggravated when the aims of a group of any size become too pretentious and exclusive, and when one group seeks to meddle with others for the sake of power rather than service and to cast its particular influence over the whole of society. Members then are forced into roles as group members rather than as citizens, perhaps to the point where they cannot live happy lives as individuals at all.

When such groups fail or fall apart their members cling fearfully to them or are cast adrift in uncertainty or disillusionment. This problem is a major reason for the fact that our highly organized contemporary society appears in so many ways to be a disintegrating society. Other chapters deal with this subject in detail, but we must note here that it is not the mere fact that society is highly organized that causes trouble, but rather the pretentious, exclusive, aggressive, and yet diminishing services of its groups which are too complicated for the supply of leaders available and for their ability to live up to their aims and principles. The politics of group activity may overshadow its service, and therefore its *raison d'être,* and, consequently, relevance is questioned, frustrations emerge, and dissentions mount. Meanwhile change comes, and groups, burdened with encumbrances, cannot adjust to it.

We have noted earlier that combined professional and lay abilities are more effective for both the professions and society than professional ones alone. Similar combinations are desirable in other groups for the same reasons. Group judgments and abilities are inadequate without individual ones because men will believe and do in groups many things which they would never consider as individuals. This applies to good things; but it also applies to evil things – from falsehood to superstition to murder – in organizations from church groups to motorcycle clubs. The more complicated, exclusive, and aggressive the group and the more individualism is subordinated to it, the more frequently group judgment and action displace individual ones. People then find themselves doing many things they do not want to do as individuals, and they either suppress their own individualism or rebel.

The work of groups also becomes less effective when it is done with one set of judgments and abilities alone – the collective. Even leadership, which depends on individuality, may be rendered ineffective. Indeed when individualism is too much subordinated, groups may become suspicious or jealous of individualists and drive them out, leaving mediocrity to take over, or become so unaccustomed to leadership that they confuse it with the exertions of demagogues, leaving the lunatic fringe to take over. Relations among groups then become less effective and harmonious because people communicate as members of something rather than as individuals, and the more complicated their organization and the more exclusive their membership the harder it is to communicate. Once more it is not the mere extent of the organization that causes the trouble, but the overly serious nature of it and the over-extension of its politics.

Group life thrives on service among members and between members and others. A service club's work for hospitals and a ladies' auxiliary of a cultural enterprise bring happiness to all concerned when that work is emphasized. Sometimes, however, groups get bored with their own work and branch out into efforts which, however good the cause, diminish or destroy their own work. A church study group becomes little more than a catering firm when its study is displaced by cake baking and bazaar tending. Or it can become a mere social club in which gossip nullifies devotions.

This getting tired of doing good is an important reason for the decline of many groups. It is often followed by indiscriminate participation and intervention in matters of which members know little, perhaps because the group has been used as a means by which some members can climb on bandwagons. Man is tempted to mind other people's business more readily than his own, and he may justify any form of participation by considering himself his brother's keeper. As we noted earlier, he gives advice more readily than he takes it, and because of a natural resistance to advice giving, which is a protection against bad advice, he has built up a general resistance to all advice. As groups get more active in other people's territory this resistance accumulates, and when it gets past a tolerable amount a negative reaction sets in and community spirit is eroded by skeptical and perhaps ungrateful cynicism. The group work will be appreciated even less if the community suspects, as it often does correctly, that curiosity, power, prestige, and publicity are stronger motives than service. Society ultimately reacts negatively to all this effort because participation has become meddling.

8

Meddling

The difference between participation and meddling must be understood if democracy is to work. Meddling needs compensation if man's postures and politics are to be natural in impact and effective in results. As chapter 7 has indicated, man will tolerate only so much participation. If he is subjected to too much of it because of the intrusions of unwarranted participation, or meddling, he will either react negatively or, worse, ultimately not react at all to any participation. Much of the world's trouble is caused by individual and collective meddling. 'Casing everybody else's joint,' observed Marshall McLuhan, 'has become a major activity ... It is just when people are all engaged in snooping on themselves and one another that they become anesthetized to the whole process.'[1]

Participatory democracy suffers from being considered an open invitation to meddlers and publicity seekers, and groups often are springboards for them. Meddlers may be defined, not simply as participators in matters of little or no direct concern to them, but as those who seek to 'get in on' something, the irresponsibly curious, who do not ask if they have any business being there. Groups and individuals are expected to contribute their work, their knowledge, and their opinion to the general effort. Meddlers, however, are inclined to drop their work, neglect their knowledge, and rush to participate with opinions and resolutions in anything but that which lies at hand. They feel an urge to straighten out other people's affairs, and easily convince themselves that they are capable of doing it. Some fit Tallyrand's description of Madame de Staël who, he said, liked to push people into the water so she could enjoy fishing them out again. Others are the chastening type who cannot resist jabbing an admonishing finger or casting a furious eye at what they cannot appreciate or understand – the self-appointed guides to what *they* think virtue ought to be. Many are social predators who, like sharks, are attracted by unusual activity, especially the smell of blood. Some may even have a sadistic streak, and, like child beaters, relish bringing misery to others while justifying their efforts as being for the victim's own good. They do not stop to consider what value their participation may have or how reliable their opinions may be so long as they become involved. They are 'do gooders,' as distinct from doers of good, excitable, bossy, energetic, and self-confident, and always ready to tell other people what to do. They assume without adequate thought that what they think good is actually good. Their effect on society often becomes like that of the scout who had trouble taking a little old lady across the street because she did not want to go: perhaps she wanted to go but the manner of taking her changed her mind.

Surely, it may be said, these people 'mean well' or 'are sincere.' Some fit this description; some do not. These attributes, not always benevolent, are not good enough. Meaning well what is harmful and being sincere in stupidity because of lack of thought or ego-indulgence are the height of folly.

Only a few meddlers can keep up their own work simultaneously; the great majority contribute little more than unproductive participation. And almost all of them hinder the work of others. Other people must endure them, do the work which they neglect, and remedy their mistakes. The more there are of them in a society the more of its community effort becomes a sterile round of participation, counter-participation, trouble making, and mistake remedying, the total of results of which are meagre in the extreme compared with the effort made. Examples are not hard to find. Great numbers of parents neglect their families in a busy round of club, church, and community work, and the community must then devote to the children much remedial effort in the fields of health, education, and social work, as well as endure the frustrations of unloved and untended young people whose youth was sacrificed to the parents' club work. In all communities there are meddlers who can be counted upon to oppose or obstruct almost any project, and 'fuss pots' who delight in making difficulties out of ordinary matters or converting small annoyances into furious resentments. Professional participators pop up in most activities and organizations: it is astonishing how regularly the same people feel they have a call to lend themselves to varying causes, and how often they fail because they are seen too much or cannot participate effectively. Authorities soon learn whether the interest and ability offered are genuine or false. If they are false someone has to devote considerable effort to sidetrack or nullify them, or else be prepared to mend the damage done.

The phenomena can be seen in the universities where certain students become involved in every issue on campus, and neither do their own work nor do much for any student activity because they are the wrong people to lead or influence others, and because their efforts are too thinly spread and too inwardly motivated. After a while an official gets tired of seeing the same person appear to talk about meals, parking, sports, and numerous other matters on which he considers himself an authority, especially when the participant talks too much and does badly both his own work and all the other jobs he tries to do. In the older generation the situation is illustrated by men and women who, sooner or later, make some connection with every community enterprise, contribute more talk than work, and badger others with ill-founded and unappreciated advice. They may justify their activity by posing as solvers of social problems. Problem solvers are certainly useful. But people who take problems and themselves too seriously tend to get to like problems and to exaggerate or aggravate them. Moreover those who would solve problems need one of the rarest of all skills, the ability to solve them without creating other, and perhaps more serious, problems in the process. Meddlers are inevitable in any society. Like fleas on a dog, they provoke some beneficial scratching. But participatory democracy may encourage too many of them with the result that society may suffer a permanent itch and spend more time scratching than working and enjoying itself.

The chances are overwhelming that the efforts of meddlers are negative and fruitless. Many of society's best projects fail because of them. Positive and fruitful efforts require ability, patience, and hard work, much of which is exercised behind the scenes, and it is usually only dedicated people who will first assume responsibility and then follow it up to its conclusion. Much community effort dies because of dabblers and publicity hunters who start things cheerfully but do not see them through. Many great causes are defeated by people who are over-confident about their own work and their place in the cause. It is splendid to aim for the just society, but fruitless without making allowance for the limitation described by Horace Greeley: 'along with many noble and lofty souls who are willing to labor and suffer reproach for any cause that promises to benefit mankind, there throng the conceited, the crotchety, the selfish, the headstrong, the pugnacious ... who, finding themselves utterly out of place and at a discount in the world as it is, rashly conclude that they are exactly fitted for the world as it ought to be.'[2]

Negative efforts are attractive to meddlers. They require comparatively little work, they bring instant publicity, and anyone can participate. Criticism is easy and cheap, it readily deludes the ego into feeling important, and, if it can be associated with some high sounding motive, it is a powerful and destructive weapon. There are, of course, many useful and courageous critics who perform a great service for society. This kind of negativism is usually a definable contribution to society, especially when it is an unpopular point of view and not a chronic state of mind. Group or individual meddlers who engage too readily in participatory criticism, on the other hand, will almost never get involved in hard, steady, anonymous, and perhaps unpopular positive work. They prefer the easier and more obvious activity, and the exhilaration and publicity which they receive from it seems to them to be sufficient evidence that preventing other people from doing things is hard work and public service. Or they may concentrate, not on settling difficulties, but on seeking someone on whom to place blame. They will never share blame themselves because, in President Eisenhower's words, 'the search for a scapegoat is the easiest of all hunting expeditions.'[3] Meddlers may also not know when to stop meddling, and keep at it despite society's verdicts. They thus endanger democracy because it cannot stand a series of attacks on its own democratically arrived at decisions. Again a mounting resistance to all community enterprises is an inevitable result. Two forms of resistance are particularly weakening in a democracy. One is the dislike people ultimately have for nests of natterers who lose their credibility as they become chronic grouchers, and the focusing of this dislike on the institutions which harbour them. People find out that meddlers, excitable under stress, are often the cause of chaos, and that most issues upset a fractious fringe that needs to be cooled down before solutions can be found. The other form of resistance is the effect of Gresham's Law: poor participators drive out good ones on whom institutions primarily depend.

Poor participators are also obstacles to progress. They obstruct in two ways: one is the tendency, already mentioned, to be against anything which they do not understand or which they think will provide excitement; the other is the depressing effect they have on the popular will. They like to stir people up, and people will react with them in public matters, not because they agree with them, but because they tend to oppose things that cause trouble. Peace at any price is a desire which many meddlers exploit for getting their own way. For example, the idea that things done against the popular will are necessarily bad is wrong. Many of society's great achievements were made against the popular will. And many great changes were prevented by the popular will, not because the people were opposed, but because they were frightened or mislead by meddlers who branded the innovations and innovators with infamy. The man on the street is probably sensible enough in matters like temperance, school questions, vaccination, and the Darwinian theory, and he can be relied on for support in starting local cultural centres and festivals. When one looks at these issues, however, one notes how violent opposition is fanned by a tiny minority who will not let the man in the street express and follow his opinions. Hurdles to truth are necessary and natural, but democracy must protect public opinion from a permanent and joyless scepticism fostered by meddlers more interested in the hurdles themselves than in truth. Contemporary unrest, including that in the universities, often illustrates the problem. Only a few of the obstacles to change are caused by the attitudes of the 'establishment.' Many of them are raised by meddlers on the lookout for trouble. Fear and social paralysis may result.

Someone must make compensation for meddlers and the state may be expected to do it, by prevention or by censorship. Yet if the state succeeds it may go too far and shut off valid negativism or encourage meddlers to plead persecution. Indeed the state itself may indulge in meddling, and meddlers are common among its personnel. Groups must take much of the responsibility themselves, and pay far more attention to their policies and their leadership than they do, that is to participatory democracy within their own organizations, before they attempt to participate outside. No one hesitates to criticize political leaders and blame them freely for real or imagined faults; but many officials of groups are protected from public criticism when they become involved in public matters, and make public statements on matters they know little about. The participation is one-way.

No students' council, for example, has justifiable claims to a share of the administration of the university if the student affairs which it controls are in a shambles or if it names weak students to committees and no one is allowed to protest. No professors have the right to demand academic freedom unless they handle their own incompetents. No church should dabble in public matters unless it is prepared to accept full and frank discussion and criticism of its policies. No demand or resolution of a social club merits the slightest attention unless it has a record of achievement behind it and is prepared to accept assessment and criticism. No group has any defendable rights of participation unless it can see both the positive and the negative, and unless it participates through people who will assume the responsibilities that go with the rights. Furthermore, the leaders of participating groups should have no more protection against criticism than those they criticize. Yet a university president can rarely attack a radical student, and woe betide a politician who answers in kind the harangues of a crusading group. Indeed when crusaders know this they often take unfair advantage of it. And it is not just society that needs protection, but the groups themselves, because people are more inclined to ascribe to the group collectively the idiosyncracies of its stupid members than the abilities of its wise ones. Our society is now so organized and its groups so involved in other people's affairs, and yet nevertheless it is such a skittish society, that group activity should be assessed with three slogans: 'credentials please'; 'what business is it of yours?'; and 'put up or shut up.'

If these questions are not asked negative meddlers may quickly undermine a whole society. They can do it more effectively now that society is highly organized. They tend to damage existing institutions, but they rarely create new ones. The result is a net loss. It takes positive and dedicated reformers to do both. Negative meddlers also ignore the fearful price to be paid for their efforts, even massive destruction and the end of rights and liberties for the many because a few sought them in the wrong ways.

We noted earlier that the state too may indulge in meddling, and not because its interventions are necessary, but because it or some of its officials like to meddle. Much worse, however, is one state's meddling in the affairs of another. It always presents what seems to it a good excuse for its meddling, such as ideological indoctrination, ecclesiastical proselytizing, business expansion, or 'liberation' – which includes a multitude of things. But the real motivation is usually a government's ambition, a cancerous ideology that must spread, internal trouble in the predator nation that requires a red herring to draw attention away from it, greed, naked aggression, or the lack of enough for a people to do within their own borders. Indeed a government may act with all the characteristics of an individual meddler.

It is natural to ask if such curtailment of group participation in other people's affairs would mean a disinterested society. Surely such ready participation is a sign of brotherly love and an assurance of togetherness. On the contrary, it is the participating society that has become the disinterested society, the society in which, as any accident or trouble illustrates, people 'pass by on the other side.'

The reasons are obvious. Much participation is mere uninformed talk, nitpicking and nattering; resolutions are so common they are paid little attention. People are restless if there is too much togetherness; they will build barriers as quickly as they build contacts among one another. They thrive on privacy as well as on publicity; too much of one causes a reaction toward the other. The individual mind thinks and acts differently from the collective mind: if one is overemphasized the other veers in the opposite direction. People get on each others' nerves if they are too much on each others' minds. Communication among groups is always impersonal; over-reliance on it forces individuals into an unnatural state of being impersonal. What is communicated among groups and individuals must be worth communicating about if the communication is to be effective; if it is not, the relevance of the very act of communicating is questioned. The effectiveness of communication depends greatly on the honesty and competence of the communicators; for instance, the least competent are often inclined to do the most talking to compensate for their inability or to cater to their egos. Excess communication reduces the work done; people complain if the service is bad. One form of communication often cancels out another form, and people inevitably wonder what the net gain, if any, was in relation to the effort. People are not as inclined to accept other people's advice and orders as others are to give them, and they do not appreciate service to the extent that those who provide it think they should. If, therefore, there is too much participation, acceptance and appreciation lag behind and the society appears to suffer from disinterest and ingratitude. Togetherness is destroyed, not developed, by close proximity and over-dependence.

The activities of meddlers may aggravate a pernicious idea that often accompanies close proximity and over-dependence. This idea holds that no one should have what someone else does not have, and sometimes goes so far as to insist that no one should have what someone else does not want him to have. The result of this idea is always a growing desire on the part first of individuals, then of groups, and finally of society, to concentrate, not on doing things, but on preventing others from doing things. Society then becomes negative, its business obstructed by too many obstacles, and the participation of its citizens frustrating and joyless.

Any group or individual can regard the affairs of any other as its or his business. What the chemist does affects the grocer, and what the Royal Society thinks has some bearing on the Chamber of Commerce. Anyone can find a close relationship with the government, with educational institutions or big business. He has a stake in their affairs and therefore is presumed to have a right to participate in them. This right is a valuable principle of democracy, so valuable in fact that it is not safe to leave it in the hands of professional participators, because professional participators, that is those who make a habit or hobby of participation, become one-way. They direct their efforts toward the business of others, but rarely permit others to question their credentials or to meddle in their business. Freedom to participate is too often accompanied by freedom from someone else's participation. Moreover participation is usually ineffective without knowledge, good faith, work, and the sharing of responsibility, a fact too many participators neglect. Anyone who has tangled with a radical protest or a political witch hunt knows how readily the rights of one group can be trampled by the participatory rights of the other, always in the name of some good. And anyone who has watched chronic meddlers in action knows that they are invariably undemocratic in their interference with others. The danger, which many participants neglect until too late, is that the right to participate can be killed by abuse or by its use by the wrong people.

The wrong people would be impossible to identify and they would vary from issue to issue. But contemporary unrest, which features the sincere and productive efforts of many reformers, also reveals three groups that endanger the right of participation by abusing it or by using the right for the wrong reasons. The first comprises people who participate for the sake of the participation, regardless of the merits of the issue or their knowledge of it. Any issue will do as long as they are part of it, and they are not inclined to examine the merits of the cause or to ask if they can make any contribution at all. If, for example, one wanted to start an agitation for the right of red-headed men to dye their hair black it would be simple to recruit an organization from society's supply of joiners, and then, with their enthusiasm suitably fired, to steer them into insisting that all red-heads *must* dye their hair. Later, if red hair became fashionable again, the same people would rush to any cause promoting it. Indeed an institution or society should be suspicious of people who ostentatiously take up too many causes. They are usually involved for selfish reasons, not for service, and their participation is not worth the trouble they invariably provoke. These people who fancy a challenge in every issue and pour forth their sympathy indiscriminately are sometimes called 'bleeding hearts.' We might even call them social haemophiliacs; bruising too readily, they make society itself chronically feverish and weak.

The second group consists of authoritarians, both conservative and liberal, both left and right. No one can plead the right of participation better than those who delight in telling other people what to do or in running other people's lives. They cannot be told there are two sides to an issue; to them there is one side, *their* side. They are angry if asked the basis of their intervention; their mere desire is sufficient justification. Any suggestion that they may be wrong is an insult to them or their cause. Participatory democracy gives them ample scope for arrogance, but, if they succeed, participation quickly dies because they urge authoritarian remedies for democratic problems.

The third group, already mentioned, includes those whose motivation for participation is a tendency to escape from their own work or to compensate for their own problems. Whether it is a parent who neglects a family for a round of social work, or a country that avoids trouble or inefficiency in its own sphere by invading another, the effect is the same – the new activity is often futile and the contributions almost always offset by the neglect of the legitimate activity. People who cannot mind their own business are rarely equipped to mind that of others and when they try they nearly always do it badly. Productive social action therefore includes the art of knowing when *not* to mind other people's business.

Some people have to be put in a position where they cannot mind other people's business, because in any activity a few can spoil participation for the many. Almost all meddlers fall into this category. An old army comment provides a generally applicable illustration. Officers, it ran, can be divided into four classes: 'the clever, the stupid, the industrious and the lazy. Every officer possesses at least two of these qualities. Those who are clever and industrious are fitted for high staff appointments; use can be made of those who are stupid and lazy. The man who is clever and lazy is fitted for the highest command; he has the temperament and the requisite nerve to deal with all situations. But whoever is stupid and industrious is a danger and must be removed immediately.'[4]

An army can remove the stupid and industrious. But they are the very people most difficult to remove in a government, a university, a church, or a professional or social organization. The more participation is featured, the less effective it will be if special provisions are not made, first to enable such people in all categories of society to reveal themselves harmlessly, and then to occupy them with activities to release their energies, sustain their egos, and render harmless their mistakes. In short, they have status and rights in participatory democracy, but they must not be allowed to destroy the status and rights of everyone else.

Some devotees of participatory democracy may say that these people need scope to participate so that their interest and perception may increase and their participation may become effective. Society pays too high a price for this fine but unworkable theory. Indeed many of the things most criticized in society are the results of the efforts of the stupid and industrious. Their interest actually needs to be reduced so that their deficient perception may be confined to what they can do well. They and their spouses, children, and colleagues would be happier, and their institutions and fellow citizens would be spared much trouble.

But, it may be asked, is this attitude not undemocratic? My answer is 'no,' because it permits other people in all categories of society to participate more effectively. Democracy is discouraged, not simply by authoritarianism, but by the kind of participation that bores, whines, frustrates, interferes, and, because society can only stand so much participation, crowds out. Democracy, like any system, must prove itself, get its business done properly, and keep its people happy, and the efforts of the stupid and industrious are not good examples of what it can do. A democratic society wishes to advance in some way. This it cannot do if it spends too much time imposing and overcoming obstacles, looking for faults and complaining, remedying mistakes, and cooling down chronically over-heated people. Furthermore, if the democratic rights of the latter are exercised in an undemocratic fashion, as they so often are, democracy itself is weakened and then destroyed.

The idea that perception can be increased by practice in participation and by the availability of information is not always true. Some people can learn from experience and profit from acquiring knowledge. For others, including the chronic meddlers of all kinds, this is rarely true. Participatory and informatory apparatus must necessarily be limited because a society can only afford and tolerate so much of it. The first category of people justifies it. But the second does not, and for them diversions are a cheaper and, because less bureaucracy is involved, more democratic alternative.

We should note again that participation always involves reactions to it. If it is taken too seriously – and social butterflies, hyperactive bureaucrats, and reformers with an itch rather than a conviction · are often guilty of presumption – participation may invoke impatience and dislike. If this reaction becomes too widespread democracy will lose first its trust, then its credibility, and finally its will to participate at all.

All this suggests that the rights associated with participatory democracy are most effective if used in moderation and if qualified. Instantly one thinks of certain curbs on its use, such as the necessity of prohibiting the right of free speech in slander, or qualifications like the right to call 'fire!' in a theatre only if there is a fire. Curbs and qualifications are not easy in social action, however, for they can be wrong just as easily as right, and it is impossible to find people who are infallible judges. Who is to shackle a profession or a group that takes itself too seriously, or is wrong or even unnecessary? Many organizations from governments to ladies' aids need to be told such things from time to time, but controls are rarely the appropriate means.

I believe one answer is the inclusion of laymen on professional boards, even, and perhaps especially, when the work is technical, so that people and organizations can talk to one another as individuals as well as groups, so that society's work can be done with a combination of group and individual thinking, and so that people who are interested in how things are done can be joined by those who ask why. If people want to participate let them pitch in and share responsibility as part of a team. Some are not prepared to do this, either because they cannot or because they prefer talking to acting. For them some colourful diversions are useful.

Another answer is two-way participatory democracy. Once one group decides to participate in the work of another group the second group should have the same right towards the first. Indeed it is only democratic that the second group should have as much right to state its case before that decision is made as the first group has to make the decision. And it is only efficient for each to ask how well prepared the participators are to participate.

When, for example, a group starts the social heather afire with inflammatory action against another group, society, especially the press, should provide the second group with a chance to state its case simultaneously. When students seek places on the board of governors or the senate of a university it should be the right of the governors and the faculty to be represented on the students' council. For parents to take an interest in the affairs of the schools is not enough; school authorities should be able to tell parents the effects of their home life on their children, a process far too many parents will not accept. People who appear before fact-finding bodies should be prepared, not just to express opinions, but also to undergo questioning. Individuals who only turn up at meetings or in the galleries of legislatures when something controversial is being discussed may well be asked where they were when business of a positive nature was being done. Social action invites reaction and, if it is not two-way at the start, the reaction will come later and defeat the original action. Furthermore, if one-way social action proceeds untested, the lunatic fringe has a heyday resenting and preventing legitimate response, what they call reactionary participation, and advocating much irrelevant nonsense and perhaps ensuring it only because a democratic response could not be made.

The right of participation is affected further by the interventions of weak people without the courage to face obstacles or the patience to complete responsibilities. Talk is often a brave front for the weak, especially group talk in which they are afraid to speak out against fashion or hysteria, and they easily talk society into impossible situations which they abandon without conscience when the going gets rough. They become quislings upon finding themselves on an unpopular tack or being wooed by oppositions that have sensed their weakness and offered popular or exciting alternatives. Cowardice is a common vice in social affairs. It causes little trouble if the cowards mind their own business. Once they venture out, however, they are as destructive as any extremist because efforts built on their support soon collapse, and leaders relying on them are so often stabbed in the back. With friends like these, many leaders have lamented, who needs enemies?

With all its virtues participatory democracy provides ample camouflage for cowards, both group and individual, and every time they betray their trust they weaken the right of participation itself. The healthiest form of social debate is that between dynamic participants of any kind who are prepared to talk and act for their causes and accept the consequent work, whether they end up right or wrong. The sickest form is that of social jellyfish who float with the tides of popularity and the eddies of fortune, stinging anyone who embraces them, and, if opposed, seeking opportunities to make martyrs of themselves. These, it must be noted, are not the uncommitted or those who change their minds with conviction; they are the betrayers whose talk and social interest can be purchased for thirty pieces of anyone's silver. It is alarming to note the part which they play in the destruction of institutions and the failure of reform. It is also sad to note how quickly they are dropped by those who use them, and how disillusioned they become, not with themselves, but with the society they have betrayed. There is a further reason for emphasizing the two-way nature of participation and the need for acceptance of the responsibilities of participation as well as the right to talk. Cowards will stick with a one-way participation; but rarely will they involve themselves in a two-way one for fear of being on the wrong side. They will flock to a talking project; but seldom will they become involved if they sense obstacles and hard work.

Cowardice is a major obstacle to effective opposition in a democracy. Cowards will always join an opposition if, like jackals, they can spring when the quarry is weak and other jackals are around. This is not real opposition. On the other hand the most effective opposition, requiring courage, is that which speaks out honestly against the clamour of the crowd, the pressure of authority, or the dictates of fashion. This kind is rare, and its rarity is one of democracy's weaknesses. To oppose the voice of the people, and anyone can pose as speaking for the people, may be called undemocratic. But the people need frankness as well as acquiescence. To oppose the voice of authority, all alone and after careful thought, is to jeopardize a career and, in some countries, to forfeit one's life. The consequences of a scarcity of courageous opposition is obvious throughout the world. The inability to advise frankly dictators and their regimes is well known, but it is no different in fact from the reluctance to advise democrats. 'It would be hard to overestimate,' wrote a well known reporter, 'the burden of sorrow carried by America in this last generation because of the advice or silence of men who didn't say what they honestly thought, who were too modest or too timid or too ambitious or too inarticulate to speak out effectively at the critical moment of national decision.'[5] It is everywhere easy to fawn or to grouch but difficult to speak with courage.

This problem destroys the confidence which is essential to progress. The public and its authorities must give their confidence to social organizations if the latter are to do their work happily and to the limit of their capability. And this confidence must be deserved. Work breaks down if confidence is lost. Loss of confidence resulting from mistakes or bad management is serious, but it can be remedied by correcting the mistakes and bringing in new people. But loss of confidence resulting from suspicions of irresponsibility and cowardice, well founded or not, is most difficult to remedy, because this kind of loss is very hard to make up. If the breaking point which exists in love, trust, confidence, and all such intangibles is reached, the loss can never be made up. No people are better at driving organizations to the breaking point than members of the lunatic fringe. This is the main reason society cannot afford to let the lunatic fringe go too far without stopping it, which it may be unable to do, or diverting it into harmless social by-passes and mazes.

The rights of participation backed by conviction and desire to share real responsibility and of participation backed by band-wagon emotionalism and meddling can be observed clashing in the contemporary media. The media are just as affected by collective peculiarities as any other profession or group. Newspapermen and radio and television personnel are made up of the same mixture of competent, mediocre, and weak people. They reflect what goes on in society and make major contributions to it. Indeed, when it comes to participating, the media must have an almost unfettered right, subject only to the law.

The press reflects society, not as a mirror, but as a set of mirrors at various times reflecting faithfully, magnifying, or minimizing. Unfortunately for participatory democracy reflecting faithfully is not always possible or fruitful. Newspapers have not enough staff or space, and readers are often bored with reality. Magnifying is much more titillating, and there is a natural tendency to minimize, or omit altogether, what is not titillating. This enormous problem has often been discussed, but two aspects of it may be presented here because they aggravate professional and group difficulties.

The first of these is an emphasis on one direction of a two-way participatory democracy – and that is the negative direction. If two people or groups speak, one attacking, one defending confederation in Canada, the European Common Market, the universities, the doctors, or a politician in trouble, the attack gets far more attention and prime space than the defence. Perhaps it is because the press is more interested in featuring as 'news' the unusual or the social knight on crusade, or perhaps it is because the readers like such diversions.[6] The simple fact is that the result is predominantly negative because trouble is featured, success is not; and attack is encouraged by front-page publicity while defence is frustrated by silence or space on the inside page. Man in society is like man in a family; if spoilt children get too much notice when they throw tantrums, and sensible children who fulfil their responsibilities are ignored, the family may suffer psychological ailments and the future of both kinds of children may be jeopardized. If one wishes to get attention from the contemporary press, it pays to throw tantrums. The world has problems, of course, but it is a far happier place, and there are more achievements going on in it, than a reading of the contemporary press would indicate.

The second aspect is the fact that freedom of the press is like any other kind of freedom; it can die because its possessors take advantage of it or gird it with professional righteousness which invites interference. Society cannot afford either the suppression of its media or a titillating approach because, in either instance, the people will ultimately believe nothing they are told which is just as bad as accepting everything. An alternative to the first is greater participation by laymen on the boards of newspapers; newspapers are too important to leave to newspapermen alone or to entrust to government control. A remedy for the second is similar to what is often suggested by newspapers for other people – an invasion of privacy in the public interest in the form of by-lines for every story and editorial contained in every paper. No group is more involved in participatory democracy than the press, and, since anonymity in other activities is usually frowned on because participants are more careful when known, the by-line appears sensible. Moreover, since there is a wide range of talents, from great reporters to casual employees, the public can read with discrimination when they know who is informing them, even when they understand only that it is not the paper informing them but just Bill Smith.

The debilitating effects of excess professionalism and pseudo-professionalism as well as ill-considered participatory democracy can be illustrated by people who, without justification, consider themselves intellectuals and members of the intelligentsia. Both intellectuals, or enlightened people, and the intelligentsia, or those who aspire to independent thinking, are in all parts of society and are not confined to scholars or professional people. The number who are true members of both groups is not great and membership is not easily defined. Their service to society is enormous.

The service of the great majority of people in activities associated with intellectual pursuits varies greatly from able to weak. Most of them work away without personal delusions or pretentions of intellectualism, although occasionally they will act too seriously as professional groups. But there are some who are neither intellectuals nor part of the intelligentsia who consider themselves as being within those select circles. They are pseudo-intellectuals, although they are insulted when that label is applied. Actually 'intellectual' is one of the easiest labels to apply or assume. It is harmless if those who bear it do not take themselves too seriously. Otherwise it disguises much nonsense and thwarts much intelligence. When it is ascribed to a whole profession, such as teachers, professors, and clergymen, the profession itself suffers delusions and the rest of the population is misled. The consequence is described in the apt French phrase *faire un pas de clerc* – to make a blunder.

The real intellectual (to use the common term for both categories) combines courage with his insights and applies his intellect most severely to his own conclusions. It takes courage to seek reality and special courage to assess oneself. The commonest mistake of pseudo-intellectuals who are overly impressed with themselves is to assess inadequately the facts of a situation in relation to their own knowledge, capabilities, and motives. Courage is especially necessary to independent thinking, which, in contrast to mere sycophancy and undisciplined irregularity, is the hardest of all attributes to master. The result of weakness and irregularity in pseudo-intellectual circles is memorialized, after the long sad experience of history, in another French phrase, *la trahison des clercs* – the treachery or treason of the intellectuals.

Real intellectuals are not inclined to treachery because they seek the philosophical explanations of underlying ideas, including their own, and their results are not based on fashion or a dependence on benedictions from any source. People know where they stand whether they agree with them or not. Pseudo-intellectuals, on the other hand, are inclined to the rationalization of passing phenomena. They can be depended upon to produce a philosophy to justify any action of authority or rebellion, any intellectual fashion, any peculiarity of society, or any whim of their own. A war or crisis reveals them as they change their ideas from master to master, event to event, and after the upheaval they and their ideas stand discredited. There are many such waiverers among the clergy and professors, as both the great wars and contemporary troubles in church and university indicate, but they are joined by counterparts in every profession and group. The problem is not lack of intelligence, but lack of courage – the courage to make up or change one's mind, and to speak or be quiet as the facts of a situation and the motives of people are clearly assessed.

The interventions of over-serious pseudo-intellectuals, always dangerous, are particularly troublesome in totalitarian systems on the one hand and in participatory democracy on the other, because there are in both systems more scope for their activity and less means of checking on them. In democracy they have the right 'to do their own thing' like everyone else. But the arrogance which often accompanies pseudo-intellectualism protects them when the participation is one-way. That arrogance may even subordinate intellectualism altogether, and, for that reason, is rarely noted in the real intellectual. When naivity, which often accompanies genius, is also an attribute of the pseudo-intellectuals, the arrogance is reinforced still more because naivety, which is excellent when it can be questioned, becomes stupidity when accepted as purity of thought.

Lack of practical experience often renders useless the theoretical ideas of pseudo-intellectual participators. The real intellectuals may produce splendid ideas by disciplined thought and observation alone. But the pseudo-intellectuals usually cannot and do not. Most know when to talk and when to be silent. But it is pathetic, for example, to see the more talkative of the highly but narrowly trained social scientists and philosophers loudly proclaiming nostrums and offering advice and criticism without the slightest experience in managing men and institutions or settling problems. Too many of this type, in Clement Attlee's words, 'can be trusted to take the wrong view on any subject,'[7] and each, according to Richard Nixon, can become 'a sitting duck for every half-baked idea or time-worn cliché that comes along.'[8] They tend to become negative in their social outlooks and pontificate smugly, like 'too many young pianists who go to concerts,' as the great piano teacher, Rosina Lhevinne, said, 'not to listen to the music but to count the pianist's mistakes.'[9] Their research, writing, and teaching are inclined to be fuzzy because, they have not tested their theories in practice and are inclined to bury their shortcomings under a mass of jargon, perhaps even under pretentions of infallibility. They may carry their deficiencies into politics. 'We had among us,' writes an experienced party whip of some other politicians of his own party, 'those deep thinkers whose mental processes will not follow the normal, sensible course of other people, lest that should relegate them to the level of the ordinary and let others forget how clever they are. Such people I find are almost always wrong.'[10] Foreign affairs is especially vulnerable to pseudo-intellectual observations. 'I am astonished,' writes one authority, 'by the arrogance of some of my academic colleagues who claim, on the basis of one-sided experience, superiority to the diplomat in both morality and the ability to discern the truth about the complex relations of men and nations.'[11] Their impact on other affairs may also be ineffective. Many of them, for example, get so flattered and flustered when asked to assist a government that they produce nonsense or tailor what they produce to suit what they think the government would like. Even when serious in their service, they are often frustrated by the fact that many of them are far more competent at analysis than at synthesis. Splendid opportunities to watch them in action are furnished by royal commission hearings and other such forums where the more irresponsible of them almost always damage the cause they have come to expound.

One may cite examples of this phenomenon in many organizations, of which the university is one. How often the resulting chaos was revealed in universities in the 1960s, not because there was dissent, but because dissent was one-way and fashionable and because the normal restraints of supply and demand were lifted for both professors and students. It was not difficult to separate the real dissenting intellectuals who took stands on the basis of judgment combined with courage from the pseudo-intellectuals who rode band wagons in opposite directions while proclaiming conflicting rights and making philosophical justifications for every passing fancy. This is one reason why dissenting students turned on their professors, having understood the treachery of certain minorities of vocal academics in confrontations with administrators, and why, when the normal restraints of supply and demand returned, governments and the public questioned academic freedom and tenure and sought to increase external controls on the universities themselves. This is also why authorities and the public became impatient with student power after it was abused by an arrogant minority who neglected their responsibilities.[12] Unfortunately the great majority of sensible professors and students, loyal to liberty and free speech, were unable to silence or divert those who abused both.

It is a tragedy that the universities, their administrators, and the majority of professors and students have had to suffer the repeated phenomena of the various revolutions, of the Kaiser's and Hitler's Germany, of the fall of France, and of other upheavals where *la trahison des clercs* has reduced the credibility of an entire profession.[13] This problem affects other professions and groups, and governments themselves, but they are not as inclined on their own to invoke pseudo-intellectualism and with it arrogance and naivety. They can always find professors, clergymen, and social activists to invoke these for them, and later they and the public can blame them when things go wrong. Intellectuals who are simply wrong are forgiven as quickly as anyone else after a crisis. But pseudo-intellectuals who are treacherous weaken permanently the foundations of the house of intellect.

They do it, not only by causing the same excessive politics and administration which the lunatic fringe makes necessary in all organizations, and not only by thoughtless interventions in the things they know little about, but also by encouraging the activities of anti-intellectuals. A society always contains a number of these. Often they are merely the suspicious or arrogant who tend to think ignorance a virtue or knowledge a mystery. But they also include many who have been aroused, not by the power of the intellectuals, but by the mischief of the pseudo-intellectuals. Whether professor, clergyman, or politician, the pseudo-intellectual teaches a powerful lesson, not when he is wrong, but when he betrays his trust. His own institution and his colleagues thereupon pay a heavy penalty, because, once more, they tend to be more readily blamed for the trespasses of the stupid among them than praised for the achievements of the wise.

It is at this point that the pseudo-intellectual becomes futile, confused, and aggressive as he defends himself. He has taken his ideas too seriously. But, what is much worse, he has taken himself too seriously by ascribing the virtues of his ideas to himself and imposing himself on others along with the ideas. This arrogance is similar to that of the dogmatist. Whereas the real intellectual takes his ideas most seriously but does not tend to promote himself with them, the pseudo-intellectual frequently destroys any chance he has of gaining acceptance for his ideas by personally getting in their way. This arrogance may be provoked by the inexperience and psychological weaknesses of the pseudo-intellectual rather than the merits of his ideas. In any social ferment it is not difficult to note what one parliamentarian called 'the never-ending guilt which plagues the conscience of so many intellectuals.'[14] It is a common and terrible thing to watch, and it needs careful assessment by those who would protect and preserve the house of intellect.

Successful remedies have not been found. Government control is always wrong because political and bureaucratic expediency are injurious to intellectual activity, and governments frequently invoke and support anti-intellectualism for their own convenience. Popular mandates are unreliable because they are fickle and contradictory. Internal autocracy is uncertain because its wisdom cannot be guaranteed. Internal professional regulation works spasmodically, and only when individualism is permitted to flourish along with collectivism. Actually all intellectuals need to be assessed with those slogans mentioned earlier: 'credentials please'; 'what business is it of yours?'; and 'put up or shut up.' When they are questioned thus pseudo-intellectuals soon reveal themselves – and inevitably to their own disadvantage. Any idea that their opinions in public matters are worth more attention because they are 'experts' in their fields is folly. They must have freedom of speech, but because some of them seem not to know when to speak, society, including their colleagues, must question rigorously their utterances. Nonsense does not become virtuous because it is professional.

There was not enough of this questioning in the 1960s, when almost any nonsense was treated as 'legitimate' in pseudo-intellectual circles and featured in the headlines. The nonsense had scope because it was not considered fashionable and democratic to talk back to assumed arbiters of fashion and democracy. Dissent from dissenters was not regarded as being 'with it,' and intellectualism itself suffered. So did democracy, because pseudo-intellectualism is not democratic when it is arbitrary.

There are two antidotes to pseudo-intellectualism. One is a supply of colourful diversions. Pseudo-intellectuals have an urge to be colourful anyway, and it is much safer for society to have them on merry-go-rounds than on bandwagons.

The second antidote is responsibility encouraged by colleagues and interested laymen. What pseudo-intellectuals say must be taken with many grains of salt because the most talkative of them usually have only narrow knowledge and experience. As in other activities, the presence of laymen within the profession is a valuable salt shaker. This presence is illustrated in universities, and the same facts are applicable in civil service departments. Scholars within academic departments can be kept responsible by contacts with those of other departments. When disciplines are too compartmentalized, however, some professors soon get so esoteric and so addicted to jargon that they can talk only to other professors in the same subject, and this intellectual inbreeding encourages the arrogance of little empires. Departmental autonomy needs inter-departmental influence. The presence of laymen on boards of governors meets the same need. The business of the universities is too important to be left to professors and students who have no higher proportion of their number skilled in policy and business than have the other professions. For them too participatory democracy must be two-way. And academic freedom is too great a principle to be misused by the small number of academics and students who consider it an invitation to license, and who take themselves too seriously.

As for intellectuals themselves, they, like everyone else, need to be questioned to ascertain whether they really are intellectuals; it is not necessary to control them, but to challenge them and screen their ideas through different media to test their integrity. It is when they are challenged that they work best, that their best ideas get accepted. Fifty professors, like fifty doctors, or politicians, or labouring men, or farmers, can be stampeded into any resolution or action when they act alone. They are typical of all groups of people in a highly collectivized society which tends to regard any participation as 'legitimate.' They often need to be reminded of that famous and essential comment: 'But the King has no clothes on.'

There is, however, a defence which all groups in any society use with vigour and vehemence. 'We have,' they proclaim, 'our principles.' This defence we should now examine.

Principles

Democracy has long featured the right to question the ideas and actions of those who organize people and wield power. This right receives recognition in several ways in the institutions of men. The reason is simple: men, ideas, and actions can be wrong as well as right, and society requires some protection against mistakes and people's tendency to consider themselves right. Questioning does not prevent mistakes, but at least it reduces the possibility of making them, and, after they have occurred, of repeating them, by forcing consideration of differing views. Participatory democracy has carried the questioning further than usual. Cherished ideas and institutions have been attacked throughout the world with persistent probing and even violence amid the enthusiasm of reformers and the regrets of defenders of beleaguered traditions. Certainly many of the excitements are vapourings of the emotional who jump on ego-satisfying bandwagons or relish mutiny. But many are deeper and more sensible in origin, revolts against greatly honoured, but nonetheless dangerous, principles which have proved obstacles to man's happiness and progress by making his politics lethal and his postures unnatural.

The principle is one of the commonest elements in all politics, and many principles are used as mere postures. Contrary to a belief that politics is distinguished by an absence of principles, it is as much an interaction of principles as of people. Sometimes people dominate this activity. Sometimes principles dominate, and that is usually when the most serious troubles occur. People can be mere servants of principles and principles mere extensions of people. Principles coexist and conflict, and can be arranged and rearranged to provide tantalizing variations in harmony and violence. The word *principle* is so overworked and principles are taken so seriously that we should consider why we have them in the first place and how they work in practice. We must ensure that participatory democracy does not succeed only in replacing wrong principles with other wrong principles. If it were also to destroy good principles in the process, it will have only unhappiness to show for the effort. Man is a negotiating species and principles are instruments of negotiation. His acts involve discussing and arranging with others and calculating with himself. While his affairs change continuously with war, revolution, and fashion, he suspects that there lies undiscovered under the changes a basic natural pattern of attitudes and relationships, like the atomic structure of matter, and a vague 'human nature' does suggest its existence. Man therefore has sought a set of fundamental laws under which humans should live. No one has found them yet. The search for such truths may be long, and man recognizes certain substitutes for them with which to make do in the meantime. These substitutes are principles, that is, codes as guides to thought and conduct.

The instinct for something fundamental prompts men to put great theoretical emphasis on principles, perhaps even to consider them actually to be natural law. But the fact that principles are still substitutes causes variation in their acceptance and use. They conflict; holders of one principle can interpret it to mean anything, even its opposite; and their impact changes with fashion. This variation makes men more inclined to proclaim, promote, and defend principles than to live by them.

Men base their institutions on principles which they proclaim vigorously and use as ideological pedestals on which any stance looks well. Government founded on democracy, economics developed on communist interpretations of history, society based on racial or nationalistic supremacy, and ecclesiastical organizations based on special relationships with God – all testify to the power of principles. This power provokes men to extremes, even to killing one another, with the mere theoretical adherence to principles perhaps furnishing the only excuse. Yet men may adhere so strongly in theory that they refuse to question or discuss a 'matter of principle,' even when they do not understand it, when they violate it in practice, or when it brings them and others to degradation or death.

One cause of this clash of principles is a tendency of many devotees to neglect relationships between theory and reality, perhaps even to be totally blind to them, in the interest of developing, interpreting, advocating, and defending theory itself. This neglect may be carried to the point where reality is ignored altogether, especially where human nature is totally unable to cope with the theory, and theorizing becomes just intellectual exercise complicated by jargon and unaccompanied by practical experience. Like playing games with the rules of games, such an exercise may be beneficial and useful in moderation. But it is dangerous if it is mistaken for game playing itself. It is often so mistaken in theology and political theory, especially by inexperienced pseudo-intellectuals. The results are disastrous when an esoteric dogma or an over-refined and brittle ideology is touted as the latest password to heaven or cure for social ills on earth, to be promoted as truth against other dogmas and ideologies and the people who hold them.[1] Indeed it is at once the disadvantage and tragedy of theories that extreme devotees turn them from useful guides to action into idols for fanatic veneration.

These phenomena obscure other reasons for principles such as the use of power, physical and geographic factors, insecurity, and ambition. 'Divine right' of leaders, for example, is both an old and honoured principle and a shrewd means of commanding obedience. 'My country right or wrong' is noble compared to 'the political ambitions of my government.' Divine auspices is declared as a principle in some form by both sides in every war and denominational conflict, not because the combatants have a sound basis for believing it, but because it is a cloak for all doubts and a better justification for action and death than the mere commands of leaders. 'Honour thy father and thy mother' is a splendid principle, but the practices which some parents use it to support for egotistical reasons cause many psychiatric problems.

Proponents may elevate mere policies, practices, and opinions to the status of principles because of the ferocity with which people will then defend them. Indeed this elevation is often a variation of the old process of 'saving face.' People dislike being proved wrong in the sense of being mistaken; but they do not mind being wrong in the moral sense if there is a principle to provide protection. If it is impressive enough, almost any means can be justified and any mistake excused in its support. This easy use of principles ultimately goes beyond the mere camouflaging of mistakes to the actual disguising and justifying of wrong doing itself. A famous clergyman and a prime minister agreed on this tendency. 'It seems to be a fact of life,' said Dr Martin Luther King, 'that human beings cannot continue to do wrong without eventually reaching out for some thin rationalization to clothe an óbvious wrong in the beautiful garments of righteousness.'[2] Lord Salisbury went further: 'Theories, though they never inspire with enthusiasm any considerable mass of human beings, are yet prized for throwing a veil of decency over the naked passions by which political convulsions are brought about.'[3] No doubt these views would be shared with regret by the very men who first proclaimed the principles if they could have lived to see how they were distorted and used.

There are, therefore, two uses of principles. First they provide codes for thought and conduct for believers to follow. This use is the one people like to think they serve. Second they provide a strategy and justification for whatever action the holder may find convenient. The difference can be noted in any issue: some people participate because they have deep feelings and sincere beliefs; others see an opportunity to serve themselves. In practice, therefore, there is sharp difference between a principle and a belief. The first is what a man says he believes in; the second is what he actually believes.

The use of principles makes necessary many compensations for them. Sometimes the principles are unworkable in practice, or their consequences are so bad that complicated action is necessary every time they are invoked. In cases of conflicting principles men may expend more energy on proselytizing and outdoing other men than they devote to following the principles, and proselytizing invokes reactions which demand still more energy. Such rivalry does not even need conflicting principles to stimulate it: conflicting interpretations of one principle are sufficient. Indeed the free use of principles and their interpretations as a means of meddling in other people's business and justifying belligerence is a tragedy of the species. An organization set up to serve a principle may grow to the point where most of its activity keeps itself going or extends its power, while the principle, always the *raison d'être,* suffers increasing neglect. At the individual level people may be unable to meet the requirements of the principles they profess and, while stoutly professing them, seek many escapes. They may not actually believe their professed principles but they do not dare to admit it. They may even owe allegiance only to a name, thus backing principles of which they know nothing; then they really have no principles at all, although they would be insulted if told so.

Principles can be divided into two categories, negotiable ones and non-negotiable ones. These categories have always existed, but the use of the word 'negotiable' in this context is recent. A negotiable principle is one that can be discussed in a spirit of explanation, justification, compromise, and agreement. A non-negotiable principle is a fixed, accepted one which is assumed to be neither debatable nor changeable and which requires no further justification. Each type commands its own kind of loyalty and makes its own special impact on men and society.

Too much theoretical emphasis on principles tends to render them non-negotiable as if they really were natural laws. Then people 'respect,' 'stand up for,' 'stick by,' and fight and die for their principles. This natural attitude may produce happiness and progress when men understand their principles, know why they hold them, live up to them in practice, and understand and respect the principles of others. It is little better than mischievous presumption, on the other hand, when men profess principles only because they have accepted them unthinkingly from other people; when they regard mere professing to be adequate loyalty and conveniently ignore the requirements of principles that prove awkward or burdensome; when they consider they serve their principles by destroying those of others; and when they insist their principles are not just principles but *the truth.* It is also little better than stupid self-delusion when men combine what is a mere habit or prejudice with stubbornness and call it a cherished principle. It is dishonest, too, if they raise a mere want to the status of a right and insist on it as a matter of principle. Indeed the more men profess principles the less likely they are to understand them and the less inclined they are to live by them. Those who *know* they are right most readily commit wrong, and the fanatic and the bigot are the ultimate enemies of principles, including the ones they profess.

The reason is not hard to find. In a given field of ideas principles that are distinguishable when moderately emphasized become alike as the emphasis increases further. A bigot is ultimately no more religious than an anti-religious fanatic. One who is on the extreme left in politics is similar in his ideas to one who is on the extreme right. Extremists on either side in most upheavals show similar values and desires. A scale of ideological differences is not linear; it is circular, and the extremes meet. They do not meet in harmony, despite their similarity, because they have approached the meeting point from opposite sides of the circle, and they pay lip service more and more to the form but less and less to the spirit of their ideologies. It is because forms clash and spirits cooperate when emphasized that 'moderation in all things' has been so ancient and so successful a policy.

Moderation is to be found in the use of negotiable principles. They are more useful substitutes for elusive fundamental truth. They do not obstruct the search for truth by assuming its guise and blocking further investigation. If they are wrong, and many principles have been so found, they are not perpetuated. They clash less violently with one another. They are better suited to men who hold principles without understanding why. They cause less conflict because they are not taken so seriously and cannot be used as readily as face savers or as excuses for evil or incompetence. As long as a principle is negotiable it can serve men as a substitute for truth and a means of reaching out further for it. When a principle becomes non-negotiable men are diverted from further search.

This distinction is the test of negotiability, which is not a flexibility encouraging wishywashy adherence to the unstable; rather it is a state of allegiance undergoing testing by contact with others and use in practice. One can revere a principle and stand up for it while improving it; or one can enshrine it by making it non-negotiable and then do both it and its possessor harm by resisting further change. The difference is indicated on the one hand by totalitarianism which tends to glorify principles in rigid unquestioning attitudes, and on the other hand by a combination of freedom and responsibility which tends to permit judgment, discussion, and experiment. The difference can also be noted in complicated negotiations among men; successful negotiators usually try to keep contestants from taking non-negotiable stands, based on principle, from which there is no retreat.

Many of man's problems are caused by allegiance to non-negotiable principles which, if they were not enshrined, could not stand up to competition with other principles or to frank appraisal of their own merits. They produce evils, rarely discussed, which on balance may outnumber or destroy the benefits. Fearful prices are paid by civilization for the glory of theories and creeds; high costs in doubt, in sorrow, and in irrationality have been the lot of countless individuals caught in dogmatic slavery. It is not ignorance that produces this phenomenon; men have been repeating their mistakes. It is emphasis on principle to the point where men sacrifice practice to myth, and court disaster rather than lose face. Then they fight over the principles. Men, like animals, will always fight. But, whereas animals usually break off before killing their adversaries in contests with their own kind, men have principles which make it mandatory to fight to the death. Indeed men do not actually fight by direct personal contact; if they did they would likely follow animal practice. They use weapons which lure them into fights, and the most potent and lethal of these is the principle.

Men bolster their status by proclaiming allegiance to principles. This support is natural and it is often sensible; it is an old axiom that it is better to stand for something than to fall for anything. But how is this bolstering done? Is it the attitude: 'We stand for our opinions of what is right; others have theirs; both sets of opinions are simply opinions in their own settings and we will mingle and let our opinions mingle and compete with one another; we will remain above the opinions?' Or is it the attitude: 'We stand for the right; we will not question it; we cannot back down if our idea of right clashes with those of others; we have a duty to impose what we think is right on others; we must protect our stand by crushing opposition and not count the cost; we will make practice fit our principles because right must prevail?' Parliamentary government makes this distinction and attempts to encourage the first attitude by admitting differences of sincerely held opinions and giving official status to opposition. Whatever its limitations in this duty, it is also designed to discourage the second attitude; its mere existence is an admission of the fallibility of rulers and the negotiability of their policies. Being able to make this admission is a major step in man's political progress.

This admission is not general in society. If it were people would attend different churches to hear a variety of doctrines, or perhaps invite clergymen of different faiths to attend their church to offer rebuttal to the regular preacher. School officials and teachers would permit alternative opinions on controversial topics. People would consider it unfair to accept a principle as a basis for opposing another principle unless they heard the other side; war, for instance, they would not tolerate after hearing only one side and their leaders' interpretation of the other. Alas, however, it is the 'hard line' that prevails; dialogue is the debating of principles rather than the assessing, accommodating, and perhaps discarding of principles. And opinion is too often not really opinion, but the acceptance of propaganda designed to reinforce principles, and of compromise designed to compensate for them.

A dangerous characteristic of a non-negotiable principle is its tendency to divide into others. A dogma readily splits into sections which energetically develop new non-negotiable principles to reinforce themselves. Rigid principles break clean. Negotiable principles may undergo the same stresses, but they bend rather than break, and if they do break the sections tend to maintain an association as long as they are negotiable. This process is evident in the beginning of all wars and in the break-up of both empires and marriages. Non-negotiable principles also increase by encouraging reactions. This is why totalitarianism in any form has never worked for long. Its non-negotiable principles create reasons for opposing ones, and thereby invite the inevitable clash.

We must return to the reluctance of men to admit mistakes and their desire to save face. Numerous political, economic, and ecclesiastical leaders and their followers have been tragically wrong, but how few have admitted it. Men may pursue a wrong action with conviction by following a principle which had never been assessed. This is different from simply making a mistake; anyone can be wrong. But permitting a non-negotiable principle to become the basis of a mistake is tantamount to using a map of Norway to explore the Congo. It also obstructs truth. The holders are prevented by the principle from consulting others before taking action, they cannot withdraw from the action because the principle holds them to it, and they cannot admit the action is wrong because they cannot admit that the principle, which they have said is the truth, is wrong. Indeed when men become slaves to non-negotiable principles they dispense with a portion of their capacity to think.

Why do men bind themselves to non-negotiable principles? In the first place those who profess the principles are fallible and they wield power. To proclaim simply a negotiable principle, that is, a 'this is our view' idea, leaves room for questioning the ability and the tactics of the declarers, for discretion on the part of those on whom the principle is pressed, and for consideration of the merits of other views. To proclaim a non-negotiable principle, that is, a 'this is right' or 'this is God's will' idea, puts the declarers in a much securer position, enhances their power because questioning them appears wrong, discourages attention to alternatives, facilitates blind obedience on the part of their followers which the followers probably like because it is easy, and in fact permits people to elevate any nonsense to the status of wisdom. Thus the degree of negotiability of principles is related to the control exercised by their declarers. If there were only one set of declarers of principles on a given subject men could perhaps endure this control without serious consequences. There are, fortunately, always two or more conflicting sets, and, if their principles are non-negotiable, the struggle among them may cause so much grief that men cannot afford to have them, especially when it becomes obvious that some, if not all, of the conflicting principles must have been wrong to start with.

In the second place those who profess the principles can thereby cover up weaknesses and demand the suspension of other equally treasured principles. A crusade provides a 'red herring' to divert attention from a group's problems and excuses for almost any persecution. It always involves the breaking of loyalties to other principles, such as those concerning killing and bearing false witness. Such dishonesty cannot be admitted. On the contrary it is made to look splendid. A predator is never an invader; he is an exponent of great principles. As for his victims, is he not liberating them from their own decadent regimes and false ideologies?

This approach to principles suggests that some of them are simply means for constituting sides in social games and conflicts, like 'cops and robbers' and 'cowboys and Indians.' They facilitate identity and discipline, even though many of the players have no idea what the labels really stand for. But these means are dishonest when the players are told they are anything more than mere categories of an activity. They are false when they divide contestants into 'good guys' and 'bad guys.' And they are destructive when used as instruments of hatred, aggression, and death. Such use of principles offsets any good they do and ultimately destroys them.

Those who accept principles may also favour non-negotiable ones to increase their personal status and to offset other non-negotiable principles they already hold. A person with no ideas of his own on a subject may avoid thought by accepting a non-negotiable principle; he will be more canny on a negotiable one. He assumes a certain respectability by declaring a loyalty and aligning himself with a group. He may find it easy and comforting to raise an opinion to the status of a principle to convince himself and others that he is standing up for principle when he is really holding stubbornly and unreasonably to a mere viewpoint. And he may play his principles against one another as convenience dictates. He may even continue the attachment to a principle long after he ceases to believe in it because, in almost all instances of non-negotiable principles, there is a stigma attached to openly changing one's mind. This problem is a weakness of many institutions when members belong for reasons other than belief in the principles involved and remain after they cease to believe because they cannot make a change. An even more serious weakness occurs when the rare people who do switch principles are forced to become supreme devotees of the new and implacable enemies of the old because the change must be accompanied by extreme efforts of justification.

Justifying conflicting non-negotiable principles therefore encourages man's worst enemy, fanaticism. Conflicting principles can never be avoided, but fanaticism can by negotiability. Few people had more experience with this subject than Madame de Staël, and few were more inconsistent in backing principles in an age of inconsistent principles. But, said one of her biographers, 'she never ceased to believe that rational men, no matter how opposed in principle, can always agree peacefully on a vast area of ideas and measures, provided they remain free from fanaticism, which sees only the irreconcilable principles, and provided they are inspired by enthusiasm, which alone can vivify the spirit. Freedom to her was above all the right of the human spirit to progress; enthusiasm fed it, and fanaticism killed it.'[4] It is significant that, in search of collective enthusiasm, Madame de Staël was one of the great patronesses of colour and culture in an age when devotees of principles were chopping off one another's heads.

Where stand the people who really believe in their principles, who hold them because they understand them, and who belong to organizations because they are sincere supporters? It is difficult to generalize, but the evidence indicates that these people hold negotiable principles and not non-negotiable ones. They tend to believe and act on the premise 'This is my belief; others have theirs which is their business; I am only human and, right or wrong, I follow what I think is right and respect others for doing the same.' They do not reveal an inclination to say 'I follow the right; others are wrong and I will do my best to ruin them.' The true believer of a political ideology, an economic theory, or a theological dogma can always be spotted. He is humble about it because he can afford to be; he need not cope with the arrogance of an assumed monopoly on wisdom or truth; he need not be fanatic because of doubt that his belief is really right or because of the presence of other beliefs. He is happier with it because, since it is negotiable, it can be reconciled with his other beliefs. He follows his principles because they are beliefs, not just forms of allegiance to an assumed monopoly.

What explains people who apparently have no principles, who can never be depended on, who 'weasel' and 'shilly-shally' their way through life, who consider no skulduggery impossible? With few exceptions they are holders of non-negotiable principles, who have so many of them that they cancel one another out so that none can operate effectively. The conscience that is satisfied with a supply of rigid beliefs for all occasions is readily manoeuvered toward any one of them and easily convinced of the rightness of any action or the lack of it. Were such people's principles negotiable they would have to justify them. Since their principles are non-negotiable they assume they are 'right' whatever they do. They will not admit that their principles conflict. They will even abandon a principle in good conscience because they have another to put in its place as convenience dictates. Such people occasionally end up in prison when they make too free with the law or in mental institutions when they break down under the weight of conflicting beliefs. Many, however, undermine society in comfort and respectability and cause it as much harm as militant bigots.

Faith is important in these matters. It is a wondrous thing to behold as a spur to inspiration and action, and it has led to much comfort and countless great deeds in the absence of proof. The word itself is much abused, however, and it may be used to cover all kinds of reliance on the outcome of events, excuses for actions for which there may be no justification, and even ways of avoiding thought altogether. This is why faiths clash more frequently than necessary, and why in human struggles faiths on either side cancel each other out. To view faith in its appropriate perspective and do justice to it (as distinct from merely misappropriating the word) we should distinguish between faith in negotiable and non-negotiable principles. The first seems real faith; the second seems unsupportable arrogance. To put faith in an outcome of a negotiable principle is to subject it to a necessary logic. After all faith does not operate without logic; it begins where logic ends. If there is no logic at all faith rests on nothing. Faith in negotiable principles is also inclined to mingle rather than conflict with other faiths.

On the other hand to put faith in the outcome of a non-negotiable principle is simply to call on some superior auspices to back a monopolistic assumption of right or to fulfil some wishful thinking. It is also an assurance of a violent clash with anyone else who does the same. Faith in God, for example, is regarded in all ecclesiastical circles as the highest of all faiths. To base it on conflicting assumptions of right or wishful thinking appears from the facts of history to be a sloughing off on God of responsibility for human problems without an adequate use of human talents. Many political troubles arise from the invocation of faith in a theory which, because it is non-negotiable, assumes rightness without an adequate examination of its practical limitations and the alternatives, and invites constant struggles with other theories. When such theory is tried out in practice and theorists repudiate evidence of its weakness and invoke faith, failure and political upheavals become inevitable. This assurance of rightness is really arrogant. Indeed arrogance is often faith in non-negotiable principles nagged by doubt and defended by bravado. It ultimately becomes corrupt. 'There are similarities between absolute power and absolute faith,' wrote Eric Hoffer, 'a demand for absolute obedience, a readiness to attempt the impossible, a bias for simple solutions — to cut the knot rather than unravel it, the viewing of compromise as surrender. Both absolute power and absolute faith are instruments of dehumanization. Hence, absolute faith corrupts as absolutely as absolute power.'[5] In this misuse of faith at least one non-negotiable principle is generally the source of the trouble.

The ancient address of new speakers of a legislature to the Crown in parliamentary government contains an apt request that the sovereign 'put a favourable construction on' the actions of a house. It is proper under this arrangement to debate opinions, issues, and laws, and even to oppose the government and attempt to drive it from office by constitutional means, without being accused of treason. In other times and systems banishment and slaughter have proved wasteful means of defending non-negotiable power; when, with responsible government, the power was given negotiable status people could hold conflicting political opinions with impunity.

Those who govern under such a system may have their political principles, but these are assailable. And the assailability strengthens the principles by requiring responsibility for them and a testing and defence of them. If the principles are wrong or deficient they can be attacked and modified or discarded. The system is not perfect and there is ample scope for mistakes, but the absence of non-negotiable principles in legislatures makes governing a much safer process. Non-negotiable authority still exists in some countries, and with it persecutions and suppressions of both men and ideas. Non-negotiable sovereignty remains in international affairs, and with it belligerence and the threat of war. Disagreements and mistakes are inevitable and natural. What makes them dangerous is the existence of too many non-negotiable principles which, experience has too clearly shown, are not really worth the loyalty given them or the consequences which follow upon their encounters with other principles.

'Favourable construction' is a necessary element in the conflict of all principles. It does not mean agreement. It means admission of the right of all principles to legitimate expression; the association of arrogance, perhaps blasphemy, with any claim to automatic or exclusive rightness or divine auspices; and the subjection of the requirements and consequences of principles and the intentions and abilities of their holders to rigorous scrutiny before defence of them is regarded as necessary or noble. The devout holder of a non-negotiable principle is not inclined to put a favourable construction on either other principles or the holders of them, yet this construction is a prerequisite to peaceful coexistence among men. As these words are written several thousand persons a week are meeting destitution and death in clashes between political and ecclesiastical non-negotiable principles. It may be comforting to think of tragedy as an inevitable consequence of good causes, the defence of 'right' against 'wrong.' Yet the price paid appears high and the question of who is right seems insoluble.

It is a phenomenon of man that religious, quasi-religious, and pseudo-religious principles are the least negotiable. Man knows least and assumes most in this field, but attempts to arrange 'favourable construction' in it have been among the most difficult of all human endeavours. It is comforting to hold that one's particular dogma is right and to produce its literature as evidence. It is not so comforting, however, to consider the variations in dogmas and their literature and to compare one's own with the others. It is exhilarating to claim the benefits of dogmas, but it is disturbing to weigh the cost and tragic consequences of the benefits. It seems right to promote the dogma by means of ecclesiastical politics; it is disturbing, nevertheless, to note (as chapter 11 will indicate) how attitudes which are characteristic of these politics tend to permeate other kinds of politics with unnatural and damaging effects.

It is assumed by many devotees of non-negotiable principles that their unquestioned advocacy is a mark of strength and an assurance of right. This egoistic belief is simply not true. It is almost always a sign of weakness. While tested principles eventually stand on their own quality, those which stand only because they are unquestioned and have some dogmatic power behind them are often respectable fallacies obstructing the truth, encouraging the cowardice of rigid conformity, demeaning those who hold them, and ultimately, after a reaction, weakening and perhaps destroying their sponsors. Wilhelm von Humboldt, after unusual opportunities for observing men of many nations, described how this problem affects people, and his comments apply to other fields as well as religion: ' ... the citizen who is wholly left to himself in matters of religion will mingle religious feelings with his inner life, or not, according to his individual character; but in either case, his system of ideas will be more consistent, and his sensations more profound; his nature will be more coherent, and he will distinguish more clearly between morality and submission to the laws. On the other hand, the man who is fettered by various regulations will, despite these, show the same variety of religious ideas, or their absence, but in any case he will have less consistency in his ideas, less depth and sincerity of feeling, less harmony of character, and so will have less regard for morality, and wish more frequently to evade the laws.'[6] These observations explain why so much evil can be done in the name of religious and other principles by their devotees.

The questioning of principles is not only a means of strengthening the principles but also a release of tension in both society and individuals. We know that humans react violently when their consciences are suppressed. Non-negotiable principles are the greatest suppressors of conscience. They weaken or disturb it when people really do not believe and cannot say so, and guilt lurks or wells up. They restrict conscience when they limit the range of thought and belief and provoke a resulting inferiority complex. People thus affected will react to the guilt by making a fetish of their principles in an attempt to support themselves, by reacting violently against holders of other principles in the hope of justifying themselves, or by compensating for the burden of the principles by either flagrantly breaking them or subsiding into indifference. Questioning strengthens principles that can stand up to it and relieves the doubts of the holders; it forces changes in stupid principles; it increases tolerance among holders of conflicting principles because it forces understanding. The more open and negotiable principles are the less conscience is restricted or diverted by the hangups which accompany devotion to what may be mere taboos and 'sacred cows.'

One of the splendid characteristics of principles in any field is the fact that they force people to take themselves and what they do seriously. This is certainly true of negotiable principles. Non-negotiable principles, on the other hand, provoke people into taking themselves too seriously. They become smug, self-satisfied, arrogant, belligerent when they apply their principles or when they rely on them without applying them. People then become over-sensitive, take to carrying chips on their shoulders and daring others to knock them off, and, because they bruise easily, over-react to other people. They invoke rights they do not deserve and as readily undermine the rights of others. They see great intentions in themselves and mischief in others. People who take themselves too seriously are found in all walks of life. When there are too many of them they wield more influence than their numbers deserve because of the assumed virtue of their principles and because priggishness is contagious. Then the collectivity looks for trouble, and if there is none it creates it. The legacy of the self-righteous is tragic – from the narrow domineering parent to the fanatic reformer to the arrogant despot.

This is why a sense of humour and a peccadillo or two are good for people, something to remind them of their own fallibility in the conduct of their and other people's business. It is a sound instinct to suspect the pretentious and the too blatantly virtuous, and to shy away from the know-it-alls. People who make a virtue of being virtuous are usually hiding a great weakness or a moral deficiency. It is human to rebel against puritanical excesses. 'It's great to live with saints in heaven,' said Cardinal Cushing, 'but it's hell to live with them here on earth.'[7] Churchill even anticipated heaven in a comment on some experienced friends. 'Yes,' he said, 'this is the sort of company I should like to find in heaven ... stained but positive. Not those flaccid sea-anemones of virtue who can hardly wobble an antenna in the waters of negativity.'[8] The judgment of the overly virtuous is usually faulty because it is untried, and they can therefore be guilty of great evil in the name of virtue. The reason is often evident: many of them fail to distinguish between being really good and being good for lack of opportunity or courage to be anything else; they raise inexperience to the level of goodness. They often have a reaction when opportunity does come and are worse than the openly bad. Arrogant principles are subject to the same forces as arrogant people, but we are too inclined to subordinate our instincts about them with obvious consequences. Social change becomes difficult and perhaps impossible. Nothing is harder on society than self-righteous reformers provoking self-righteous establishments into fights over arrogant principles.

The worst of all the characteristics of non-negotiable principles is their punitive nature. Men are inclined to punish others for many reasons, including revenge, jealousy, and a desire to enforce obedience. But their most dire penalties they reserve for the enforcement of their assumptions of right. A totalitarian political party loves a purge, and it invariably describes the victims as subversives or enemies of the state or the people. A revolutionary group may take its crusade so seriously that it will punish 'reactionaries' and its own moderates and backsliders, and be carried away by a desire for self-justifying revenge. A church may assume that divine recognition carries with it divine delegation of powers to punish, and ecclesiastical retributions have ranged, and still range, from character assassination to boycotts to slaughter. Punishment of this kind assumes the righteousness of those giving it, and the less negotiable their principles the more ready they are to punish severely. The reason is not so much the disciplining of ignorant people or enemies of the state as catering to vanity and an urge to control. Cruelty is a feature of dogmatism of any kind, and excess virtue has always been a cloak for persecution and revenge.

The cost to society of non-negotiable principles results not only from their direct effects but also from the way they disrupt other forces of life. A person may be so involved in a particular and demanding loyalty to a principle that he has no time for other significant loyalties and activities. The principle should be relevant to his life to deserve a large share of it. It should also be in harmony with his other principles so that in devoting himself to one he does not neglect others of equal or greater importance. Yet how many people are forced to devote a major part of their lives, indeed their very lives, to principles which push aside desirable experience and other principles! A mixed marriage may thwart love and cause grief out of all proportion to the significance of the conflicting dogmas. Indeed love is the most frequent victim of dogmatism. A fiery reformer advocating great nostrums may give up everything worthwhile in life and discard many of his principles to become a slave to his cause. Indeed any cause will do as an excuse for some people to abandon life's responsibilities or as a vehicle for their own ambition. Peddlers of all-embracing political ideologies usually demand total loyalty which may include giving up work, home, family and friends, even to the point of betraying them, as well as devotion to other beliefs and conscience itself. Ultimately they will demand genocide or war as righteous instruments of their cause. Peace, love, work, thought, and leisure are so important and the time for them is so limited, and life offers so much opportunity for experience and service, that it is remarkable how people deprive themselves and others of these benefits in favour of narrow and exclusive allegiances which they are unable or unwilling to question and for which they are expected to make any sacrifice. The freedom to do something in an age of causes includes the tendency to give up freedom altogether.

A negotiable principle is much less demanding and exclusive. If it conflicts with peace or love it can be adjusted. If it means mortal confrontation with others it can be assessed. If it takes more time or money that it deserves it can be altered or abandoned. Since it has not been sanctified by alleged rightness it can be changed with less loss of face. Meanwhile a person may devote a disproportionate amount of his life to it, but it is his choice; he is not a slave to it; and it is harder for him to enslave others through it. It is certainly a far less potent reason for a smear campaign, a vitriolic confrontation, a revolution, a war.

Parliamentary government has placed all political phenomena in the negotiable category and there seems no reason other phenomena should not be so treated. Man's eternal quest for freedom requires that the individual and society be able to negotiate all principles and to question ruthlessly any principle which carries any arrogant pretentions. And the search for truth, fundamental law, or whatever may be the natural social structure which men have long sought can only be carried on if the boundaries set by principles are continuously being changed and extended as life's experience directs.

10

Church politics

'The spectacle of what is called religion,' said Prime Minister Nehru, 'or at any rate organized religion in India and elsewhere, has filled me with horror.'[1] This rare frank statement on the subject of religion by a politician is an informed example of the contemporary disillusionment with ecclesiastical organizations and the growing understanding that they include many postures and politics which are not appropriate, indeed not safe, for man, and not relevant to religion itself.

Church activity is an extreme example of participation in society, but not of democratic participation. It is relatively easy to become a clergyman or layman in a church, and the extent to which churches and their personnel participate in affairs of every kind is unrivalled. No other activity of man better illustrates postures and politics, the extent and nature of allegiance to principles, the lack of a 'favourable construction,' professional protection, and the effects of social and political participation. Religion plays a small part in this activity, but the rest is devoted to principles and practices which distinguish, accompany, empower, and promote countless sects and the people and organizations which comprise them. The variety of operations is endless. From cabinet formation to bingo playing, from war to school administration, the conflicting politics of churches pervades every corner of society. Men periodically wonder what all this activity has to do with religion, especially when they see tragedy result from it throughout the world, and it is not surprising that religion itself must take the blame for flourishes carried on under its auspices.

Religion is concerned directly with the personal recognition and service of God. Its impact on man's behaviour has long been affected by other encroaching phenomena which are occasionally related to it but which often obscure and contradict it. These are church dogma, ecclesiastical power and organization, and denominational participation in political and social affairs. They are not religion although they operate in its name. They may serve the cause of religion; they may violate it. They bring dignity and happiness to man; they also bring him with appalling ease to sorrow, degradation, and death.

This conflict follows upon a failure to distinguish between man's relation with God and his allegiance to organized churches and creeds which are two completely different things. The first is awesome and demanding, yet simple; it takes humility and courage and does not require elaborate credentials and manipulations. Allegiance to church or creed, on the other hand, is easy and comforting, yet complicated. It is not difficult to be born into or join a church and profess a creed, as distinct from the greater exercise of living up to the obligations of that creed. It is therefore easy to mistake mere allegiance to a creed for the service of God, to confuse religious men and mere denominational politicians, and to compensate by raising up official belief, ritual, regulation, and activity to make the allegiance important and respectable. The result sometimes serves religion itself and sometimes does not.

Church dogma and activity breed a potent form of politics. They have a long record of dividing men into opposing factions, and the more they are emphasized the more divisive they are. The success of a faction is often judged by the number of its members, the proselytizing done, and the political and social power won. Direct and sometimes exclusive divine sponsorship is assumed and vigorous claims to 'the truth' are made. This loyalty is regarded as 'standing up for what is right,' which action would appear laudable only if one has made a careful scrutiny of his stand and of alternative views. In this scrutiny church people do not as a rule indulge. Consequently the dogmas clash, and much church activity is devoted to the defence of the dogmas and the power of the factions. This activity flows with ease into the political, economic, and social concerns of men, always in the name of religion, but inevitably in the interest of power. The result is usually disastrous.

We must therefore distinguish between the effects of church dogma and activity on religion, which is a theological subject outside the scope of this discussion, and the effects on public affairs, which are not religious, and which theology often ignores or tolerates. This chapter and the next deal with the politics of churches, not with religion itself; and church politics is a powerful yet frightening influence in any political system. In this connection we will use the word 'church' in its broadest sense to denote any organized ecclesiastical body of any category or denomination, despite the fact that churches differ greatly in the power they wield and in their interest in political and social affairs, and despite the inclusion in the term of so many diverse groups throughout the world.

Relations between man and the God he believes in are a fundamental part of his political, economic, and social activities. This does not mean, however, that the dogmas and endeavours of churches are necessarily relevant or desirable in these activities. Nor does it mean that people cannot pursue the right and the good in these activities without the participation of churches, or even that such participation will necessarily be beneficial. Theologians disagree on the relevance of church dogma and activities in religion itself. Their impact on men and society is even less reliable, and it should not be taken for granted that their impact is positive simply because the auspices of religion are claimed.

The impact of the churches in political and social life is reinforced by their assumption of divine auspices. Other institutions boast sponsorship too; political parties invoke the people and political philosophies; other groups speak in the interest of good health, justice, education, the cause of labour, and the like. None of these, however, can match the stated or implied sponsorship of God with which churches and clergy of all varieties justify their interventions, reinforce their opinions and demands, and quarrel with one another. Despite the obvious fragmentation of this sponsorship and the conflicting interpretations of it, it is a powerful weapon, and the churches, the clergy, and church laymen use it with telling effect irrespective of other justifications or the lack thereof for their opinions and actions. Those against whom it is used find it the most difficult of all political phenomena to deal with because they incur automatic suspicion of irreverence or bigotry; disagreement with a church or a clergyman is too easily interpreted as opposition to religion itself. Counterparts of Henry II and Thomas à Becket are numerous in the affairs of men.

Functions clearly and directly concerned with religion, that is with the recognition and service of God, may support claims of divine auspices despite the many conflicts among such claims. Other functions do not. The dividing line between these sets of functions is rarely clear. Churches and clergy push this line out into non-religious activities, and those concerned with non-religious activities may pull the line towards them to gain the respectability of religious auspices. Churches tend to assume that the further out this line is pushed or pulled the greater is the influence of religion. History contradicts this assumption. Evidence from the crusades or missionary activity among primitive peoples may indicate church power but certainly not religious influence. Church intervention in contemporary politics provides similar evidence at the local and personal level. Religion is not a problem of history. The politics which surrounds it, the careless assumptions of divine auspices, and the stretching too far of the line described comprise the real problem.

Two further characteristics of church politics compound the problem: the assumption of 'truth' and the bitterness associated with the defence of this truth. The tenacity with which one can hold a church dogma and the feeling that there is something indecent about questioning or even discussing it are unmatched among loyalties to other theories. The assumption that one has the right, perhaps the exclusive, approach to God and the ruthless appraisal of other approaches must surely violate the most fundamental tenets of religion itself. Certainly no arguments or wars are more bitter than those which are unjustly attributed to religion when they are really just defences of 'our side' and invasions of 'the other side.'

The direct impact on men of these conflicts has been bad enough, in Ireland, the Middle East, and India, for example. The indirect impact is also evident as the line between the church and other interests is pushed out. Church politics mixes with other kinds of politics and it rarely mixes well. It often brings bigotry, viciousness, and shame to otherwise peaceable situations, and where those situations are not peaceable it almost always aggravates them. Nothing confuses government more than the activities of 'our side' in church matters; economics and church politics are an explosive and most costly mixture; and denominational factions are the most quarrelsome in social affairs. 'These bloody people – they're like animals,' said a sergeant during the Irish troubles of 1971 in which the factions were two branches of Christendom and the issues concerned political power. 'Women spit at you. The kids have a high time of it when they throw rocks at you. The men snipe at you and think they're heroes. They laugh about it. These people only know one thing – hate.'[2]

'Of all the factors dividing Canadians in their political outlook and behaviour,' state two authoritative observers, 'religion is uppermost in importance.'[3] Consequently church affairs cannot be given in practice the same free and frank public discussion and legislative debate which other affairs can expect in a democracy. Churches take advantage of this fear. Public funds for a public institution, for example, can be thoroughly discussed; public grants for church institutions, however, are generally arranged furtively behind the scenes and given consent by a 'gentlemen's agreement.' 'We have never had,' testifies a British politician, 'a political controversy about the Catholic Church for twenty years, because they have got their church school bills through without any discussion in Parliament. This is the height of lobbying.'[4] It is not, however, the height of democracy. These tactics are motivated, not only by struggles between church and state, but also by rivalry among churches on both theological and non-theological matters – what the Bishop of Auckland called 'a cycle of sectarian epilepsy.'[5] Unfortunately, however, a bad example is set, and, as chapter 11 will indicate, what is acceptable in church politics invites similar tactics in other kinds of politics.

For these reasons man must question openly and without fear of reprisal the role of churches in his society and question with the same freedom with which he questions other institutions. There has always been questioning of churches; indeed many of them were founded on some form of it, and numerous great religious leaders were protestors. But this questioning has been fitful and hysterical, and it has been costly in terms of money and suffering. Today, however, the world's problems are too serious for any major human activity to be exempt from frank and fearless discussion. The growing admission of this fact is an important force in contemporary debate about the role of the churches in society and the place of church dogmas among the ideas of men. It is also one reason why the ranks of the clergy have been decimated, and empty pews and declining interest in church matters testify to the extent of the departure of the faithful. The basic problem of the churches is not the message of the creeds as it concerns relations with God, but the power of the churches and churchmen as it relates to numerous activities of no relevance to religion itself and indeed often contrary to it. This is not easy to admit. 'Shortage of vocations,' said Cardinal Heenan, Archibishop of Westminster, results from 'a lack of religious faith and the spirit of self-denial,'[6] a remark with which few departing priests agree.

Some clergy and laymen turn to the ecumenical movement to bolster this faith and spirit; but it seems that many see ecumenism as a buttress for shoring up church power dissipated by division. 'The ecumenical movement,' said an executive of the Baptist World Alliance, 'is needed to bring Christianity to the entire world.'[7] Other denominational groups would scarcely applaud. Ecumenism without a change in the power structure of the churches and the political activities of churchmen will not help the cause of religion in the slightest, and may even weaken it further and endanger society if it creates super churches warring with one another or operating on religious compromise and enormously increased political power.

History has often recorded how dangerous is this increased power. 'Unfortunately religion became more intolerant as it became more unified,' write two historians. 'Persecution spread; and the cry for orthodoxy became [in Hume's words] "the most furious and implacable of all human passions." Philosophy ... was compelled to become the servant and apologist of the faith of the masses ... merit and "salvation" were more and more divorced from virtue and attached to ritual observance and unquestioning belief. In consequence educated persons became either martyrs or hypocrites; and as they rarely chose martyrdom, the life of man was tarnished with lip service and insincerity.'[8] Voltaire's observation of this phenomenon is applicable today in many countries. 'If one religion only were allowed in England,' he wrote, 'the government would very possibly become arbitrary; if there were but two, the people would cut one another's throats; but as there is such a multitude, they all live happy and in peace.'[9]

The influence of church doctrine declines with the increase in church politics because they are contradictory. There is not room for both in any case because churches do not have the time or the personnel for both. Politics always affects doctrine by making it irrelevant, even suspect, except insofar as an allegiance to it is necessary to belong to 'our side.' It turns a church into a political party. The average adherent of any church would therefore be hard pressed to answer were he asked the difference between his doctrine and that of others. Indeed he may not be able to explain his own, and were he told some special feature of it, he might disclaim belief in it. Even the clergy may not believe their own doctrine. Monsignor Giovanni Musante, a retiring member of the Pope's household, testified that of priests who follow the rule of celibacy because they believe in it, 'there are few, these are rare.'[10]

Unfortunately, however, people who want to believe in things relevant to their relations with God and cannot find them in their church, or who believe in things knowing they believe merely because 'our side' subscribes to them, know that something is lacking in their faith. They remain in the church conforming but not really believing, or making up for lack of faith by engaging in hyperactive political and social activity in the name of religion, or they leave the church. Thus the religious image of the church is dimmed and the credibility of both its doctrine and its churchmen is weakened. The Aga Khan, himself a religious leader, testified to the difficulty of freeing Islam 'from the many superstitions and from the many semi-idolatrous ideas and practices which – contrary to the true tenets of our faith – have been fostered in Iran by the ecclesiastical lawyers, who thus kept the people ignorant, their own interests secure and their power supreme.'[11] He confessed 'experience which for the rest of my life has given me a certain prejudice against professional men of religion – be they mullahs or maulvis, curates, vicars or bishops.'[12] In the consideration of church problems should not this one have highest priority? In discussions about political power and social activities should not this one be treated openly and fearlessly?

The principles and intentions of an institution are of limited value in assessing it. They are simply labels and guidelines. How they are carried out is the vital evidence. 'What a man believes,' wrote Shaw in *Man and Superman,* 'may be ascertained, not from his creed, but from the assumptions on which he habitually acts.' Assessment must also include the use of power, the character and training of the men who exercise it, and the effect of that power on the people and the institutions who feel it. 'Belling the cat' illustrates how excellent plans can be too great for those who make them. Reforms of governments have included both impossible schemes suggested by inadequate people and numerous attempts to limit the power of officials. Church controversies involve the same things. We sometimes justify them as struggles for great truths, but they are really based on the fact that the powers used in church politics are far beyond the ability of most humans to wield. For this reason the status and power of the clergy and church laymen deserve the same appraisal so often given to other people.

Clergymen too can be divided into the competent, the mediocre, and the weak. In devotion to the service of God and fellow men there are many great clerics and great souls in all ranks of churches. The good they do is incalculable. The other two groups, also in all ranks of churches, are, however, different men altogether, and their effects on society can be doubtful in value or devastating. Unfortunately the distinction is not made; ordination gives all of them an accolade – in some sects they assume it themselves – and, whatever their qualities, all carry the auspices of the church into their activities. Even the newest ordained immediately secures a precedence, a deference, and the salutation 'reverend,' 'father,' or 'rabbi' which gives him a status and power far greater perhaps than his personal qualities deserve. Other professions enjoy distinctions too, but the stated or implied divine auspices enjoyed by a 'man of God' is far more significant and potent in its effects. 'The context of Divine partnership in which a clergyman is viewed,' writes a well known rabbi, 'especially by avid female devotees of the faith, surrounds him in an emotional aura, a poetic, other-worldly afflatus that sets him apart from other men.'[13] This aura, helpful no doubt to the distinguished, is a dangerous shield to the weak and a cause of disillusionment among the faithful when it is taken advantage of or not lived up to.

The professional preparation of the clergy encourages the weak. They are not trained in theology, but in their own theology. They are not prepared to enter a calling; they become agents of one category of that calling, and, with few exceptions, birth alone has determined that choice. The 'our side' attitude is thus reinforced. The theological aspects of this training are too numerous to examine here; but we may venture the opinion that ecumenism can hardly be effective without. some change in it. The non-theological aspects of the training are also numerous, but a few are particularly significant in this discussion.

The system of training affects both the number and the quality of those entering the profession, as well as the work they subsequently do. 'As things are now,' writes an Anglican bishop, 'a sub-standard ministry may not merely not be doing much good; it can easily do a great deal of positive harm.'[14] There are not enough good students; with rare exceptions the standards of admission to most theological courses are low; almost anyone who applies is welcome and is assumed to have 'the call'; virtually no one is failed. Church-directed training, rather than a theology-directed training, combined with low standards, discourages many able students. It also attracts many mediocre and weak ones who are encouraged, perhaps comforted, by the pre-arranged theology of one church, who find theology the only alternative open to them, or who have previously measured the amount of power and prestige to be gained in relation to the requirements. There is simply not enough screening of the prospective clergy. Many teachers and students, myself included, have watched over the years the number of the inadequate who drift into the churches. However high a church sets its principles and intentions, they will be frustrated by men unable to handle them. Woe betide the other institutions on whom these men bestow their interest, as they often do when theology proves too much for them. Jane Austen's Mr Collins, Wilde's Canon Chausable, and Sabatini's Father Cosimo were drawn from life, and their counterparts in modern churches who react eagerly to participatory democracy are among the chief causes of discontent and trouble in society and of loss of credibility in the churches.

Scholastic ability is not the only factor in competence. Character is obviously vital but too often overlooked. Character is difficult to define, but it and the lack of it are obvious if one compares the examples just cited with the Reverends Hilary Laurens and David Lyall in Agnes Turnbull's novels, *The Bishop's Mantle* and *The Gown of Glory;* Miss Turnbull reveals clearly how character enables clergymen to give unique leadership by powerful example. Without this character clerical leadership is dangerous. The hyperactive egocentric, for example, who rushes in wherever he thinks angels should tread will consider himself an angel because he treads there, and yet he will contribute little but confusion. The vacillating parson who cannot make up his mind, who has not the strength to stand up for what he knows is right or against what he knows is wrong, or who cannot be depended upon in a course of thought or action will undermine his church's principles and intentions more quickly than the most active opponent and will weaken any cause which may draw him into other institutions.

Such weakness, which is evident elsewhere, is more dangerous in church politics because of the cloak of respectability and power that may camouflage it, and because of the protection from direct and open personal criticism which may shield it. I believe the churches lose more members and prestige through the actions and example of weak clergy than through any other single factor. Their zeal may be substantial, but their actions are too often stubbornly futile or wrong, especially when they get in other people's way. 'The greatest danger in times of crisis,' said Tallyrand, himself a bishop experienced in clerical intervention in public affairs, 'comes from the zeal of people who are inexperienced.'[15]

The 'call,' the challenges of theology, and the love of ecclesiastical service no doubt motivate the men of ability and character and the men of character alone who enter the profession. Those deficient in such attributes, whom we will describe as weak clergy in this discussion, may cite these motivations too, but other reasons frequently determine their choice. Sometimes even the choice itself is not theirs; too often parents have made it for them by compulsion or suggestion. Of the other reasons the one which concerns us here is the desire for power. The aura of respectability makes that power attractive to even the weakest of men who could find no comparable power in other professions. There are fools and rogues in any field, but most institutions do a more rigorous job of screening, criticizing, or firing them than do the churches. An Anglican advisory committee for postulants to holy orders suggested a need for psychological appraisals to 'assist both the church and the man to make the right decision ... It is not helpful to either party if the man is unsuitable.'[16]

This subject is sensitive, and I must emphasize that I am not attacking the clergy. I am assessing the effects of weak clergymen. This anyone can do with relative impunity in respect to other occupations, and it is done regularly and openly by the press and the public and by clergymen themselves. But no comparable assessment is made openly of the clergy, which fact enhances clerical power beyond reason, even today when there is some questioning of churches. This protection diverts criticism from individuals to the churches as a whole because the power and prestige of institutions are always weakened by an excess of powers and immunities enjoyed by people in them. Among church personnel, prospective theology students are the first among whom assessment, now reluctant, should be most rigorous. In discussing this subject I have used examples which are documented or which I have seen often in actual operation.

One cannot stay long in a theological college residence without feeling great respect for some theological students and disgust at the thought of the ordination of others. Of the latter one encounters those who have already revealed their deficiencies in other faculties and are seeking a soft alternative. One also encounters people with moral and personality defects that would kill their chances of successful careers elsewhere. Universities and university students are often accused of being anti-religious, irreligious, or indifferent; there are various reasons why this should be so, but many students have their first doubts about churches as a result of acquaintance with theological students. Gresham's Law applies here. Poor students drive out good ones, and theological colleges help perpetuate the shortage of good candidates while there are waiting lists for entry to other professional faculties imposing careful selection and rigorous training on their candidates.

It is a shattering experience to see clerical power reposing in weak hands. One sees that situation arise very quickly after the graduation of the theological student. Suppose, for example, two priests or ministers or rabbis share a graduate seminar with a dozen other students and a professor: one is a first-class person respected by all, and the other one quickly earns the contempt of everyone. The first will shed any church auspices or protection, the students will associate and argue with him with complete freedom, and the professor will appraise his ideas frankly and critically. The other will quickly assume an air of clerical privilege and piety, the students will exclude him from their exchanges, and the professor will be deferential about his criticism. Graduate dissertations and theses of clergymen often are treated less rigorously than those of other students, and their transgressions are passed over more lightly. Delusions of competence and privilege commence early under such conditions.

The serious study of theology is long and arduous. Some able students embark on it and combine with it a training in another subject such as philosophy or a professional discipline. The result is evident when men of character with this background preach or participate in a social service. Such men rarely become what Victor Hugo called 'stage managers of sanctity.' Unfortunately, however, the lack of such a background distinguishes other clergymen. The basic theological course for them is short, usually following a general bachelor's degree and readily adjusted in content and time to suit 'special cases.' Most courses in such circumstances are elementary, and the majority of these students graduate with a limited acquaintance and little training in any field of scholarship.

As for practical matters like preaching, churchgoers who hear many clergy can judge the effectiveness of homiletics by appraising the quality and delivery of sermons. When weak clergy preach the gospel or make pronouncements on public matters they invite scepticism for themselves and their church. 'I think almost anything said by clerics is bound to be nonsensical,' said Malcolm Muggeridge; 'I'm very keen on Christianity and not even the clerics can completely obscure that.'[17] 'The best advice an officeholder can get,' wrote Harry Golden, 'is to see that, in general, the ministers are not on his side.'[18] The prospect of social service lures many theological students into the social sciences. They usually have time and patience for only a few elementals and rarely undergo the discipline of these subjects or gain practical experience. 'Post ordination training,' one clerical principal has testified, 'is in all dioceses totally inadequate and in most dioceses is unbelievably amateurish and ineffective.'[19]

Men so inadequately trained may become a danger to society when, fortified by respectability, they advise people and groups on the basis of superficial experiences, and when they take or refuse to take stands on issues. They also weaken theology itself when they dilute it with thin social science instead of strengthening it with serious thought and, wrote A.N. Whitehead, 'a rational understanding of the rise of civilization, and of the tenderness of mere life itself, in a world which superficially is founded upon the clashings of senseless compulsion ... The defect of the liberal theology of the last two hundred years is that it has confined itself to the suggestion of minor, vapid reasons why people should continue to go to church in the traditional fashion.'[20]

This social science approach mixes verities and conveniences to the confusion of both, and it hamstrings social action, from the abolition of torture and slavery to the study of drinking and sex. 'Religion should be studied for what it is,' wrote Gunnar Myrdal; and again, unfortunately, it is religion rather than church politics that takes the blame, 'a ritualized and stratified complex of highly emotional beliefs and valuations that give the sanction of sacredness, taboo and immutability to inherited institutional arrangements, modes of living, and attitudes. Understood in this realistic and comprehensive sense, religion usually hits as a tremendous force for social inertia. The writer knows of no instance in present-day South Asia where religion has induced social change.'[21] In countless other localities churches exercise an effective veto power over social action. Experience throughout the world indicates that social change that must have the benediction of clergymen is doomed to delay, distortion, or prevention, not because of religion, but because of the conflicting needs of church power and politics.

The resulting impact of weak clerics on society can be seen in practice in the collective influence of groups of clergymen and the influence of individuals. The collective influence is almost always bad when it is brought to bear on political and social matters, even where such matters concern religion and morals. This phenomenon is similar to what happens when parents interfere in disputes among neighbourhood children; they invariably aggravate them, making them harder to resolve, and then they retain ill will after the children have ended their quarrel. History records such influence in numerous large issues such as the crusades, prohibition, and education, as well as in countless reforms against which the clergy were the first and most enduring obstacles. The evil is not wrongness – every social group has been wrong periodically – but the difficulty of criticizing and combatting clerical power which compounds error and makes it difficult to correct. Consequently the name of God has been invoked by clergy for every crime in the calendar without anything like the assessment which others incur in contemporary accounts and in histories. Despoilation of natives or burning at the stake in the name of the faith, for instance, were praised; those engaged in such atrocities who received punishment or death from those persecuted were regarded as martyrs or even saints. Modern counterparts of these coercions, like political intimidation and the destruction of personal reputations and careers, are equally protected from criticism.

This collective influence is being questioned, nevertheless, despite the protection. The questioners face an unequal battle because of clerical respectability, and turn to probing or ignoring religion itself. The stand of the Roman Catholic Church on priestly celibacy, the attitude of the Jewish religion on questions of citizenship and political power in Israel, the role of the Anglican Church in public affairs in Britain, and the influence of religious leaders in India and the Middle East have aroused concern about clerical judgment and power. They also cause embarrassment to public men who cannot afford to take stands less they be considered anti-church and are forced into compromise or inaction.

This situation bedevils education, for example, and both church influence and the fear of it paralyze action and reform.[22] A bishop importuning a newly elected premier to include more members of his faith in a cabinet, an archdeacon rousing his colleagues to public protest because of the absence of a representative of his clergy from the head table at a state dinner or because his church's representative was seated further down the table than that of another church, or a rabbi who cannot admit the difference between anti-semitism and disagreeing with Israel cause public acrimony and damage the credibility of the churches. Indeed of all professions the clergy is the most sensitive to protocol and its place in it. The private correspondence of politicians and experience with appointing public committees and arranging events testify eloquently to the ease with which clerics bruise.[23] Other people bruise too, but it is safer to ignore them, and they can rarely make issues of such matters.

The state has little protection against the collective influence and sensitivity of the clergy. If the public ignores clergymen politicians cannot. The people and their political leaders will not hesitate, for instance, to question the collective ideas and actions of doctors or military officers, and many have done it openly and with relish. Their suspicion of collective professionalism is a protection against its mistakes. But very few people and only a rare politician will take on a church or a clergyman in public or carry on an open campaign against a diocesan policy. To do so is to invite ruin. A president of the United States can combat a powerful army commander or a steel combine and be admired and supported for it, but a church or prelate is, in effect, beyond his capacity for even mild public reproach. Anyone can publicly castigate a president, but not a cardinal, on Viet Nam; a prince, but not a caliph, on Arab warfare; a politician, but not a rabbi, on Jerusalem; a premier, but not an archbishop, on Quebec or Ireland. There have been commissions of enquiry into almost everything but churches. A local newspaper can criticize a mayor, the police, or a school teacher; for it to reprove or question a church person is, however, beyond the scope of freedom of the press. Frank debate on church activity is almost impossible in a legislature.

The mixing of religion and church politics is the reason for the reluctance to criticize. Church intervention is readily considered religious rather than political, and to oppose it is generally considered to be obstructing what is good or holy or even God himself. People who do not understand the intervention and the opposition rarely hear both sides in an issue and perhaps even fear hearing them. The only practical way to oppose church intervention in public affairs is to do it behind the scenes. Because it is dangerous it takes time, patience, and subterranean politics in the form of arguments behind closed doors, rallying those who are frightened of denominational conflict, visits of emissaries to prelates, compromises, and gentlemen's agreements. A church-supported school question, for example, is like an iceberg to the public view; only a fraction of it is visible. Moreover such a matter is so sensitive that it disrupts public business, breaks political partnerships and personal friendships, and almost always involves pounds of political flesh in money, patronage, or other advantage as features of compromise. Such arrangements are sometimes dishonest: it is not uncommon for a church to insist on a 'right' policy when it is in a minority and later advocate the exact opposite when it becomes a majority. The existence of the issues is not the basic problem; they are inevitable. The problem is the protection of churches and clergy against the free and open processes of democracy. Indeed without this protection many church interventions would never take place because they could not withstand open and free discussion from either other churches or public forums.

Two kinds of weak clergy destroy the collective influence of the churches, the activists without sufficient knowledge and character to make wise contributions to projects which attract their interest, and the waverers without the strength to take a stand on anything. It does not take too many of them in a diocesan meeting or ministerial association to ensure the production of nonsense in the form of resolutions or the avoidance of a stand on an important issue. It is a disconcerting experience for public men to have distinguished clergymen apologize privately for the action or lack of action of such a group.

It is interesting to observe, for example, a clerical group dealing with a complicated issue such as the picayune tussle which took place in Canada in 1958 over the award of a Canada Council grant to the Dominion Drama Festival whose highest award was the Calvert Trophy. A crusade developed when certain clergymen protested the granting of public funds by the council to the festival because it awarded a trophy donated by the liquor company which financed it. Those crusaded against were angry, but they could say little. The crusaders made free and unfair observations on the council and the festival, and sent protests to government without having ascertained the facts from either body or considered what alternative help there was for the needy festival. Wafflers did not take a stand. This combination inevitably produced trouble for all concerned and surreptitious visits by embarrassed clergy apologizing for the action of their fellows. If the council, the festival, and the liquor company could have replied with impunity to the clerical group as they could to any other, or questioned the competence of the crusaders to express intelligent opinions on the matter, the whole issue would have been more carefully considered by the clergy, more satisfactorily debated by the parties involved, or, what is more likely, would not have arisen in the first place.

Some clerics are clearly motivated in social action by opposition to evil. They are not the only people so motivated, but they do enjoy the widespread association of church action with the search for good. 'Good' and 'evil' are relative terms, however, and under no circumstances are they the exclusive prerogative of any one church or of churches generally. A dogma or policy of a church may seem good to its adherents simply because the church states it; its wider application may be evil in its effects because this limited interpretation may ignore realities, consequences, and the views of others, or because it may be entirely wrong. The ancient slaughter of infidels seemed good to its church sponsors, but it was evil nevertheless; the good intentions behind prohibition were more than balanced by the consequences of bootlegging and gang warfare; the advantages of the compulsory education of children in church schools are trifling compared to their unhealthy divisive effects on Christianity and on the democratic society.

A church can be right or wrong on such an issue like any other organization, but the difficulty of criticising the church guarantees that it will make mistakes. Society suffers the mistakes because it fears the passions of denominational conflict. Many church dogmas and policies are therefore tolerated as necessary evils rather than accepted as personal convictions. The consequences to society are obvious enough, but the patience of people runs out sooner or later as the mistakes become intolerable, and with it, unfortunately and tragically, often go many allegiances to the finer church dogmas and policies. Or people realize that the mistakes have nothing to do with religion and leave their church or support it without personal conviction. Religion itself suffers grievously, although erroneously, when church political mistakes accumulate to the point where the church is considered irrelevant.

This situation suggests a comparison with parliamentary government. As we noted earlier, one of the latter's greatest achievements was getting accepted the distinction between the state and the government, between treason and opposition, and between the interests of the people and the advantage of politicians. Without parliamentary government these distinctions disappear to the temporary glory but ultimate destruction of governments, and to the disastrous disadvantage of the people. It is not difficult to wonder if the troubles of religion are caused by the lack of similar distinctions between religion and churchmanship.

All professions must consider the advantages and weaknesses of professionalism. The advantages are well known and openly admitted: control of the admission and training of new members, supervision of standards, exchange of information, encouragement of research, fostering of professional pride and public relations, and providing a voice for the profession in dealings with other groups. The weaknesses of professionalism are less understood and are admitted with more reluctance: the tendency to build a power structure which, when unchecked, may subordinate service to the public in favor of the prestige of an organization; the inclination to elaborate administration and regulations which, when unchecked, take up more of the time and effort of the participants than the service for which the organization was originally set up; and the conservatism which defies criticism, discourages innovation, and ultimately punishes dissent. These advantages and weaknesses have often been discussed in conflicts between the professions and other authorities, such as unions in labor matters, doctors in issues concerning socialized medicine, teachers in school and university matters, and officers of the armed services in both war and peace. The literature on professionalism is large and the subject is a familiar one in our society.

Little is known, however, about the effects of professionalism among the clergy. The assumption that all clergymen are devoted 'men of God' working humbly in His service and that of mankind has been well established; the literature of the churches features the power and duties of the clergy and is interpreted by them; the clergy preside over many of man's significant individual and group ceremonies; they enjoy a respectability which protects them from public criticism; and deceased members of the profession are often canonized by their successors and are considered to have special powers in the next world. This arrangement the members of any profession or group would gladly have; some, especially politicians, have aspired to it (and many of history's most sensational upheavals were concerned with preventing them from getting it). This professional aggrandizement almost invariably boosts church politics. There are two ways in which it operates: one is the unique ease with which the clergy get involved in secular matters; and the other is the transfer of their ideas and attitudes to other people and groups who in turn, fortified by example, sponsor them in society generally.

A major share of clerical activity concerns rivalries among the clergy themselves. This is the ultimate in professional weakness; it is a characteristic of power that the more power a group has the more will the group suffer internal struggle for it. This struggle unfortunately spills over into other groups called on for help in the respective causes. The reason societies set up ways of making power responsible is the need, long illustrated by history, of preventing its confinement in individuals and groups and the subsequent involvement of others in the resulting explosion. The extent to which clerics have involved others in their rivalries has been one of the saddest experiences of men.

This involvement usually starts innocently enough with a bureaucracy. Churches, like other organizations, enjoy building bureaucracies. The personnel are subject to all the common weaknesses of civil servants and specialists, and require the same kinds of responsibility that are arranged in other bodies. This responsibility is not often evident, however, and the number and power of ecclesiastic officials have grown. 'Recent years,' says one church writer, 'have seen move after move to concentrate power in the hands of the central bureaucracy both in Church House and in the diocesan headquarters. The Church Assembly's Advisory Council for training the Ministry is steadily encroaching on theological colleges and bishops ... Pastoral reform ... is eroding individual liberty and making the diocesan planners more powerful.'[24] Two facts are unique about this development. An ecclesiastical bureaucracy enjoys its church's assumption of divine auspices and respectability which afford it more protection than its counterparts in the other bureaucracies enjoy. And in addition, while church bureaucracies include some able clerics who sojourn there for experience between appointments in distinguished careers, they also include men with little or no experience in pastoral work, as well as weak persons who are failures in pastoral work and cannot be otherwise disposed of.

Bureaucracy always encourages politics. A partnership of some kind between the clergy and the politicians in the management of public affairs is always sought by ecclesiastical bureaucrats and has been a common practice. The idea presumably is to include moral practices and traditions in government. Thus the tribal chief shared authority with the witch doctor, the ancient king with the high priest, the colonial governor with his bishop, and leaders of established churches with sovereigns and ministers. Senior members of the clergy, alone among the professions, even enjoy places on governmental precedence lists. History has long since shown that this mixture of power leads to a division of the loyalties of laymen. Few have understood why temporal authorities alone may not sponsor moral practices and traditions in public affairs. Each side in the partnership has tended to disclaim responsibility for the other's jurisdiction and to indulge his own interests, failing to accommodate its administrative practices or religious principles to the political facts of this combination of power. Generally the clergy have found the power too much for them, and their religion has suffered because it has been diverted into the quicksands of politics where it is submerged by the fear of the faithful rather than supported by their conviction.

Peter the Great was forced to deal with the Russian Orthodox Church which had been great in the fifteenth century but was corrupt by the seventeenth. The views of one of his biographers, Ian Grey, are as relevant to contemporary church politics as to the church politics of Peter's day. Peter, he said, revised the clerical structure in 1721 through 'a revolution of customs and institutions, not of doctrine and ideas,' concentrating on making the clergy mind its own business instead of using it to meddle in public affairs and on making public respect for the church a matter of religion rather than of politics. It was not just the old problem of separating church and state; it was also the need for the church and the people to realize that, while they must distinguish between what is God's and what is Caesar's, they must also understand that Caesar can serve God on his own through his own actions without the church telling him what to do. It took time and authority for the Czar to make the point because 'simple people do not know how to distinguish the spiritual power from that of the autocrat, but struck by the glory and splendour of the highest pastor, they think he is a second sovereign with like powers, or even with greater powers, and that the spiritual rank is a different and higher state.'[25] The same conflict causes wonder to those in any town where 'the palace' houses in splendour the local representative of the carpenter of Nazareth.

The assumption that politicians are unable to do good things without the promptings of the clergy persists in our own time. 'In Quebec, until the middle of the Duplessis era,' wrote Hugh MacLennan, 'the true power was not the Legislative Assembly but the Catholic Church.'[26] 'Religious authority,' writes King Ibn Saud's biographer, 'existed in parallel with his own secular authority, and he always had to take care that it was on his side.' Religious power lay largely in the hands of the Ulema 'who directed the observance of the Wahhabi interpretation of the precepts of the Koran ... To satisfy the more bigoted of these fanatics sometimes strained what little patience Ibn Saud possessed.'[27] Saud, like numerous counterparts, would no doubt have readily dispensed with his clerical partners, not because he was insincere in his faith, but because both public business and the faith would be better served if they stuck to serving the latter. There is no evidence whatever in either history or contemporary affairs that politicians serve God any the less in their spheres than do the clergy in theirs, or that interventions of the clergy in secular matters either increase the good or decrease the bad processes in those matters.

The ultimate link between the church and politics arises when a clergyman holds political office. This is an almost impossible combination of roles because the clergyman may hold fast to, and use, his church policies to the exclusion of those of other groups; or he may be so anxious to please everyone that he has no policies at all and his personal advancement becomes his main interest. Politicians, today as always, find Wolseys and Cranmers to support anything. Actually the combination of roles readily brings out the worst of each. A political mandate from the people, plus the trappings of power, plus power itself are a heady enough mixture for any human being to bear without adding to it the respectability and protection assumed by an alleged 'man of God.'

The problems are easily found in biographies of clerical statesmen like Richelieu and Mazarin, and the ease with which both religious and political principles can be juggled was shown by two episcopal chameleons, Tallyrand and Fouché. Even Richelieu, the most dedicated of these, envisioned power and a political career in the earliest days of his priesthood and used men for his own advancement. Yet 'whenever he found it expedient he was to deny his old friends, to betray them to exile and imprisonment, to send them even to their deaths at the bidding of political necessity, which for him meant Destiny too.'[28] A peculiar psychological factor is also found in men who combine political and church power, and it is frequently seen in the proponents of contemporary protest movements. Stefan Zweig describes such a figure as one of 'those strange personalities that always come to the top in times of rapid change, one of those individuals animated by pure and ardent idealistic faith, and one of those who do more mischief with their faith and bring about more bloodshed with their idealism than the most brutal of realists and the most savage of terrorists. We always find that among revolutionists and reformers it is the man of quasi-religious temperament, the ecstatic, who, with the best of intentions in the world, gives the impetus to murder and havoc which he himself loathes.'[29] A man may show this tendency not only because he wants to persecute enemies, but also because under stress 'he is afraid of being disapproved of as a moderate.'[30] The ecclesiastical potentates of political history have their counterparts among modern churchmen who assume political functions as office holders, advisers, or advocates. When men like William Jennings Bryan, William Aberhart, Father Coughlin, and Archbishop Makarios invoke religion in politics, it is difficult for an opposition to oppose them or for a society to control them. It is not surprising, therefore, that the 1971 Synod of Bishops in Rome recommended that 'priests should stay out of partisan political activities and may never hold political office unless in rare circumstances, and then only with their bishop's permission.'[31] It is not unreasonable to apply the same rule to other churchmen, including lay preachers. A very few benign churchmen assume political responsibilities and avoid mischief; for the rest the intoxicating dose of two kinds of power and respectability proves too much.

On the gravestones of most of them might well be placed the couplet which appeared on that of one:

Passant, n'est-ce pas chose étrange
Qu'un demon soit près d'un ange?[32]

Many contemporary politically minded or power-orientated clergy by-pass direct participation in affairs of state in favour of service in social organizations. Sometimes they stop there; often they go much further and participate in the politics which social service involves. This work may appear more modern than that of clerical politicians and advisers, but it is essentially the same in that it involves political power and tactics reinforced by respectability and religious auspices. A minister or rabbi can become a politician when he joins enough committees; a priest often rivals local political officials in actual political authority. Able clergy may occasionally do this kind of work well when they understand the misty area between religious and political leadership and the limitations which one puts on the other. Their weak brethren, on the other hand, usually get lost in the misty area and wander around unguided by either the insight of the religious leaders or the skill of the political ones. Indeed participatory democracy encourages them. They can ruin an institution with shocking ease, and their credibility is often destroyed with it.

There are many vantage points from which to watch this phenomenon: a board of directors or a committee of a community enterprise is one of the best, especially a board which must deal with some controversial matters. Difficulties commence with the appointment of clerical members which, on the whole, tends to favour weak clergymen. Such men are inclined to look for the posts, and it is harder to resist them than other weak people. The able clergyman rarely seeks appointment; he is too busy with work and study, and must be sought after. This is a common occurrence among all appointees in such enterprises, but it is reinforced, in the case of the clergy, by the way in which they are nominated. They get on boards through church nomination to membership because the church tends to favour safe men or professional committee members, because able clergymen are too busy, or because the church wants to give recognition to a man who needs a favourable gesture or something to do. They also get there through nomination by a public authority because it either consults the church or selects those active in social circles. They get there also through nomination by other clergymen from different denominations. A weak clergyman is sought after by stronger rivals, particularly when the business concerned is controversial, such as education, because a weak social activist can be directed or flattered into any decision if he is given some importance and power, and the waffler will agree to any pressure in the interest of harmony. The best way to get an able clergyman on a board is for the board itself to make the selection; it usually considers nomination in relation to the interests of the board and its work. A minister, a priest, or a rabbi who takes his place as a result of one of the first three types of nomination almost always emphasizes his position as a clergyman over his duty as a member, and the two roles often conflict. This trouble is less evident when the cleric is invited by the board itself.

The able clergyman whom the board has been successful in securing participates effectively, like the other good members; the weak one clothes himself in respectability and soon seeks to exert authority. The chair defers to him, and he is forgiven transgressions intolerable in other members. The odds are heavy against a member who argues with a monsignor; the chairman must try to accommodate a rabbi; and a guilty feeling prevails at a meeting if a minister records a dissenting vote. If the issues discussed are vital and controversial the clerical wafflers will disrupt the search for decision by their natural instability; other kinds of wafflers can be shamed into a stand, whereas clerical ones make a virtue of evasion which is difficult to deal with.

Nowhere is this impact of weak clergy more evident than in appointed offices appropriated by them outside of their churches. Chaplaincies in schools and universities furnish examples, and also illustrate a reason why young people leave the churches. Their service in hospitals and the armed services are similarly revealing. Able clergy do participate as chaplains in the field of education and perform distinguished service. They are almost always men who are sought and named to their offices by the institutions themselves. When a church or government appoints or nominates chaplains it often selects inexperienced novices, elderly men, or men who have proved to be incapable of parish work and have to be given something to do. Often enough such men are appointed only in a vain attempt to lend a touch of respectability to an enterprise.

These men cause trouble when they prove bad examples to those to whom they minister, or do little or nothing because they cannot, or do too much because of a need for self-vindication. It is a sad occurrence for an institution to ask for the transfer of a chaplain and be advised by his superiors that there is no other place for him. It is tragic to watch a chaplain alienate his constituents from his church while seeking an increased influence in the institution which he cannot justify. Chaplaincies are attractions to weak clergy; the social activists among them see them as centres of power; the wafflers see them as centres of respectability. Neither realizes that direct ministering to youth requires work, honesty, selfless devotion, and personal example in excess of that required in regular parish work. In any community, however, weak clergy are often the first to volunteer for chaplaincies, usually because they are not making their mark elsewhere, and institutions must be tough in refusing their blandishments and in seeking instead the talents of the abler clergy who are much less forward in offering their services. If an able full-time clergyman is not available for the post it is better to do without one and invite the services of suitable parish clergy when the occasion requires.

Unhappily, however, the proverbial woman scorned has no fury like some weak chaplains over whose heads a parish clergyman's services or a bishop's intervention are invited in dealing with special problems. A university can refuse the services of a professor or an administrator; it can even decline the proferred talents of retired politicians or businessmen who think their experience would be useful. But if it declines the help of a prospective chaplain it must risk charges of being 'godless' and political manoeuverings among church and university authorities. Such experience adds yet another group to those disillusioned by the church. The problem requires the same examination recommended by a rabbi for hospital chaplaincies: 'There must be a re-evaluation of chaplaincy services,' he is reported as saying, '... in setting standards and selecting suitable, trained candidates.'[33] This kind of examination, valuable in any profession, is a protection to the church as well as society, because reaction is bound to set in, in extreme if not normal form — for example, a proposal made by a disciplinary committee to the General Synod of the Church of England by one of its own lay representatives, to deal with 'unruly, permissive and undignified behaviour of increasing numbers of clergy.'[34]

There is a roundabout method by which the clergy can get appointed posts. Many clergymen leave their parishes to return to university for special training in social work, especially youth work. Some of these men are able, and their entry to this field is laudable. Some, however, are failures in parish work. Neither the churches nor the universities erect barriers against this second group, and the courses in this field are among the easiest available. This combination of backgrounds can help able clergy to do much good in appointed jobs; it can enable a few weak ones to do useful work after they are freed from parish work for which they are not suited. For most of the weak ones, however, the result, reinforced by protection and respectability, can be a calamity for any authority hiring them or for any young person who must suffer their ministrations. To cite only one of many instances, I once listened to such a clergyman, who had taken special training in 'alcohol education,' give a lecture on the subject to an auditorium full of students. It was an arrogant, yet pitiful, performance, and a group of students told me they never felt more like drinking than they did after the lecture. The result was the same wherever the man spoke on his nationwide tour. Most colleges refused to have him back on his second tour, after which experience he reported to the local clergy and his superiors that the principals and professors were not cooperative and that the students were indifferent to his message. It took much behind-the-scenes politics to get him off the circuit, but not, unfortunately, before he had spread much ill will for which he blamed everyone but himself. The medium was a bad message.

Churches and clergy concerned about the alienation of people from religion should ask whether it is religion or church postures and politics that repel people, and whether or not they are themselves part of the problem. 'There is an anticlerical movement in our church,' said a moderator of the United Church of Canada, 'as if there is something suspect about the ordained ministry.'[35] Certainly the churches have declined in influence in their rush to be part of a social service age. They should examine whether or not their social and political work detracts from their spiritual work, either because they cannot handle both, or because they send the wrong men equipped with the wrong kind of authority and protection to do work for which they have little justification or talent.

11

The impact of church politics

When churches gave dogmas to the world they gave hostages to fortune. The history of many dogmas indicates that fortune has not received them kindly. It has played them off one against another, and made them the bases of complicated politics and internecine quarrels. The politics of the dogmas mixed with other kinds of politics with striking impact, and the quarrels belied the dogmas themselves. The reason is not difficult to find: while religion does splendid things for men, church politics has a schizophrenic effect on them. This effect has been strikingly illustrated by the political activities of church laymen and clergy throughout the world.

The activities of church laymen provide both motivation and opportunity for politics. Indeed simply being a layman may affect profoundly a man's activities outside a church. There are two categories of laymen. One comprises elders, members of official church bodies, officers of church societies and fraternal organizations, recipients of church honours and titles, and other prominent participants in church work. The other category comprises rank and file members and adherents. The first category is what we will mean by laymen in this discussion, that is, those who participate actively in the affairs of churches.

The layman's interpretation of his relationship with God is an ancient and controversial subject. It can be humble and honourable. It can also be blatant and egotistical, and include an assumption that a special relationship with God of a personal and intimate kind exists automatically and confers special status on the layman in public life. The more seriously a layman takes himself as distinct from his religion, the more grandly he tends to deem the auspices. To him his work readily becomes God's work, his decisions God's will. Instead of humbling him, this relationship may make him arrogant and hard to advise and criticize, and prompt him to leave too much to faith – not really in God, but in himself – with disastrous consequences.

Two concepts get mixed up in this assumed sponsorship: the humble servant of God and the egoist who boasts divine patronage. Power tends to turn the first into the second. 'I regard my whole position as given to me direct from Heaven and I have been called by the Highest to do His work,' declared Kaiser William II. 'Remember that the German people are chosen by God. On me as the German emperor, the spirit of God has descended. I am His weapon, His sword, His vice-regent.'[1] And millions cheered. Republicanism may not dilute this arrogance. 'God ordained that I should be the next President of the United States,' the Kaiser's enemy, Woodrow Wilson, informed an astounded Chairman of the Democratic National Committee who had just helped him get elected. 'Neither you nor any other mortal or mortals could have prevented it.'[2] This kind of reverse idolatry is common among over-serious officials down to the humblest clerk. A political party, indeed a whole nation, may assure itself of the same distinction. This attitude is usually regarded as being religious rather than blasphemous, despite repeated evidence that the use of God's name and sponsorship in this manner is suspect and could be discouraged with much benefit to public affairs and religion itself.

In local politics the layman's activities are not necessarily motivated by religion. Some are; some are not. It is commonly assumed, nevertheless, that what a layman does in the name of his church is therefore religious. Indeed some use church auspices to justify any idea or action however good or bad it may turn out to be. It may also be assumed that being a church layman automatically puts one into a state of grace or respectability. Sometimes it does; sometimes it does not. When it does the attributes of the layman are obvious assets in his work in other organizations. When it does not they can be disastrous. In either event a church position confers respectability on a man in and outside his community. Some men never take advantage of it to secure prestige or power in other activities. Some, however, use it as a claim to status, a protection against trouble in employment, a means of securing advantage in politics or contacts in business, or a tactic in applying pressure or securing patronage. This kind of strategy is particularly evident in smaller communities, and the smaller the community the more it shows up in political and social life. Indeed church politics is so pervasive in many small communities, in the Maritime provinces of Canada, for example, that it is a factor in the migration of people to larger centres.

The competent churchman devoted to religion needs not use his church affiliation for advancement. But the weak and over-serious one, perhaps conscious that it is his only mark of respectability, uses it with vigour. The latter type is only too obvious. 'Unfortunately,' writes one clergyman, 'volunteer work within the administrative structure of church and synagogue ... does not always attract the most generous-spirited, compassionate, and "civilized" members of the community.'[3] Both community service and the church suffer every time the church is used by such people as a bridge to public service. The church is often so used, unfortunately, because it is the one institution in which mediocre men can quickly attain a respectability which will both cover up their deficiencies and facilitate community recognition.

Ecclesiastical political patronage facilitates this kind of recognition and is a well trod bridge to public service. Political appointments must always allow for church affiliation. Both clergy and laymen keep count of the number of cabinet ministers of their persuasion and protest vigorously if there seems to be an imbalance. 'The turn,' that is, one vacancy for this denomination, the next for another, is evident in numerous categories of public appointments. Confessional appointment may even be open and compulsory, as in Lebanon.[4] A balanced membership among able men is an advantage, but in frequent instances where there is a dearth of good prospective appointees talent is displaced by denominationalism. However irrelevant membership in one church as distinct from another may appear to be in either religion or politics, it is a common means by which weak men secure political prefer- ment, often over much stronger candidates. The reason is simple: able men make their way on their own talents and achievements and no one regards them as denominational appointees; weak men may rely on church affiliation, and in sensitive situations it is difficult for governments dependent on votes to resist this kind of pressure.

A prominent churchman will act in one of two ways when he takes poli- tical office. If he and others know that he was successful in gaining office on his own merits, if he did not use his church affiliation in seeking appoint- ment, and if he maintains credibility as a successful office holder in his own right, he will rarely allow his affiliation to affect the performance of his duty to all the people he serves. If, however, he and everyone else know that his was a denominational appointment, if he used his church work to help his election, and if he maintains political advantage with church influence, he will become an agent for his church and he will be inclined to regard his public duty from the viewpoint of 'our side.' It takes only one such man to make a government factious, to make colleagues frightened of denominational pressure, to render decision making unduly compromising, and to increase the amount of backstairs manoeuvering needed in government. Such a man is hard to argue with and almost impossible to dismiss or demote because his church status is a formidable protection.

Why should church affiliation, it may well be asked, be a less desirable determinant than other kinds of affiliation? The answer lies with the same elements of respectability and protection noted earlier as advantages of the clergy. These elements are hard to deal with when prominent church laymen use them in politics, and anyone who combats them must tread warily on sensitive ground, mined with emotion and bitterness and fortified by non-negotiable positions. One can argue vehemently with spokesmen of labour or agriculture, of business or the professions, and remain on friendly terms. One can tell the sponsors that their spokesmen are incompetent. A group can discuss problems in these areas openly and frankly. Once, however, a church matter comes up participants rarely can say what they think. A Knight of St Gregory or a Clerk of Session has a sensitive constituency he can report to. The result is either unwilling accommodation and compromise managed by militant churchmen or the shelving of issues or action to avoid confrontation. The charity and humility which people want to associate with religion are rarely evident when church politics is played in this manner.

Fairness and efficiency are rarely evident either. Church patronage prevents the operation of the law of averages – which does not operate in rotation – and thereby often brings the wrong people forward at what is the wrong time for the right people because the chances of getting the best men available from a given church at given times are not great. The practice is also unfair to other categories of men – occupational, professional, racial, and age – which might be equally deserving of recognition, and especially to men in the church categories which cannot be considered out of turn. As long as church laymen and affairs are protected from open competition and frank public discussion, church affiliation is an irrelevant and dangerous determinant in political appointment and status as well as a weakness in the churches themselves. It should have no more consideration than the height of a man or the colour of his eyes.

But should not churches participate in expressing opinions and deciding policy on public matters just like any other organizations? The answer is 'yes,' but only if they are prepared to have their participation regarded as political, and to have their opinions, actions, and personnel treated in the same open democratic fashion as those of other organizations. If there is any suggestion that their representatives form a party or pressure group, or that they are expressing a denominational or political viewpoint in the guise of a religious one, it soon becomes obvious that religion fades into the background. For this reason the fact that there may not be a desired number from one religious group in a cabinet or a legislature (for example, Protestants in Quebec or Spain, or Roman Catholics in Northern Ireland) is a cause, not for increasing denominational representation, but for abolishing it altogether. The mere fact that there is denominational representation encourages denominational dividing lines and friction, hampers cooperation in all public business, and has no relevance either to religion or to public affairs. Church representatives are human; they can be right or wrong like everyone else; and their doctrines and ideas are numerous and contradictory. Any indication that they have special auspices on a monopoly on rightness or that they can be opposed only at peril is not only arrogance; it is also, as history frequently indicates, an unreliable foundation for either the brotherhood of man or religion itself.

Bigotry is the ultimate problem in the mixing of church and other politics. It is tragic that bigotry should be associated with religion at all, because it is not a consequence of religion; one never sees it in a truly religious man. It is a result of church politics, especially of struggles for respectability and power. One nearly always sees it in the more egotistical of church politicians. Examples of it are legion from mighty contests for the power and wealth of empires to picayune bickering over the limited prestige of a backwoods parish. Wherever it raises its head it strikes fear in man, confuses issues, and disrupts public and social life. Its ecclesiastical protection is hard to combat. Its worst feature, however, is that it is accompanied by an even more odious element, reverse bigotry, which always involves fear and betrayal. One eminent American had to weigh the effects of bigotry in elections: '... would a Catholic candidate gain more from his kinsmen's inclination to vote *their* past, or would he lose more from the Protestants' inclination to vote *their* past.'[5] At the same time his opponent faced reverse bigotry: 'I was getting it from both ends; Republican Catholics were being urged to vote for Kennedy because he was of their religion; and Republican Protestants were being urged to vote for him to prove that they were not biased against Catholics!'[6]

The foregoing suggests that church political attitudes tend to overflow more readily into public and social affairs than religious attitudes. This is especially true of dogmatic assertiveness and the urge to command and control. He who has a rigid dogma to proclaim will be content, not with persuasion, but with command. Once he becomes accustomed to command in church affairs he tends also to command in other spheres, perhaps using his church auspices as an unassailable defence. In turn those who become accustomed to being commanded in matters of dogma take little coaxing to accept the same command in non-church affairs. This approach introduces into public life under special auspices elements undesirable in politics and psychologically crippling, albeit acceptable, to the people.

One of these elements is the 'hard line,' blindly followed and rigidly defended. No organization is more encouraging of hard lines than a church. It teaches men from childhood that its dogma is truth and, by implication or instruction, that other dogmas are wrong. Once the mind is trained in this way this attitude is readily adapted to other categories of ideas. Another element is belligerence. Sometimes the quickest, but in the long run the worst, way of getting something accepted is to couple advocating it with making an evil of its alternative. Churches use this method frequently in dealing with ideas and men that are not evil at all, but only different. Indeed the auspices of a religion or a church are the most powerful weapon for combatting anything one does not like. Churches can make an individual or institution 'godless' or disreputable very quickly, perhaps very quietly, and people will not want to defend the victim or be associated with him. Churchmen given to this tactic often carry it into public life where it is tolerated because of its sponsors and where it serves as a bad example to others tempted to use it. It is always unfair and undemocratic, and its results are invariably unsatisfactory.

The work of church politicians therefore needs careful assessing. He who is known favourably for his church work alone can be regarded with extreme caution; in his concentration of effort his outlook and techniques tend to be narrow. He who is excessively and openly devout should be avoided altogether in public life because he may have something to hide or compensate for. Most dangerous of all is he who invokes religion in fights, for he destroys the very soul of man. 'Say how is it,' runs the caption under a contemporary cartoon, 'you're never out sniping, planting bombs, burning and fighting, O'Rangatan? What are you, some kind of atheist?'[7]

Church politics is a barrier to religion in public life. People who are encouraged to act politically according to their religious categories bring to public life the same problems of bitter antagonism as groups that church politicians do as individuals. Of this fact the politics of Ireland or Latin America, for examples, must surely provide sufficient evidence. 'What is insisted on in India,' writes a distinguished observer about a solution to the problem, 'and constantly preached by those intellectual leaders who support the modernization ideals is that religion should be relegated to private life; it should not influence those in public life.'[8] Once more we see religion blamed instead of church politics. Furthermore there is nothing new about the modernists' plea. 'A bishop ought to abstain completely from mixing himself up with politics of the day ...' wrote Prince Albert to the Dean of Westminster. 'As to religious affairs, he cannot but take an active part in them, but let that always be the part of a Christian, not of a mere Churchman ...'[9] Half a century later the French government had to increase drastically the separation of church and state after fanatical church participation on the side of injustice and anti-Semitism in the Dreyfus affair and other celebrated issues of the day.

One reason for all this trouble is common to countless issues. Whereas religion is a splendid agent for showing man his significance in the world and encouraging his love of other men, church politics is a powerful agent for convincing man he is better than he is and for provoking his hatred of his fellows. Another reason is the use of denominationalism as a passion to feed other passions, from national aggrandizement on the international scale to political supremacy on the local. It is difficult to control ordinary passions, but it is impossible if they are backed by denominational ones. A cruel psychological condition seems to be encouraged in the form of a subconscious childish jealousy that seems to seek a favoured position in the eyes of God at the expense of others of his children. It never varies, and is the same now in the Middle East and India as it was in the Crusades. This jealous rivalry which, if encouraged in a family, can wreck it, is tragically aided and abetted in denominational life. But, it is so often said, should not God be involved in all men do? The history of denominational conflict must surely answer that his presence is neither assured by church politics nor prevented by lack of them.

Zealous political activities on the part of laymen and clergy have undoubtedly been among the main reasons for the playing down of church affiliation in contemporary life. Applications for jobs and admission to universities in some parts of the world now rarely contain a question about 'church affiliation,' and in some lands it is no longer a social stigma to have no church affiliation. The rightness or wrongness of this trend is a matter of opinion. But one thing is clear in meetings, in classrooms, and in social events. When men's church membership is evident a group often suffers embarrassment, timidity, and discord. When men are unable to make impressions with church memberships, indeed when they neither know nor care about one another's affiliations, they do better work and get on more harmoniously. Another thing is becoming even clearer. There is no evidence that the increasing numbers of people without any church affiliation lead any less good or productive lives or make any less devoted citizens, or indeed are any less religious, than those with it. Religion would no doubt be encouraged if this trend were continued to the point where denominational labels applied only to forms of worship, where, outside worship, they meant no more than 'red-headed,' 'soft-spoken,' or 'plump,' where a man would be automatically dismissed for seeking preferment on the basis of how he worshipped, and where the terms 'Jew,' 'Catholic,' 'Protestant,' 'Muslim,' 'Hindu,' and 'Buddhist' disappeared from local politics and international relations. Were these categories regarded as irrelevant to everything else, they would become more relevant to religion. And other activities could be carried out more peacefully.

Such a trend would not be 'away from religion.' It would support religion by preventing the political conflicts of churches, which cancel one another out, and protecting churches from their greatest enemies, other churches. We too often forget that churchmen exert influence not just for their own churches but against other churches. Such conflicts arise among factions in other fields too, but there it is easier to take sides and assuage acrimony.

Problems affected by church rivalry too often must be left unsolved. Or they must be dealt with by unsatisfactory compromise and a high price in duplicated facilities or payoffs, or by the marshalling of men in emotional power struggles that lead inexorably to persecution and death. There is some advantage in interchurch conflict when astute people can play several churches off against one another, which tactic can be infinitely better than bearing the unchecked pressure of one church or several. Unfortunately, however, someone using this tactic will incur sooner or later the separate wraths of all the churches, because they will tend to blame him rather than one another when he ignores them all; or to prove his 'religion' he may be forced to take an undesirable stand for one of them or be ruined. When that stand is taken tragedy is so often the inevitable but unnecessary consequence.

This kind of rivalry is a major cause of criticism of churches. The criticism can rarely be expressed adequately, however, because church propaganda is so formidable. If two factions are involved, the big one with ample sources of support, perhaps on a world scale, can overwhelm the other to the point where only one side of the argument has a chance of becoming the 'solution' to the difficulty. There is never a real solution, of course, as old problems are left to fester and religion itself is degraded still further by the power politics involved. What profits a church if it gains the political power of a nation or a parish and loses its soul? The good of the loser is crushed, while the winner has gained a political inch and lost a religious yard. And the community loses through the turmoil which probably would never have taken place if the churches had kept out of it. Church affairs in this century, Christian or other, have not altered the melancholy conclusion of Gibbon at the end of the eighteenth century that 'Christians, in the course of their intestine dissentions, have inflicted far greater severities on each other than they experienced from the zeal of infidels.'[10]

This sad situation is caused in part by the tendency of man, already mentioned, to justify wrong in the name of right. Prominent churchmen are afflicted by this tendency like anyone else, and they will murder, steal, lie, and destroy the reputation and careers of other men in the alleged defence or promotion of a church interest, or in the accumulation of political power or personal advantage. Such men are often most zealous in dispensing communion, attending mass, saying prayers, or observing fasts; they appear to assume that the performance of such duties and offices gives a special dispensation for any conduct. The idea that wrong is right or tolerable if done by or in the name of a church, or is excusable if the wrong doer performs church duties or attends services regularly, is the result of the respectability and protection mentioned earlier. The latter will discourage free speech, questioning, and discovery, even in the face of overwhelming evidence, and often results in the persecution of enquirers. From Galileo and Copernicus, hounded for the heresy of discovery, to a contemporary history teacher condemned by a local church for assessing the clergy reserves and Bishop Strachan, the consequences of discussion are perilous if a church is bent on opposition. Even the clergy may be victims. In one well known issue a Canadian parish forced out of his office and his ministery a clergyman charged with a serious offence, and, although pledged by its dogma to mercy for even the most wayward brethren, the church tolerated vicious persecution before and during the trial and did not make amends even when the Supreme Court of Canada quashed the charges.[11]

Even such essential religious elements as love and forgiveness may be deliberately ignored. When Sir Charles Dilke tried to re-enter public life twenty years after his celebrated scandal, it was church leaders, including the Bishop of Southwark and the President of the Baptist World Alliance, who led the protest which rejected him and discouraged political leaders who were willing to give him a second chance.[12] This attitude is no less deplorable than the impulse of the Irish women who in 1971 shaved the head of, and tarred, a young lady who was to marry a British soldier of a different faith. The incidents themselves are as anti-religious as they are impossible to punish, but it is the example they set that is most dangerous to society.

There are so many examples of this kind of persecution that bills of rights which include freedom of religion should also include freedom from church persecution because few other forms of persecution have resulted in a greater loss of rights.

The most undesirable of all church political attitudes which overflow into political and social affairs is puritanism. We noted earlier that man is at his most dangerous when he gives free rein to his puritan tendency. The extreme strictness of puritanism becomes authoritarian because of the demands of control, and then vicious as excessively narrow conviction subdues the inevitable reactions to it. When church people advocate morals and live up to them they proselytize by example. But trouble inevitably arises when they proclaim moral values as truths, and treat them with such deadly seriousness that they take themselves with similar seriousness, and seek to impose both their morals and themselves on others. Such people are usually wrong, not because the moral value is necessarily wrong, but because they associate its virtue with themselves whether they deserve to or not, and because they readily ride roughshod over other people's virtues when touting their own. When dogmatic assumptions of right meet other assumptions of right the latter must become dogmatic too in self-defence. The rampage then begins: love and joy are pushed aside; life ceases to be fun.

A form of selfishness accompanies puritanism and makes it drab. Overly virtuous people, perhaps with a tendency to masochism, often dislike seeing other people enjoy themselves. So-called kill-joys are common, and many of them use their alleged virtue as a weapon. Their subdued emotions remain, however, and explode sooner or later, perhaps in individual crises, often in confrontations with others. This is the striking lesson of Somerset Maugham's *Rain.* If, therefore, a puritan, who has had his puritanism encouraged by doctrinal security in church affairs, carries these tendencies into political and social life, he will cause, not only drabness, but a kindling of dangerous aggressive instincts. He will also promote one of the most vicious of all social arguments, that no one should have what he does not want or cannot have – an argument that rarely contributes to social welfare or progress because it is negative and restrictive. The prevalence of this argument in many affairs is a major reason for the disappointing results of numerous social developments. This puritanism is yet another reason why there must be freedom from church aggression in a society concerned with civil rights.

Not only do churches make use of laymen in political and social activities, but laymen also use churches for their own purposes. Many men climb to prominence on the backs of churches; a few do great service to the churches by so doing; most do them great harm. The service is usually obvious; the harm, however, is hidden because few can discuss or admit it. Each time a church gets caught in a power play, for example, and its name is used in the alleged interest of religion, people wonder and have doubts, the church's reputation is besmirched, and religion itself is condemned. Every authoritarian or weak man who uses or betrays his affiliation as an aid to politics adds to the wonder and doubt. Every clergyman who feels he must support a weak man for an important office because that man is a churchman, or oppose the dismissal of an incompetent who has established himself as a representative of the church, tarnishes his church's image. An accumulation of such incidents outweighs much of the good done by able laymen and produces a cynicism in those for whom they are a regular experience. As one of the most active media for social and political participators, a church can do society much good by carefully assessing who uses its name and how.

Many of these problems arise from a basic characteristic of church work: it caters, not just to the religious and charitable instincts of man, which is its real function, but to his political, thespian, ideological, and predatory instincts as well. 'The actors want praise and the politicians want power,' said an Anglican primate. 'There are elements of both in the Ministry.'[13] No field other than politics itself offers more scope for politically inclined people than church work. And no interest adds more to the basic tasks of public administration than churches, both on their own business and on the business of opposing other churches. From Jewish-Muslim and Hindu-Muslim struggles on the world scene to the securing of patronage in public departments on a local scene there is a vast quantity of church politics. As for thespian and ideological instincts, the church is the next best place to the stage and platform for the would-be actor and philosopher; there he can expound his ideas before a captive audience without fear of unfavourable reviews in the newspapers. Henry Cardinal Manning, who was once an Anglican archdeacon, was a striking combination of politician, actor, and ideologue. Archbishop Errington whom he outmanoeuvered, Cardinal Newman whom he subdued, and his opponents in church consistories had reason to consider him a predator as well. Manning's counterparts thrive in less exalted roles in all the ranks of every denomination and in the laity as well.

Power is a major lure and motivation for such men in churches, as it is in most other institutions, and many activities are devoted to its justification. History has revealed no reason why churches should be freer than other organizations from the ancient and vital need to make power responsible for the sake of both the effectiveness of power and the welfare of men. Two church-related functions are so protected by respectability, however, that they make church power difficult to control: one is the function of preaching, teaching, and proselytizing; the other is dispensing charity.

Telling other people what to do is a popular activity and many professions indulge in it. We have already noted that people are not as inclined to accept advice, however, as others are disposed to give it; and that this is fortunate because much advice is bad, and a certain amount of natural resistance enforces responsibility. When this natural resistance is prevented, by a dictator or tyrannical parent or teacher, for example, bad advice tends to increase because it is less responsible, and the judgment of the recipient either atrophies or becomes enslaved. He who likes power always aims at diminishing this natural resistance to enlarge his opportunities for telling. Such strategy prospers for a time, but not usually for long, because that resistance returns and because the power wielder's unchecked mistakes inevitably require remedy.

Preaching, teaching, and proselytizing on behalf of a church and its doctrine and working in the interests of its politics are inclined to diminish this natural resisting. A politician, however capable, must marshal many forces to convince people of the merits of tight money or social welfare, and his opponents can marshal many forces to oppose him actively and freely. A church doctrine or action has as much chance of being right as wrong (opposing doctrines themselves indicate that all cannot be right), but any clergyman or layman, however capable or incapable, may present the doctrine or action with an assumed sponsorship which no one else would dare to invoke, urge its rightness over all other alternatives, and thereupon put any critic or opponent in the position of seeming wrong, even wicked. Dangers arise when authoritarian or weak men use this power in political or other fields, and trouble follows when people turn what is really a secular political struggle into a question of religion so as to give it added respectability, to make it a more acceptable and less assailable 'matter of principle,' to place opponents in the wrong more easily, and, above all, to frighten politicians into action to which they might otherwise not agree. Whether such tactics are successful or not, religion always suffers along with public affairs. 'There is the profoundest of wisdom,' wrote a Washington correspondent, 'in the Biblical injunction about rendering to Caesar the things that are Caesar's. As an old political writer I have never known a politician given to making stirring moral judgments out loud who could be trusted very far. It is not that all these fellows are cantridden; it is only that at best they operate in a hopeless confusion of purposes. Their's is the worst of all public sins – ineptitude.'[14] Carlyle was even blunter: 'It is a sad but sure truth,' he said, 'that every time you speak of a fine purpose, especially if with eloquence and to the admiration of by-standers, there is the less chance of your ever making a fact of it in your own poor life.'[15]

The dispensing of variously defined charity is accompanied by similar dangers. Kindness, help for the poor, and compassion for the afflicted are everywhere regarded as benevolent, and countless examples enrich the life of man. Yet a serious question about charity was raised at the World Synod of Bishops in 1971: 'How does it happen,' asked one archbishop 'that after two thousand years of uninterrupted preaching of Christian charity, the Church must admit the scarcity of the results attained in shaping the conscience of its members?'[16] The answer is not hard to find: with all its merits charity can be used for what are really political and uncharitable aims, such as the satisfaction of the ego of the giver, or the ultimate control by the giver of the receiver.

Parents who spoil children as a compensation for neglect are common cases in point (and also causes of much youthful discontent), as are missionaries who distribute spiritual and material favours only to those who attend their institutions and accept their doctrines. Moreover people tend to be exclusive in claiming charity as a prerogative of their own because of the good will and power associated with its distribution. This is why governments in a federal state quarrel among themselves over which shall distribute social services. Furthermore people will justify the most dire punishments and rigid controls on the ground that they are good for others. From heretics to the victims of child beaters, from oppressed colonists to students forced into professions by parents, countless victims of good intentions have endured misdirected charity. When this charity is forced or used as a bribe it may be considered immoral. 'But no one will say,' said an eminent leader of the Salvation Army, '..."we've done all this for you, don't you think you ought to ..." That would be considered immoral as far as we are concerned.'[17]

The use of the ecclesiastical powers of preaching and of dispensing charity and the results of their acceptance as respectable are well documented on a large scale in many parts of the world. Where such activity has been purely religious it has been a splendid saga; where it has been political it has been a sordid story.

The Marquesa Islands in the Pacific furnish a typical example. Missionaries, recounts R.C. Suggs,[18] entered a society with its own history, culture, and religion and began friendly relations with a few natives. Soon with the help of military forces they armed these unsuspecting friends and used them as mercenaries against other natives. Conversion was followed by obedience to the new masters. Then the friendly missionaries were replaced by tougher men who exercised control by encouraging rivalry among chiefs and their followers. Converted chiefs would be urged to invade their neighbours in the name of the new gospel. If a chief proved stubborn the church would encourage his overthrow by tempting his rivals with prospects of power. Native cultures and customs were respected at first, but gradually they were denounced and suppressed, and ultimately replaced by alien substitutes. The diseases of the invaders accompanied their gospel, and illness and death took over and invited even more control. Disillusioned with the loss of old traditions and doubtful about the new ones, grieved by the loss of independence and of life, the remaining natives took to debauchery and self-destruction and tried in vain to revive the tribal values they had been forced to exchange for the dogmatic 'truth' of the aliens. A vigorous population of around 110,000 dwindled to a pathetic remnant of 1500. 'Christianity had triumphed,' says the archeologist, 'but at what a price.'[19]

Such a process of telling and dispensing is regarded as positive action beneficial to both the churches concerned and the people they attempt to serve. Even the ridicule and destruction of existing interpretations of life may be regarded as employed in a good cause. 'Somehow,' wrote Vilhjalmur Stefansson, 'it seems that one of the first things an Indian learns in school is contempt for the ways of his ancestors; but after all the ways of his ancestors are the only ways that can prevail in that country.' He comments on the ease with which the northern Indians lost their enterprise and became over-dependent on the missions, and on the growth of their graveyards which accompanied the advance of 'civilized' ways. As for the Eskimo, wrote the explorer, 'it appears that the spread of Christianity among the Eskimo was as the spread of a habit or a fashion,' and was difficult to deal with. 'This was our first conflict with Christianity, and we had come off second best, as many others have done who have set themselves against the teachings of religion.'[20] Again we note that it is religion that suffers from being identified with church politics, this time in the form of church colonialism.

However much this colonialism may be justified as a professed desire to bring glad tidings and convert, the real motivations are too often an urge to control and the political and economic interests of the sponsors. Humboldt on one side of the world was appalled at 'seeing the symbol of the Cross wielded with the savageness of gun and whip,'[21] while Moorhead on the other side recounts how missionaries with 'the crucifix in one hand and the dagger in the other' brought the natives 'to ignorance, hypocrisy and a hatred of all other modes of faith . . . once foreign to the open and benevolent character of the Tahitian.'[22] The control may be almost blatantly political. In China the local gentry were confronted by missionaries who claimed privileged status and 'would-be rivals in the performance of their social functions,' among whom the bishops 'assumed a quasi-official status with much pomp and ceremony.' 'In retrospect it seems plain that the missionary's purpose, however he expressed it in terms of succor and salvation of his fellow men, was inevitably subversive of the traditional Chinese order.[23] In the Sudan the government passed a Missionary Societies Act in 1962 restricting the activities of missionaries because it suspected that they were 'not merely anti-Muslim but also active agents of a western policy of separatism.'[24] Chaos followed.

This use of church power operates often on a local scale in exactly the same way. There is the same diplomatic approach by the friendly clergyman or layman, invariably to weak men first, followed up, after a few unsuspected and secret commitments, by a take-over of the strategy by tougher advocates who replace the original commitments with harsher demands and force destruction and, almost inevitably, disillusionment. Men may be defamed and careers destroyed in the process, but it is in a 'good cause,' and it is impossible to oppose it with a comparable force. This is why politicians will do almost anything to avoid a confrontation with a church. This is why it is the politics of churches which takes hold among people rather than religion itself. In the slums of Glasgow, for example, 'not one in ten thought of his religion as anything but a label or a banner to fight under. They were contemptuous alike of God and their fellow men.'[25]

When a contempt of churches arises it is church politics which promotes it, not religion. It arises especially from a feeling that religion is being used merely as an excuse for the acquisition of power, and that such use harms religion and any secular activity touched by church politics. For example, the combination of mysticism, faith, and non-negotiability encouraged by man's ecclesiastical attitudes spreads readily into other fields and is used to establish and defend other ideologies and practices and give them a respectability they may not deserve. Man always has trouble when he invests a political ideology or institution with religious or quasi-religious trappings. The wrong kinds of emotion and fervour are thereby introduced into political processes, and discussion and responsibility are hindered by them. Any political or economic quack can combine a pseudo-religious attitude with a mesmeric or messianic approach and lead a multitude to disaster. The tendency to depend on faith in non-negotiable principles is so transferable that it can be invoked by any demogogue and freely indulged in by any group. Man does not need a 'truth' to support this fervour; the validity of Hitler's dictum 'the bigger the lie the better' has been only too amply demonstrated. Indeed people may not want to know the truth at all lest it disturb their existing ideas. They may prefer comforting make-believe, for which non-negotiable principles are solid buttresses.

It is not religion itself which has this effect on other fields. Most gospels stress humility, tolerance, the inheriting of the earth by the meek, the precedence of the soul over wealth and power, and the turning of the other cheek. How splendid life would be if these doctrines were only followed! It is their opposites, which are mistakenly associated with religion, that are the bad examples for other activities. Ecclesiastical history and current church politics throughout the world pay eloquent testimony to the attractions of arrogance, intolerance, money, and power, and the inability of many churchmen to handle them and to appreciate their consequences. One wonders, for instance, how non-Christian faiths would react to, and what fearful politics would result from, the ecumenical monopoly of Christendom in world religion suggested by the executive of the Baptist World Alliance already quoted. [26] When the faithful on various sides are expected to give their support without question, and when public officials dare not criticize, it should be no surprise that ecclesiastical tactics are adopted in political, economic, and social projects. As soon as they are adopted nations weaken and crumble because the wrong values are emphasized. From experiences in India and Pakistan 'and from collateral ones with the Catholic nations of Europe and the Arab states of the Middle East,' James A. Michener, again confusing religion and church politics, concludes that 'religion is about the poorest base for erecting a nation and the least to be depended upon. Almost any other vital force seems stronger.'[27]

Not only do such tactics weaken public projects; they are themselves weakened and rendered ineffective. 'What happens,' asked Aldous Huxley, 'when good men go into power politics in the hope of forcibly shoving humanity into the kingdom of God?' He quotes the pamphleteers of Ratisbon: 'Sacrilegious are the arms wielded by a sacred hand. When the mitre commands the soldier, it is the soldier who commands the mitre.' 'The whole political history of the church,' he concludes, 'is summed up in those phrases. Again and again ecclesiastics and pious laymen have become statesmen in the hope of raising politics to their own high moral level, and again and again politics have dragged them down to the low moral level upon which states- men, in their political capacity are compelled to live.'[28] I have seen this happen frequently in politics, but contend that church politics can often be at a lower level than other kinds of politics, that church politicians will drag down as readily as other kinds, and that the regular politician is often the innocent victim in such encounters.

The 'this is right and non-negotiable' attitude is the principal tactic which spills over from ecclesiasticism into other fields. It can be used to reinforce and excuse any theory or policy. Thus when the principles of Arabs, Jews, Christians, Hindus, Muslims, and the tactics supporting them, are associated with politics and economics, not only do the latter become chaotic but religion does not triumph. It is common for clerics to assert that God and the moral values of religion should be a part of all activity, but non-negotiable principles and accompanying tactics impede this salutary process. They do it by circumscribing the fatherhood of God by their limits and his impact on men by their influence. If the churches would drop these principles and tactics, they would have more time for the cry of countless thinkers through the ages which was enunciated by Diderot: 'enlarge and liberate God.'

We should refer again to parliamentary government for illustration. If a politician were to express his opinion on trade or transportation and invoke any suggestion of right, faith, or divine sanction for his stand he would be laughed at, argued with, criticized, told in no uncertain terms that he could be wrong. He is in a negotiable position. If on the other hand he is concerned with anything that interests churches, from local education to international affairs, he may then present his church's dogma or policy, or threaten its intervention, and he is considered to be taking a stand on a matter of prin- ciple. He assumes the protection of non-negotiability, and opposing him is regarded as an insult. Ecclesiastical principles have proved wrong over and over again, and many of the world's greatest tragedies are ecclesiastical ones (*not* religious ones), and yet man continues to treat them as non-negotiable and mix them with his economics and politics. If the followers of sects could be argued with openly and frankly so that creeds and church tactics could have the same discussion as economics and politics it would do the sects much good; they would get along better, and the cause of religion would be promoted. As for political and social action, one suspects that society could avoid many evils by asking its churches a variation of the old wartime question: 'Is your dogma really necessary?'

The answer is not only important to political power and social action; it is vital to religion itself. Church politics cancels out or renders inoperable much of the good done by churchmen. Religion itself suffers grievously every time a foray made in its name destroys people, institutions, and practices for the sake of group or personal power, every time a shield of alleged sanctity is used to deflect criticism or resistance, and every time a political, economic, or social advantage is sought or opinion expressed on the basis of denominationalism or special divine auspices. When General Amin announced that God instructed him to banish Asians from Uganda, and when a group campaigned in a Norwegian referendum on the slogan 'a vote for the Common Market is a vote against God,' one suspected, not adherence to principle or divine auspices, but a blasphemy which lowers the credibility of religion. The widespread damage which results is being increasingly admitted. Churches still persist, however, in being political parties and denominational 'sides' are evident in the world's conflicts. Because man is forced to assess his diminishing resources and increasing tensions, he can no longer afford institutions and politics which are accepted with insufficient questioning and which may cause further disaster. If one surveys history and contemporary life, it is not difficult to conclude that religion is far too important to man to allow the churches or churchmen to use it for political purposes.

12

The personnel of universities

The university is a natural place for human diversions and social and ideo-logical facts and fashions to display themselves in spectacular ways. To it come young people with varied upbringings and professors with all sorts of experience in numerous fields of knowledge. Indeed a university is a social laboratory in which forces, ideas, abilities, and experiments are combined in a limited environment and tested for their applicability to the community as a whole. The good university is an ivory tower – it has to be – but the com-munity affects what goes on in it, its denizens reflect the characteristics of the citizenry, and its leadership and influence in society are beneficial, and immense. Everything said about other organizations applies to universities too, and most assets and problems in the academic world prevail everywhere else as well.

Postures and politics and participatory democracy are admirably il-lustrated in universities, although no more so than in other organizations. There professional people are trained and others obtain various kinds of education; much literature, research, and countless ideas come from them; they provide experience, example, and challenge to youth; and they are part of the cultural and economic fabric of their regions. Good universities provide society with service of a value far beyond what is spent on them. This service is not straight-forward and automatic – education never is. The quality of universities varies like that of most other institutions. Some are distinguished assets to civilization; some are national and local benefits of the first rank; some are useful places for study and experience; some are brave but mediocre mills of indifferent routine; and some are travesties not worth the time, the money, or the effort spent within their walls. Their habitués vary from geniuses to frauds, and their work similarly. Each, therefore, is a kaleidoscope of unpredictable people, unlimited ideas and skills, and sensitive relationships. When the components are colourful the resulting educational patterns may be rich and stimulating.

These people, ideas, and relationships must be variables if a university is to thrive. It cannot be organized like a processing plant, turning out people from an assembly line, or like a mint, stamping them with recognized values. The ideas it deals in cannot be standardized. The organization of a university is, therefore, of a special kind, suited to the mixing of people and ideas in the proportion suited to education. This mixing is like muddling fresh concrete, or stirring the batter of a cake after fruit and nuts are added; there must be just enough mixing so that the elements will mingle properly, and not so much that the texture of the finished product is destroyed.

Everyone knows the categories of people who comprise a university or are involved in its operation. Few, however, appreciate the variety of talents within these categories. Students may vary from able, experienced, and happy young persons of character and integrity to naive, shallow, discontented, dishonest fools with neither common sense nor an appreciation of life. Professors may be wise men, brilliant scholars, splendid teachers, and popular personalities, or only one, or none, of these. The kinds of administrators are as great in number as the functions everyone expects them to do well. The office and maintenance staffs show all the characteristics of bureaucracy everywhere. Politicians and civil servants who deal with universities exhibit similar variations and can solve or cause problems as much as the others. And pressure groups with conflicting interests in education can provide helpful assistance or create frightful obstacles. It is remarkable how every official publication and policy on university education expounds on the place and duties of these participants, and how little allowance is made for their variety. Many contemporary troubles in the universities are the strange but inevitable consequences.

Let us commence with the board of governors, which is not very different in character from professorial, student, or political bodies. It is the corporate entity exercising an indispensable over-all authority, and its collective and individual activities on behalf of the university are of immense value. It is usually a lay body which provides support for, and alternatives to, professional opinion. It is also a committee with all a committee's virtues and defects. Its ability varies greatly with the quality and characteristics of its members, especially the chairman, and those who elect or appoint them can name both godsends and liabilities. Board members can be deeply concerned about the welfare of the university, or overly dominated by the interests they represent, and the two approaches may conflict. There is, consequently, a routine which the board, like any other body, must find which will enable it to do its duty, keep out of mischief, and allow for the idiosyncracies of its members. In this routine it is mandatory that the board be almost anonymous. The chairman is its front man who speaks for it before other authorities, receives attention at ceremonies, and is the confidant and colleague of the president. Even he, however, must be a grey eminence; otherwise he will get in the way of the chancellor, who is the exponent of the colour and dignity of the university, or the president, who is its chief executive officer.

The board members in the background act as a group, and the results of their deliberations should be negotiated, implemented, and talked about only by their chairman and their chief executive officer. Busy people in their own right, the members have not the time to handle details well or even to keep themselves informed on ever-changing university affairs. Policy is their province, and it is all they can do to attend to it. A board soon knows its own able and weak members, of which it is bound to have both. If all the members were well known and considered officially active, the weak, talkative, and meddlesome would be the first to become energetic and the board would be vacillating and cliquish. The principle of anonymity keeps the weak ones in the background where they should be. Then the board may expressly designate qualified members for special functions and contacts, such as financial work and public relations. Official anonymity prevents the dilution of leadership, but not the exercise of it.

Surely, it may be said, all members of a university board of governors are able, prominent citizens who should be both obvious and busy in the life of the university. Surely democracy requires all of them to participate actively. This laudable theory is no more true in a university board than it is in a cabinet, a legislature, other boards, or in a faculty of professors or a student council. The board is subject to the characteristics of committees already described. The supply of competent available board members in a society is not great. The process by which members are appointed or elected is not infallible. Allowances must be made, therefore, for both their qualities and the necessity of teamwork. Indeed, if every one was a member of the highest quality, the same principle would apply because, as in the cast of a play or the membership of a cabinet, the more prima donnas there are the more they must subordinate themselves to the action. Anyone who has sat on a board and watched a powerful potentate, an excessive talker, a temperamental egoist, or a narrow representative of an interest group, has been thankful that their contributions are collective and are confined to the boardroom, or, if board meetings are open, to behind-the-scenes politics.

Meanwhile the university equivalent of the ancient triumvirate – chancellor, chairman of the board of governors, president – provides basic services. Each of the three complements the others, and it is not safe to let one infringe on the prerogatives of the others. The chancellor in many universities performs dignified, decorative, and symbolic functions similar to those of the

Crown in the state. As in politics, it is sensible to keep these functions away from the president because he, like a head of government, is generally unable to handle both administrative and symbolic functions without getting arrogant, and away from the chairman of the board too, whose eminence must be grey rather than bright if he is not to become a nuisance. Similarly the chancellor should be a constitutional head who, except for rare emergencies, should act and speak only on the advice of the board and the president. Both chancellor and chairman should leave most functions of leadership to the president. A trinity of perfect incumbents in these posts is rare in any event, and the division of authority provides powers in manageable packages and the checks and encouragements most leaders need. It also provides flexibility so that power can be rearranged to suit the qualities of varying incumbents.

Other institutions within a university operate in a similar fashion and according to the characteristics of professors and students. Endless debates take place about the function of senates, councils, faculties, departments, committees, and student organizations, and the complicated network of relationships among them. Certainly the number of institutions is great, and it takes skilful politics to deal successfully with them. Some do not work at all, as university affairs have always indicated, and the reason is obvious: they are comprised of professors and students whose idiosyncracies are frequently neglected in the urge toward administrative change.

It may seem obvious that professors are like everyone else in the variations of their character and ability. But professors, like the students and the members of all professions, political parties, unions, or groups, do their best to hide the fact. Devotion to teaching, scholarship, knowledge, and research suggests esoteric auspices for their activities and special distinctions similar to the clergyman's aura of sanctity and the politician's servitude to the people. One needs to get behind these auspices and assess the professors as people, allowing for both the devotion and the people in organizing and operating academic institutions.

The human ability ratio mentioned earlier applies to professors. In relation to the standing of the university approximately one-third are competent, one-third mediocre, and one-third weak. It is as naive to look for a better ratio in most universities as it is to expect a better one in a legislature, a chapter of clergymen, or a labour union. All studies of professors that assess scholarship, teaching, research, committee work, and relations with other staff members and students indicate a wide variety of desirable abilities; to a command of all of them only a very few attain. Some are skilled in only one or a few of these functions and yet serve well. And some are skilled in none. The competent include many professors who are among the nation's greatest leaders, and countless public benefits are the result of their work.

Unfortunately critics of academe often expect all who are entitled to wear cap and gown to be paragons of scholarly and pedagogical virtue. Students sometimes rebel when professors show the same variations in ability which they, and everyone else, exhibit. Meanwhile professors must suffer gladly the fools within their ranks and, as in most groups, find it easier to extol their collective rights and virtues than to eject or discipline their weak. This situation is natural and in practice difficult to avoid, but as in other bodies of men it must be admitted, understood, and provided for.

Students, for example, must learn early to study despite professorial differences, if they have not already become accustomed to similar variations among school teachers, parents, and friends. If they can work only when a professor 'turns them on' they will not learn much, because in any course of study the major effort must be made by the students. If they do not make it even the best of professors can do little for them; if they do make it even weak professors can teach them much or they can master the subjects themselves. This fact can be verified in any registrar's records. The marks of good students are consistently good in all courses from all varieties of professors; the marks of mediocre and weak students are just as consistent, and even the best professors make appreciably little impact on them. This is not an excuse for weak professors, but an emphasis on the paramountcy of student effort. The social service outlook, which regards education as something dispensed by teachers rather than worked for by students, is as fallacious in universities as it is in schools. Similar fallacies are evident in the home where children are too dependent on parents, in the church where parishioners expect their religion to depend on their intake from sermons, and in most areas of life where individuals get in proportion to what they put in.

Defective communication between a professor and his students is not, therefore, always the former's fault. Weak and offensive students can 'turn off' a professor just as easily as good ones can 'turn him on.' Indeed the presence and negative attitude of some students can depress a whole class. And a class may vary in effectiveness from year to year according to who takes the course; almost always it is a few individuals who make the difference. Furthermore the difference is usually one of personality and behaviour rather than of ability. Political audiences, service clubs, congregations, and other gatherings draw out in similar fashion the best and worst in those who address them. The adage 'people get the kind of government they deserve' is not a truth, but it does indicate that politicians cannot be blamed for everything that goes wrong. This fact is often overlooked, both in the advocacy of participatory democracy and in the appraisal of the impacts of a communication.

Indeed it is good for a student to encounter a weak professor or a difficult communication from time to time. He can learn from the bad examples in educational as well as other institutions; he can be thrown back on his own resources and learn to develop his own initiative; and he can appreciate the best professors all the more. He also learns much from observing bad examples among classmates. This approach may seem negative, but it actually works, provided a student does not encounter too many weak professors and fellow students. If he has any gumption at all, the experience sets him questioning, assessing, probing, dealing with incompetence, appreciating standards, and making judgments on his own. He must do the same at home, in church, at play, and at work. Much of his future success will depend on living and working with all kinds of people, on making allowances for his own abilities and weaknesses which other people, in turn, must recognize, and on assuming his share of the communicating, which must be two-way to be effective.

A vital but perplexing question inevitably follows. How does one define the 'best' or the 'weak' professor? Oratorical skill, scholarship, and getting along well with students are qualities commonly attributed to good professors. It is not difficult to arrange a questionnaire on student reaction. But are these attributes of a professor any more easily assessed than those of other people? Brilliant lecturing is an obvious asset. But some of the best teachers are poor lecturers who have to be listened to carefully, or unusual lecturers who, like certain wines, are an acquired taste. Some of the worst teachers are good lecturers who make little lasting impression, either because the manner is more impressive than the content, or because they and the students confuse entertaining with imparting knowledge. Indeed it is often some years after graduation before a student recognizes and appreciates the kind of teaching he receives. The same is true of the utterances of clergymen, politicians, and salesmen. Moreover skills in the lecture room are different from those in seminars, and only a few professors possess both kinds. Scholarship is obvious in some men, but not in all. It can be covered up by other personal attributes; indeed some men make a habit of covering it up because they are shy, or because they cannot express it without offending others, or because many people actually suspect scholarship. Furthermore some excellent actors can assume a guise of scholarship as readily as others can feign piety or public service. Popularity with students is as nebulous and subject to fashion as is popularity everywhere else, and it is shared equally among all types of professors. These qualities, together with other personal ones, vary greatly in their impact on students because the latter vary in their tastes, and teaching methods change in fashion and popularity.

Other characteristics of professors affect the work of the university because it must be a self-governing community of scholars and because academic independence and freedom are vital to higher education. These principles, however, are ineffective in themselves; they must be accompanied by postures and politics which compensate for the characteristics. Professors of all abilities, like most categories of men, include both wise men and fools, and university business must include mechanisms for featuring the former and rendering the latter harmless. In any university, as in any organization, it is not hard to ascertain who has good sense and integrity, who is foolish and unreliable. In any project one quickly notes who will do his share of the work and who will not, who can bear responsibility and who cannot. In any discussion the merits of both an individual's talk and of his appreciation of other people's talk become obvious. Certainly everyone must have the opportunity to participate and talk, but the opportunity requires safeguards against unworkability and abuse.

Participatory democracy must be selective if it is to work. There is no point, for example, in giving Professor B a task which most colleagues know he cannot be relied on to perform, or in appointing Professor P, who is a compulsive talker and poor listener, to an important and busy committee. Yet these are often the very men who most want to participate, and they must be kept contented or they will cause trouble out of resentment. A few colourful but unimportant committees and positions may provide them with useful busywork and means by which they can talk and feel important. Like similar mechanisms in a legislature, these cannot be talked about out loud, but they are as important to teamwork as they may seem irrelevant to the sceptical observer or incongruous to the democratic theorist.

A general sharing of responsibility for policy, vital in participatory democracy, is built into the university faculty structure. It is recognized in both theory and practice, and rightly so. But what the theory says, practice must modify, because many men — professors included — are incapable of contributing to policy making. Some have too narrow a view; some have little sense of what is practicable; some have not the strength to make tough decisions and work with the consequences; some too readily subordinate the welfare of an institution to their own interests. Their opportunity to participate must be absolute, but it must be offset with obstacles in the interests of others and of the institution.

A faculty council illustrates the process. A large, cumbersome faculty council is an excellent instrument for honouring democratic theory and compensating for its weaknesses. It can be most productive if the agenda and procedure are planned so that two types of people are featured. Astute leaders should have ample opportunity to do work and rally supporters beforehand and to make appropriate comments and motions at meetings. As in a good chorus, the soloists must be selected and prepared with care because important business is jeopardized if it falls into the wrong hands. Stupid people must have similar scope because, in a faculty as in a legislature, they must be given every opportunity to reveal themselves. They can be encouraged to speak openly and long so that they can show their weaknesses and bore everyone else. If, despite such manoeuvres, some stupid action seems imminent, someone can talk it out past the time for adjournment, or it can be made to disappear in a special committee. Afterwards the secretary can send long and elaborate minutes and other documents to all faculty members, many of whom were absent from the meeting because of other duties, and few of whom actually read the communications. The real policy makers will meet frequently and by themselves later, as work must get done, but meanwhile the others will have at least a sense of participation. Indeed a faculty council operates just like a party caucus in a legislature.

All this is neither a waste of time nor a travesty of democracy. It is human nature at work, and little else can be expected in practice. Nor is it inefficient, because the *opportunity* for all to participate is just as important as the work of the few who must do it. Few actually avail themselves of the opportunity, and many who do do it badly. But it is there, if they can measure up to it, and it is effective if there are appropriate compensations for incompetents. Without the compensations it is not effective. Furthermore it is essential that the few who do the work be subjected to the inclinations of the others. They will be more responsible if they and their policies are subject to possible scrutiny, if they must hear ideas from all quarters, and especially if the procedure reminds them that they are trustees, not masters. These procedures are needed in all levels of the administrative structure, from the senate to the academic departments to student organizations.

Much politics results. There are two kinds of it: the manoeuvrings needed to get the work done, and those required to handle the complicated network of relationships among participants. The second, that often-neglected feature of administrative organizing, is difficult in large universities because academic work is divided into numerous disciplines handled by presumed experts. More prima donnas are therefory encountered than in most organizations, with the exception of government and the churches. The necessities of academic freedom provide even the newest lecturer with a small personal empire which he quite properly cultivates and defends. These little empires can be criticized readily, especially when their work seems incomprehensible, but only with extreme caution, because they are perfect spawning grounds for literature and philosophy and discoveries in science, as well as sources of numerous studies which society requests of them. Who knows when the shyest and most incomprehensible professor may inspire a splendid student, as such men often do, or shock the world with a great discovery? Some professors are eminent men whose work has wide significance; all the others have a similar environment in which to work; their potential, whatever it may turn out to be, is usually dependent on the character of that environment.

It takes skilful politics to deal with these scholars. They need prodding but not interference, direction but not control, coordination but not supervision, and criticism but not censorship. Under the theory of university self-government they expect, and are expected, to handle their politics themselves. In fact only a few among them are skilful in this delicate task, and no one outside the university can be safely entrusted with it. Consequently we have yet another reason for accompanying academic democracy and freedom with practical safeguards.

Safeguards are essential, not only for the university, but also for the professors themselves. Without safeguards the desirable and useful privileges of all may be sacrificed to the irresponsibility of a few. The matter of sabbatical leave is an example of what happens in universities as well as in other institutions. Sabbatical leaves with pay and income tax reduction are most productive, and splendid projects of great benefit to society have been carried out because the sabbatical made them possible. Most professors do not have to be reminded of their responsibility to make use of a sabbatical, or to be checked up on afterwards. But at a time when a scarcity of professors coincided with a widespread emphasis on rights and participation, some professors misused the privilege, which they considered a right, and no one was able to question them. The cold facts, as when an academic family relaxed abroad for a year, sending postcards home to their hard-working and tax-paying neighbours, and, on return, produced nothing to justify the venture, invited ridicule and public assault on the principle of sabbatical leave. Everyone, including society itself, became the losers in this regrettable development.

Universities provide examples of how any institution in a society, from labor union to political party, may endanger its rights, let alone its privileges and fringe benefits, by tolerating abusers of those rights. Rights are rarely lost because they are undesirable. It is unwise use of them that kills them, and often their staunchest devotees inflict the fatal blows. Impolitic people invite opposition to their rights; this is really a means of opposing the individual, not the right. People who invoke rights too much wear them out. People who flaunt rights endanger them by raising resistance and jealousy. People who abuse rights lose them. It follows that, in the universities and everywhere else, there are three ways of safeguarding rights. One is to deserve them by fulfilling the responsibilities that go with them. Another is to be politic in using them. A third is to use appropriate postures that make them acceptable to others. Why not entrench them? a constitutionalist will add. The rise and fall of many constitutions provide the answer. They or whatever they are entrenched in will not last if the three tactics are not followed, because they will eventually become honoured in theory without being tolerated in practice.

University politics are complicated still further by the obvious lack of political skills in the great majority of professors. Even in departments of political science the politically naive are everywhere evident. It is not difficult to find countless examples to back the experienced observation of President W.J. McGill of Columbia: 'It seems to me that a university community is the most politically conscious and one of the most politically inept groups in society.'[1] This discrepancy between political interest and political skill is one of man's basic problems in all fields, and damage by unskilled and inexperienced enthusiasts is done to all forms of government. The way in which the backgrounds of professors prepare them for university affairs illustrates how the discrepancy may arise, not only in academic life, but also in other organizations. Some professors are excellent scholars who have had colourful lives, much practical experience, and numerous contacts with people in other walks of life; these men went into academic life because they wanted to and because they were attracted by the challenges of some discipline. This group furnishes the overwhelming majority of professors who prove skilled at university administration and politics.

Some scholars, on the other hand, were bright students to whom study and prizes came easy, who were encouraged by parents and teachers and financial scholarships through the BA, the MA, and the PhD, and were then snapped up by a university. Many of these worked long in solitude, never knew much of practical affairs, and did not have any real alternative to academic life for which their cleverness predestined them. These people, distinguished in their own fields, often prove deficient in their knowledge and experience of affairs and of people. They frequently become inept politicians on campus as they dart out from the confines of philosophy or chemistry to participate in political activities. They do not do great harm, however, if more politically competent colleagues have the opportunity of informing or restraining them. With enough experience they may even become skillful politicians because, being able people, they have a strong, if narrow, base from which to participate.

A third group is much more dangerous. It comprises professors who are able in their fields but with psychiatrically doubtful backgrounds, or who are not able but have secured academic appointments at times when the universities expanded rapidly and professors were scarce. The bright youngster who was a spoilt child, for example, is difficult to handle when he goes into any employment; but many jobs carry their own corrective procedure by which such people can be handled — threatened with dismissal or put through tough crises, such as encounters with suffering and death in medicine, or rough work in engineering. It is hard, however, to take the ginger or naivety out of them in the necessarily independent and tenured academic posts where their egos have ample range. Indeed academic life can be almost as comfortable a berth for the insecure as theology, because they can get continuous attention and satisfaction through telling other people what to do. When they exercise political power they expect to get their way, and their temper tantrums or stubborn inexperience can throw a university into the same turmoil which their families suffered years before. This kind of person is often slow at making the change from youth to adult, and, when he gets his first teaching appointment, his constant contact with young people encourages him to adopt either immaturity as a means to popularity or autocratic methods as instruments of personal control. There are many sincere, stable academic politicians in universities, but any period of unrest provides a heyday for the inexperienced and the active neurotics, even psychotics, who are almost always compounders of trouble and obstacles to the solution of problems, and who invite negative reactions from governments and the public. Their antics in the 1960s, when funds for and good will toward higher education were plentiful and academic jobs were easy to get, were prominent causes of the widespread feelings against the universities which developed in the following decade.

Inexperienced or incompetent professors thrive in a sellers' market, and public authorities must recognize that in the university, as in all institutions, the services of just so many competent people are available. When a system expands in size and functions beyond this supply, more and more incompetence appears. Society is fortunate that, after two decades of university expansion, the proportion of competent professors is still high. Nevertheless there are many who secured posts who would never have been considered in steadier circumstances, and their effect on the universities is like the effect on government of inferior members of a political party who won election during a landslide. Indeed their presence is a main reason for the contemporary questioning of academic freedom and tenure. For them too the universities must compensate; otherwise they will try to make in campus politics the personal reputations denied them in scholarship, and they will damage the valuable rights of the whole academic community. With rare exceptions these people are ineffective in politics too, which fact frustrates them so that they become permanently temperamental.

Incompetents and psychotics flourish in every field, but they may have special leeway in universities because they assume status as educated men, work in the crowded, shifting realm of ideas, and seldom have to put ideas into practice. Some of them indulge in the antics of pseudo-intellectualism already described. It is easy to become irresponsible in such a situation, especially when the weak can enjoy the same opportunities of freedom and the protection provided by tenure which their abler colleagues need and justify by their actions. Consequently the university furnishes an excellent example of that great dilemma of society – how to establish and protect essential rights and privileges while preventing the abuse of them and interference with their enjoyment by the lunatic fringe and the incompetents. A large proportion of the administration and politics of universities, and of other organizations too, is now devoted to this dilemma.

Everything we have said about the members of the board of governors and the professors also applies to the students. They show the same individual variations and they perform no differently in classes and in residences, on committees and in student activities. There is the same evidence of outstanding ability and of gross incompetence. I have not seen or heard of a single student comment on the faculty or the administration that cannot be applied to the students themselves. There is more idealism and less experience among them, but their officers in student government, athletics, and social activities reveal the same abilities, weaknesses, and methods of administration as appear in presidents, deans, and department heads. We have already indicated that students are just as variable in class as professors, and that their variability is the more significant in learning. Popular topics for discussion such as relevance, communication, rights, participation, and the like are as applicable to study and the conduct of student affairs as they are to other university functions. Some student councils, for example, are highly successful, some are dismal failures, just like similar bodies in 'the establishment.' Indeed students will form establishments of their own,[2] and their presidents reveal exactly the same variations in opinions and skills as heads of political organizations. Moreover one can hear the same kinds of debates and watch the same tactics in a students' council that one finds in a legislature. About the same proportion of students take an interest in their affairs as does the public at large in its business, and they do their work in learning in about the same ratio of competent, mediocre, and weak as most people do in other activities. As to postures and politics, students are no more and no less concerned with them than those on the other side of that ill-defined, and perhaps non-existent, generation gap.

Countless reasons have been put forward for student unrest. I have arranged several student seminars for discussions of the reasons, and what follows is an accurate indication of the conclusions reached. Three of these reasons are of basic significance: the social service approach which features giving instead of getting education; the loss of identity resulting from impersonal accommodation to anonymous numbers; and the collective and political instincts of governments in their patronage of universities.

These causes are accompanied by three other less obvious reasons. The most important is a growing understanding of the dangers of the non-negotiable principles described earlier. Good education encourages students to question ideas and opinions, and, in the climate of worldwide difficulty with civilization, it is inevitable that assaults should be made on principles which aggravate that difficulty. Because some of the principles being questioned concern fundamental matters like sex, religion, and human relations, it takes a great deal of unrest to get their protectors even to discuss them. The value of the discussions often becomes obvious only when change reveals how bad the principles were in the first place and how negotiability provides better and more truthful ones.

The second of the less obvious reasons for student unrest is a limited allowance for variations among students. The state, parents, the university, and the students themselves should admit openly the variations and make allowances for them in studies and extra-curricular activities. An able student is an able person regardless of his age. A fool among students is still a fool. And he who was picked up too often when a baby will cause trouble later. The university needs many activities and diversions for each of these kinds of people.

The third reason for the unrest is the lack of colour in the rapidly expanding universities of today. When student bodies are numbered in the thousands many concessions to human nature must be made. For instance, planners will defend as economic the transition from refectory to cafeteria; nevertheless a poor meal – the butt of countless disturbances – can be served in the refectory and evoke far less complaint, and students will mingle better there and engage more effectively in stimulating conversation and friendship. Opportunities for sports, concerts, plays, and making friends and exerting egos have increased slowly, and in some places decreased, while the numbers burgeoned, and this discrepancy has provoked much dissatisfaction. Leacock's smoking-room theory of the university has a practical place in the affairs of even the largest, and to ignore it is to ignore the humanity of those in it. Years after graduation it is not the serious work that one recalls with nostalgia and brags about to one's grandchildren, but the friends, the fun and mischief, the discussions and extra-curricular achievements, all of which form part of one's education and give it savour and character. Without them a feeling of being cheated of something valuable is inevitable.

There is yet a fourth reason for student unrest which I have often heard discussed by students and seen in operation – incompetent leadership among the students. It is rarely mentioned publicly, while other reasons have received enormous publicity. The variation among students noted earlier is as evident in leadership as in studies. Some of them display in their university careers all the skills of wise statesmen and shrewd politicians; they rival or surpass the administrators, the professors, and their parents in ability and common sense and make splendid contributions to university life. It is a joy to watch them operate, and to benefit, as everyone does, from their work. Next to them in value are the shrewd, experienced, sensible, hard-working students of whom there is a large number. These are effective leaders when they can be recruited for student activities. But they are often hard to get for two reasons, both of which I have heard often from students who declined campus jobs or requests to run in student elections. One is the difficulty some have in combining extra-curricular work with studies, especially if that work is too demanding and perhaps thankless. The other reason is the existence of a third type of leader.

The third type, the incompetent, is always around, but he can usually be compensated for by others in normal operations. But some peculiar interpretations of participatory democracy have caused abnormal operations which prevent this compensation. The lowering of standards, encouraged by society and the government, particularly the dropping of certain rules regarding keeping up with studies and the end of 'Christmas graduates', have made way for the staying on (and in many cases on and on) of students who do little or no work at all. These often fill their time with politics, and, in the absence of achievement, personal aggrandizement based on politics. Others who are clever students with rampant egos have been forced by the lack of colourful activities and extra-curricular interests to release their urges and emotions in campus politics for which they have no skill. Both groups have caused much turmoil and, because they are not representative of most of the students, many mistakes and much public misunderstanding. Their mistakes have affected the students most of all because they run student institutions, newspapers, and activities badly thereby causing much dissatisfaction with campus life. For example, in the seminars mentioned above there was almost unanimous criticism of student newspapers and a general opinion that few readers took them seriously. Again Gresham's Law has operated; poor leaders by their example and their mistakes have driven out good ones.

The nature of incompetence among student leaders is the same as that among any other leaders. This point is important because many critics think age and lack of experience to be the main handicaps. In actual fact many students have more experience than many of their elders, or are more skilled in getting facts and seeking advice for the work they do. Incompetence in student leaders which results from inexperience is no greater than that among inexperienced elders, including their parents and professors. The incompetence invariably results, as it does in everyone else, from the following: the arrogance of the egoistic who get swelled heads on attaining office and become authoritarian; the irresponsibility of the financially inept who cannot handle their budgets; the meddlers who feel an urge to get involved in everything; the lazy who like authority but not work; the selfish who promote only those activities which interest them; the politically stupid who have no skill in dealing with the authorities or with other students; and the shortsighted who do not plan ahead for the years after they graduate, when future students must suffer the consequences of their incompetence. None of these weaknesses are purely youthful ones. They are the limitations, found in all age groups, that require compensation in the administration of communal affairs.

The youth cult is an inevitable result of emphasizing age and neglecting limitations. It is no different from any other cult, and just as undemocratic. All cults start with self-aggrandizement on the part of power seekers, especially the mediocre and weak who have little else to stand on. A political party, like the Nazis, will create a cult if it can. So will age groups such as 'wise old elders.' Competent people in any group do not need a cult to establish their superiority. The weak do, and it is always pathetic to see an incompetent or stupid person presenting himself as a privileged person because he is a member of a cult.

As for youth, there is nothing new about young people assuming major responsibility. Musicians in their teens and politicians in their twenties have always been common. So have student leaders who contributed advice and work to university affairs, even at the higher levels of administration. Increased student responsibility is no doubt desirable, and many able students justify it. The cult is not necessary, however, to inject new blood into these affairs, but, in the absence of alternative work and colourful activities, to accommodate restless energy, political ambition, and status seeking on the part of virtually anyone who wants to participate. Inevitably the new kinds of interventions tend to be no more democratic, liberal, or indeed youthful, than those of older people or earlier kinds of student leaders. Anyone who thinks only the old can be reactionary or narrow should sit on committees, not with 'students', but with incompetent or excessively temperamental students. The cult which dictates that a student should do this or that is no more reliable than that which features a professor, a politician, a clergyman, or a 'anyone else.' And no theory of democracy will work any better among students with incompetent leaders than in any other badly led group. The ultimate danger of the cult is, however, that the damage done by the mediocre and the weak spoils privileges for everyone else, and the cult dies. Once more we note that, while the rights of all to participate are essential in a democracy, there must be appropriate postures to reveal ability to participate and to compensate for the lack of it.

The university furnishes an excellent example of how politics complicates an expanding administration and how excess participatory democracy makes it harder to get people to administer. Difficulty in getting university presidents should not be surprising, in view of the open season on them enjoyed by any kind of hunter with any kind of weapon. Selection committees for deanships encounter many refusals because of the amount of paperwork and the number of meetings involved. And no longer is the headship of a department sought by professors who wish to be teachers and scholars rather than office managers. In student affairs it has become increasingly difficult to get good students to lead organizations, serve on committees, work for the campus newspapers, organize events, and run in student council elections; as a result many student activities break down altogether because of the poor leadership mentioned earlier. On the other hand when good student leadership appears it is startling in its effectiveness, and the whole campus reflects the spirit it generates.

The amount of administration and committee work is not the only reason for the reluctance to serve in administration. Nor are the alleged problems of the universities; indeed it is often the existence of problems that stimulates interest in administration. The real reasons are the use of administration and its politics as a means of escape from real work by incompetents and psychotics, encouraged by the theory of participatory democracy but not restrained by its safeguards, and the frustration and acerbity which always accompany their participation. The professional participator in campus politics is, like his counterpart elsewhere, particularly troublesome if he has no other outlet. Campus politics is essential, but it is inefficient if it is the only instrument available to the participant for personal relationships and ego satisfaction. The member of the hockey team or of the drama society, for example, who keeps up his studies, contributes more effectively to a committee or an activity in the necessarily limited time at his disposal than the student who can find unlimited time for politics and has no other outlet for his energies. The Rotary axiom that it is the busy man who is most dependable applies equally to students and professors. But good people will not take administrative posts, from the presidency of the university to the chairmanship of a student social committee, if they feel it is a waste of time. Beyond a given point, unfortunately, administration does become a waste of time and, with complaining at a premium, it becomes thankless. Furthermore, as every academic and student administrator knows, 90 per cent of the frustrating duties of administration is devoted to that 10 per cent of the professors and students for whom it is impossible to do much under any circumstances.

Connections with government complicate further the task of administration and the politics associated with it.[3] We should state immediately that the reason is not the need for money. This need is not unique. It is always present because no organization has all the funds it thinks it should have. One special problem is the elaborate ritual which bureaucracy requires in return for its support, especially when that bureaucracy is the sole patron. Another is the fact that governments display the same assets and weaknesses we have already described, and these are added to the already complicated maze of university politics.

To most people centralized support from one authority appears the most efficient solution. Actually it is not, because the single patron provides less money, spends more in administration, devotes more time to management, takes less real and positive interest in the work being done, interferes more readily, makes more demands and mistakes, and displaces more initiative on the part of the people involved and more interest on the part of the public than does a group of patrons. Furthermore a single patron must be cultivated, coaxed, placated, and flattered to such an extent, and his whims and prejudices so anticipated, that those dependent on him are forced to adopt his outlooks and procedures, and these are not necessarily appropriate to the dependents' functions. The impact of several patrons is more informal and interested. Indeed it is much more appropriate to participatory democracy. The inefficient impacts of several patrons, on the other hand, tend to cancel one another out, and the institution they support experiences less negative interference from them and less need to cater to their lunatic fringe. And several patrons can add patrons; when one dominates others shy off. The difference in the amount of interest and involvement between the single patron and the group of patrons is illustrated by the Community Chest programme. Despite the undoubted efficiency of a centralized collection, there are still numerous charities which remain outside it; the giving to charity becomes as coldly impersonal as it becomes indirect; and numerous workers give up close, benevolent contact with good causes which did them and the recipients much good.

The Canadian experience with university grants after 1966 illustrates how administration and politics rise as the single patron takes over. Before that date the universities got money from both federal and provincial governments, as well as from private sources. Federal funds were given on a formula basis with no conditions imposed. Provincial funds were given by means of the usual budgetary procedures of the local government (then not very complicated), and the separate universities urged their claims like any other beneficiary. Private sources remained interested, although taxation steadily discouraged them and government support tended to displace them. Meanwhile the differences in quality and needs among universities remained recognized.

In 1966 the federal government gave its money to the provinces to distribute. The universities then came under the influence of a single patron, the provincial government. Federal support was soon forgotten by the public because the provinces did not feel the need to acknowledge it, and private donations dropped sharply. While it seemed that the provincial governments were increasing greatly their aid to universities, they were actually distributing three existing sources of funds, only one of which was their own. Then administration and politics mushroomed. New offices and even new departments sprang up in the provincial civil service, and university grants commissions were established to act as buffers between the dispensers and the recipients of funds. University administrators formed themselves into new associations and committees, while the national association of professors established provincial chapters. Coordination committees flourished and university-government and inter-university liaisons sprang up. Meetings increased a hundredfold. Immense amounts of reports, questionnaires, submissions, minutes, regulations, and correspondence appeared. The ultimate in administrative inefficiency was reached when the provincial administration became so chaotic that councils of ministers and of other ranks with accompanying paraphernalia were set up in an attempt to offset the effects of government intervention and earlier decentralization. All the interventionist, decentralizing, and centralizing apparatuses then remained and expanded to complicate enormously what was once a more efficient enterprise, to multiply costs, and busily to solve the problems which they themselves created.

Meanwhile a large office structure had to be established in the university to handle all this business. Officials covered the academic field with the paraphernalia of bureaucracy. Administrative officers were obliged to divert much of their time from running the university to negotiating with politicians and officials, getting decisions from conflicting jurisdictions, attending meetings, preparing and reading documents and statistics, arranging budgets, filling out forms and questionnaires, and explaining the complicated operations to their faculties. The latter, in turn, interested in participatory democracy, found themselves involved in a great increase in committee work with obvious consequences for their teaching and research. Students then found that their affairs had to compete with an increasing network of business and, indeed, that student activities themselves became highly complicated and bureaucratic. While all this was going on, a sameness in management, architecture, facilities, and policies developed among the universities as they bowed to the pressures of outside standards. They became increasingly local, too, as their identity with their provincial governments increased. This was perhaps the unhappiest consequence of all at a time when Canadians required national unity and understanding, for which the mobility of young people is one of the best stimulants. Provincial governments gave preference to their own young people in admissions and scholarships, thus encouraging parochialism and destroying the easy migrations which had earlier been so valuable and which, from the financial standpoint, had cancelled one another out.

Investigations always follow such administrative tangles. In Canada commissions of inquiry – federal, provincial, and professional – solemnly investigated the situation and usually found ways of blaming somebody or something. In not one instance was the administrative apparatus questioned, and there were no studies of its effect on education. Science policy furnishes one example of the consequences. 'The greatest enemy of progress in science and technology in Canada,' said Nobel Prize winner, Dr Gerhard Herzberg, 'is bureaucratic control. The interference of politicians, accountants, and committees in the free development of creative processes in the scientific laboratories of the country is becoming more severe every year. If allowed to continue unchecked, this tendency is liable to stop all real progress.' But administrative activity shows no signs of ceasing. 'Now it appears that for every working scientist there are four persons spending their time deciding how and where and when he should work.'[4]

An increase in politics accompanied all the new activities. Strategic university leaders, for example, had to lobby with some governments to ensure that they spent enough of their own money on education rather than diverting it to other activities when they got federal funds. The same leaders had to remind governments of the differences in quality among universities, something which it is hard for politicians to admit publicly. It takes great skill to maintain effective contacts with politicians and educational officers, and governments require even more subtle personal influence than do other patrons. Preventing stupid policies in advance became just as important as devising good ones. Remedying political mistakes became more important than rectifying academic ones. Getting general agreement among such large numbers of authorities is as difficult as discouraging the efforts of the inevitable czars who seek to get power into their own hands. And, because universities are as competitive as every other group of organizations, they had to watch one another to ensure that no one got the exclusive ear of the government. Meanwhile a whole new group of officials outside the universities were supposed, in theory at least, to make and keep up an acquaintance with the intricacies of higher education, something only a very few could do. Officials with little or no understanding of universities were a tough problem complicating the whole business. They had counterparts in faculties and student bodies, who also did not understand the vast new administrative maze, and protested. For example, an unimaginative government official would tell the university how it had to construct and finance a residence; some students were appalled at the results; but it was the university and not the government that got the criticism and bad publicity, and malcontents occupied the office of the president rather than that of the government official really to blame.

It is easy to cite constitutional and administrative reasons for this change and to plead a need for coordination and standardization. These reasons are, however, all debatable. The simple fact is that a Pandora's box has been opened, and whatever merits they may have must be balanced against the effects of the new phenomena. Certainly the change of 1966, which transformed a fairly simple process into a huge bureaucracy and several sources of support into a single patron, produced costs and complications difficult to justify as desirable, relevant, or efficient, and in the process increased the size of the government and changed the character of the universities. And there crept in, gradually but inexorably, one of the strange paradoxes of democracy: that people who would have served independent organizations free or at a modest cost now expect extra pay for their efforts or higher prices for their goods simply because the government provides the money. This paradox itself provokes increased demands for personnel and funds and makes it harder to curtail them. Under all these circumstances it becomes too easy to keep on expanding without counting. For example, one has only to consult three reports on Canadian education, all of which recommended enormous structures with the resulting work and politics. These reports, from the Commission on the Relations Between Universities and Government,[5] the Committee on Aims and Objectives of Education in the Schools of Ontario,[6] and the report of the Universities Commission of Ontario of 1972, should be assessed by a count of the number of committees and officials and the network of political relationships they recommend, as well as answers to the question of where all the people are coming from to do all the work proposed.

Almost all the phenomena described in this chapter are illustrated vividly in the office of the university president. His duties as executive officer and academic leader are well known. His political duties, however, are largely unrecognized, but it is they which cause him the most trouble and, in so many cases, lead to his downfall.

There is nothing about the president's policy and administrative functions which differs greatly from those of other heads of major organizations. The constituency he deals with, however, is unique, and it requires politics of a special kind. He is blamed when things go wrong, like the captain of a ship, although, unlike the captain, his power of command is severely limited. He therefore must lead efficiently while steering with agility and delicacy over and around academic and political shoals. On the other hand he may avoid danger by doing little and taking few risks, in which event the university will suffer, and there is no doubt that the caution of some incumbents has caused a legacy of trouble for those who follow them. Participatory democracy prevents the president from becoming an autocrat, while at the same time it does not relieve him from the responsibility for unpleasant tasks which others will not assume. If he does not assume them he may be accused of being weak; if he does he can expect rough treatment: in both instances it is those who assume pleasant functions but not unpleasant ones who are his first critics. These peculiarities are the results of inflated administration and politics and are a cause of the current abnormal turnover among university presidents.

The president's constituency includes a potpourri of talent and influence. The governors with their varied backgrounds and interests must be kept happy with the right amount of deference, initiative, reports on progress, and explanations of difficulties. The professors, experts in every conceivable subject, of every shade of opinion and degree of competence, are supposed to be a smoothly working team sharing among themselves the duties of captain and coach. The students, in their infinite variety, are looking for an education, and have varying ideas about how much work they will devote to it and about the conditions under which their work should be carried on. Both academic and student administrators control small empires which the president should be assured are operating efficiently, but with which he must deal cautiously, if at all. Officials of the government with diverse ideas about university education devise policy, administrative procedures, statements, questionnaires, channels of communication, and correspondence, and are coy and playful as they perform ritual dances around university budgets. The public, in turn, draws an immense number of valuable services from the university and makes numerous conflicting demands on it. Dealing with all these forces so that their combined effect is salutory and in the interest of higher education is a monumental task which the president is expected to perform with confidence and dispatch.

One of the president's major tasks is explaining university phenomena and personnel to governors, government officials, and the public, and professors, students, and politicians often make his task difficult. The image of some professors and students is beyond comprehension, because a similar image is more readily tolerated in other professions. Whether it is the absent-minded recluse at one extreme or the slovenly dressed undisciplined egoist at the other, they draw attention to themselves and to the university by establishing an image which, in the interest of the academic freedom of the great majority, the president must either explain or make valiant efforts to submerge among the activities of other more understandable personnel. The party leader has the same types in his ranks, and the arts always feature them, but society accepts these and their chiefs rarely have to defend them. The university president is expected by his sponsors to do something when they become troublesome, and other professors in many cases will not help him. If he does not act, he is deemed to be losing control; if he does, he is accused loudly and publicly of interfering with academic freedom.

Everyone knows about 'odd-balls' among professors and students. But few are aware of the impact on the university of similar characters among the politicians and civil servants. If a minister is stupid, and it is a fact of government that cabinets consist not of Solomons alone, the work of the university president is greatly complicated. If a civil servant who is a spinner of webs becomes involved in university business he can cause endless trouble and expense. Both types like to have people responsible to them, and, to a far greater extent than their more sensible colleagues, are inclined to meddle and fond of regarding themselves as 'representative of the people.'[7] Neither can be explained publicly when they make their contributions to the difficulties of university education.

It takes much skill and time to solve this dilemma, which split many universities asunder in the 1960s. A high price was paid for the academic freedom and rights of a tiny minority and for the interventions of officialdom, and countless presidents wistfully wondered what happened to *their* freedom and rights and their authority. Once again we note the reluctance of an organization to discipline or make provision for its lunatic fringe, wherever it may be situated; only in this instance a new phenomenon appears – the administrator as a sacrificial victim to appease the gods of academe. As universities grow and governments become more involved in their affairs, academic freedom, which is vital to higher education, is in danger of being lost altogether because a few in both universities and government have been permitted to abuse it. Although some presidents could be accused of autocracy, in practice it is usually the president, standing alone or with a couple of deans, like Horatius at the bridge, who defends academic freedom against authorities and the public who do not understand it or become impatient with its abuse, and against those who plead its benefits but will not assume its responsibilities. Meanwhile associations of professors have too often rightly defended their members against arbitrary administration, while wrongly neglecting to support administrators against their arbitrary members, and thus weakened the scholarship, leadership, and management without which academic freedom becomes a myth. And democratic politicians have too often given up democracy for bureaucratic control. Like many trade unions, professional associations, and governmental organizations in similar situations, the universities have proved once again that participatory democracy cannot be one-way, and that special postures and politics are necessary to make it work.

13

Campus politics

The variety of personnel and the amount of administration in university affairs require enormous quantities of inner politics. Everyone contributes to the politics. A president, for example, simply does not have all the skills associated with the numerous duties expected of him, and, like anyone else in such a position, he needs back-up support, and perhaps occasional reminders to use it. On the other side of the educational process the tides of politics do not always cast up competent ministers of education, and, in any event, a set of manoeuvers is always needed to secure maximum benefits from the minister's personal assets and protection from his liabilities. In between these potentates are many functionaries, each with prerogatives and ambitions. They combine and divide in the elaborate patterns of institutional participation, and it is not possible for them to do it harmoniously and productively without some stimuli and precautions.

It must not be supposed that this uncertainty is confined to university personnel. Observers often make this mistake. Instability in any institution is frequently the consequence of excursions into its affairs by participators who come from outside its ranks. They can cause as many problems as benefits, especially if they are not directly associated with its work. A clerk in a treasury office, for example, can be the source of constant manoeuvering, friction, and financial chaos if he is the narrow meddling type. A crusading do-gooder who seeks publicity, a minor politician looking for patronage, or a representative of an interest group wanting to get its work done for it can be expensive and troublesome nuisances. Tenure is an excellent example of the problem; professors require it largely because of the meddling of crusaders for whom persecution is the answer to something or someone they do not like. There is no doubt whatever that countless people from outside the university contribute enormously to it in funds, support, work, criticism, and encouragement. Indeed it could not thrive without them. Nevertheless the great value of much outside participation should not preclude some precautionary apparatus to protect against negative participation. While we will be discussing the kinds of apparatus needed by professors, students, and politicians, we must not confine the need to them.

The university has all the characters who appear in other organizations. There are many who blend efficiently and well into its operations. There are also academic prima donnas, both brilliant and incompetent, who display the same kinds of temperament noted on the stage or in politics. There are meddlers and there is a lunatic fringe. And others are present of whom that is about all that can be said. It is as impossible to treat them all alike as it is to expect them all to participate in regular or effective ways. Indeed that is half the fun and educational benefit in a university.

Nevertheless these variations are only fun and beneficial when they can be permitted to direct themselves into productivity or harmlessness as they deserve, without impeding other variations or the work of the institution. They cannot be so directed; they must be given the opportunity to direct themselves, which is a different and much more effective strategy.

The politics of this strategy, accompanied by ample postures, can be noted in simple activities. Rather than censor directly a professorial or student nuisance – he may be right – it is often practical to appoint him to an innocuous advisory committee. If he is right his ideas will be assessed and encouraged. If he is wrong, or if he is simply attempting to satisfy too large an ego, he can be appropriately flattered and silenced with enough harmless work, or athletics, or social activity to keep him busy and out of other people's way. Prime ministers often use the junket, and bishops chaplaincies and memberships in study groups or evangelical projects, for the same purpose. A common alternative is to play one nuisance off against another by putting them in a harmless position where they can waste each other's time and energy while other people are freed from their hindrance. Both these tactics are also useful for dealing with able people who are good at some things and incompetent at others but cannot themselves make the distinction. Indeed in universities, as in government, many committees have originated to keep nuisances busy and happy.

Entertainment is another useful means of dealing with temperament. A good meal smooths the ruffled feathers of a prima donna who feels neglected; and nothing helps the process better than inviting the prima donna's wife to pour tea at a party. Fulfilling this same kind of role is one of the many useful functions of a faculty club. The malcontent and the bore can get complaints off their chests at the club and thus diminish the impact of their tensions on administrative and academic bodies. As for student malcontents and bores, those who can shout themselves hoarse at a football game or dance to exhaustion at a ball on Saturday night are not very interested in occupying a dean's office on Monday morning. A careful appraisal of most successful organizations reveals numerous such devices, unpublicized but nevertheless effective, which operate as escape valves for pent-up humanity. And organizations often explode for the lack of them.

The significance of colourful activities in the universities can be illustrated by convocations. One of the great mistakes of so-called practical people, including those professors who absent themselves from such ceremonials, has been to regard convocations as mere show. On the contrary they are valuable events in many practical ways. A well staged convocation is unrivalled in its impressiveness and the entertainment it provides, and it has all the characteristics of a dramatic performance along with the attractions of a good political meeting. Nowhere can human nature with all its assets and vanities be better displayed, and nowhere is there more scope for both solemnity and a sense of humour. But it must be well staged; as in any other performance a mediocre show is inadequate.

This spectacle has several uses. It provides students with a final climax for their years of study and an excuse for some accompanying parties, both of which they will remember all their lives. It gives officials, professors, and visitors a chance to celebrate and parade. It gives society a chance to reward deserving people with honourary degrees. It provides the parents and friends of the students with an opportunity, perhaps the only one in a lifetime, of visiting a university, of sharing their pride in their young people's achievements and in the university itself, and of meeting the professors at receptions after the ceremony. A convocation costs nothing; actually it is an excellent money maker for an occasional honourary degree can open a benefactor's purse. It is also an efficient means of public relations; indeed for many university personnel it is the only means.

This last point has been well illustrated in recent years. Some professors with a peculiar form of inverted snobbery have eschewed efforts to enjoy themselves at university functions and to display themselves to advantage before the public, and in many cases have prided themselves on being absent from convocations. For this attitude, among others, they and the universities have paid a fearful price in over-seriousness, in the cultivation of a public reaction which says in effect 'who do these people think they are?', and in the compensating rise of other and more expensive forms of public relations run by PR men. Professors, like other people, need to cultivate their own public relations by means of both work and postures. One of the best opportunities for cultivating rapport between them and the students and their families, public officials, and the alumni is furnished by convocations.

A good attendance by the professors gives a student and his fee-paying and tax-paying relatives much pleasure. It indicates what a community of scholars looks like, shows that the professors care about sharing in one of the most important events in the students' lives, and enables the student to introduce his family to his professors at the reception. Indeed the work of only one professor in thus meeting parents and guests may be worth several weeks of highly paid effort by a PR man. Conversely few things have contributed more to the dark side of the public image of a university and received more adverse comment than the poor attendance by professors at convocation and the resulting experience of the students and their parents who stood around after the ceremony with no one to meet. It is wrong for them and the public officials present to have to ask where the professors are on such an important public occasion. Convocations need not be dull. With a judicious mixture of solemnity and gregariousness on the part of the faculty, some acting skills among the administrators, and two or three imaginative stage managers in the form of marshals and hosts, the university can put on for its own benefit and the public's enjoyment what Barnum and Bailey would no doubt call 'the greatest show in academe.'

As organizations grow the number of these escape valves and colourful activities may become insufficient, perhaps because of administrative tidiness or budget cuts. This is precisely the time when the number should increase, because the organization becomes impersonal and the people feel anonymous, neglected, or irrelevant and become skittish. Much of a university's trouble is caused by this discrepancy. It is just not possible to keep 20,000 students and 2,000 professors happy in conditions of administrative and academic sterility. Colourful business is too practical to be dismissed with impunity, and a steady programme of higher learning is not enough to satisfy human beings, however dedicated their efforts, however brilliant their minds, and however principled or practical they may be. Moreover the government, as principal patron of the universities, cannot expect the universities to do without colour any more than can the government itself, which requires methods of satisfying the more esoteric of human needs in its own ranks.

One of these needs has been neglected as the universities have expanded – the needs of students away from home for the first time. Some regard the university as in loco parentis, and consider that it should watch and guide its charges, while others feel that the students should be able to stand on their own feet. What happens is a continuation of the politics of the family. Some young people are taught early to be independent of their parents and to face life and its problems with initiative. They are usually encouraged to express their opinions at home, and generally they have summer jobs and other experiences by which they encounter practical realities and human nature. Others, being sheltered too long, are not as fortunate. Their mothers may dominate them and their fathers discourage independence, with the result that they reach eighteen with comparatively naive ideas and reluctant or frustrated initiative. Still others have parents who have neglected them altogether in busy rounds of occupational, social, or community work, and come to university confused and perhaps bruised.

These young people, in varying stages of preparation for life, meet at university, and their backgrounds have a bearing on the process by which they get an education and on the activity of the university itself. Indeed the state of initiative of the students is as important to the students and the university as their academic preparation. Some over-dominated and neglected students thrive immediately on their new freedom. Some, however, are lost in the challenging environment and become shy and withdrawn. Others become intoxicated with the new freedom and cut loose in lively fashion. The experienced, independent ones, on the other hand, usually make the adjustment easily. This mixture of behaviours, altogether apart from academic considerations, requires special arrangements so that the faculty can deal with the problems of the students and the students can influence one another.

It is a traumatic experience, for example, for an over-dependent person to arrive on a big campus in an unfamiliar city, knowing no one, rooming alone, lining up for hours to register and to buy his textbooks, eating by himself, and perhaps for the first time at a cafeteria, listening to lectures in crowded theatres, undergoing exhortations from valiant welcomers at packed freshman rallies and orientation programmes, and finding his way among courses in which he is a number, regulations which are a mystery, and strangers who ignore him or greet him with the desperate salutation 'some rat race, eh!' It becomes obvious at an early stage that some students meet this challenge with cheerful skill, savouring the new experience and picking up friends in the process. They know how to ask questions, seek advice, and get help, and they are not afraid of either the professors or the administrative staff. They are not on their own for the first time and they do not expect someone *in loco parentis* to assume their responsibilities or push them along. Others, however, start off badly, and some never adjust to the university spirit and routine. For this problem the university is only partly to blame; family experience or the lack of it is the primary cause.

Interaction among students declines in the huge, expanding university. Classes, seminars, dining facilities, lounges, and commonrooms become too crowded and impersonal for the discussions and arguments which are so important to education. Students teach one another by example and even by horseplay. A series of good bull sessions is as valuable as an entire course, and, as for horseplay, there is nothing like a cold bucket in a residence waterfight to humanize the stuffed shirt or the spoilt child. Indeed new worlds of personality are opened up at university for the students, especially when they encounter for the first time those of other lands, races, or religions, even those from other parts of their own country.

The causes of an impersonal atmosphere are not just related to size; small universities can be dull too. Another reason is the growth of an administrative apparatus connected with both internal management and relations with government without a corresponding growth in colourful business and personal contact. For instance, extra clerical help at registration time cannot do as much to make the new students feel at ease as a provost and several professors able to entertain new arrivals at intimate small gatherings. A hundred gallons of sherry and some kegs of beer dispensed with appropriate hospitality at these gatherings will stimulate more education and settle more personality problems than a guidance counsellor and cost less money. Courageous, however, is the university that puts that item on its government budget. Putting on a musical is another example: it gives the participating students an interest and a memory which will add a glow to their college days and last a lifetime. Yet it is difficult for a large university to get support for one musical, when actually it should be producing ten. Intramural sports are just as valuable as intercollegiate ones and they involve more people; and the necessary equipment, which seems a frill to a budget official, pays handsome dividends in spirit and experience. Incomprehensible as it may seem to a purchasing agent, an oak table provides a better atmosphere for a seminar than one of vinyl and plywood, and the oak is far more economical in the long run. A panelled room makes either eating a meal or listening to a lecture more interesting because it is warmer than plaster and linoleum, and it is no more expensive. Periodic faculty or class dinners in appropriate surroundings with entertainers or distinguished speakers provide memorable occasions for undergraduates. Noon-hour concerts or art exhibitions by students for students are an encouragement for the one and entertainment for the other.

It is neither right nor efficient for students talented in various areas to pass four years at a university without being featured several times in campus enterprises; yet the waste of not encouraging such students to seek the enjoyment participation would offer is great. And the talents of professors, especially those in art and music departments, should be similarly employed, free of charge and often. As for residences, they should not be mere dormitories; they are home for most students for several years. Living in them is an education in itself, particularly for the students who have had little opportunity to mix with other young people, of which there is a surprisingly large number. Everyone cannot live in residence, but everyone can be a member of one with the privilege of using its dining and lounge facilities. One of the great mistakes of large universities has been to build residences with no dining facilities and provide huge central cafeterias for everyone, instead of following the more suitable, and in the long run no more costly, plan of providing good residence or college dining halls which non-resident students could use. The provision of scattered vending machines is the greatest folly of all; they encourage hasty and lonely snacks. We could discuss many similar means of making the students feel a part of a university, mixing them in small groups and featuring friendship and individuality. These means, valuable in themselves, also provide an effective and necessary change from mass instruction in large classes as well as from the other mass activities in society. They are also the best antidote for loneliness.

It is not easy to discuss these matters with governments. Politicians and civil servants consider them frills, and instead favour formulae involving square feet, numbers, hours, and dollars. Such standards of measurement are important and practical, but they are not enough without other standards concerned with fostering that mixing of people and ideas which is unique in the university. It is simply not practical for a department of public works to apply the same design to an academic building that it would use for a government office building, or consider a residence and a hospital in the same terms. Yet how often this happens on campuses, and how expensive it is in terms of both money and human relations. Nor is it practical for a department of government to set policy for providing residences, classrooms, or social facilities, whether they do it directly or through a grants commission. Aside from the department's tendency to establish immediately another bureaucracy to do the job with its own costs and network of politics, the interference and standardization which inevitably result cancel out the advantage.

Costs will not justify departmental control. It costs vast sums and countless man hours of administration and politics simply to have the control. Every clerk in a department adds some red tape, and his red tape causes work and expense for other people. Moreover governments tend to be penny-wise and pound-foolish. Their political approaches to the awarding of contracts, indeed the very fact that they are awarding the contracts, often adds a substantial fraction to the cost of a building.[1] As for minor matters, the most expensive way for a university to secure furniture, for example, is to order it through a government purchasing agent or in accordance with standards laid down by him. Furthermore the result is in accordance with governmental outlooks rather than university ones, and the entire atmosphere of a university thereupon becomes wrong for the functions it is supposed to serve. A student lounge which looks like an airport waitingroom or a study area which resembles a hospital utility room will not be efficient for fellowship or study.

Can we suggest more suitable alternatives? At the government level control should be general only, just enough to exist but not enough to require a bureaucracy at both ends of the control. For instance, it is really not difficult to determine the cost of a residence for a given number of students. That amount should be given directly to the university and it should be able to spend it in any way it likes. The formula should involve the long-run amount but not the details. If the university wants oak tables in the dining hall at $250 each, instead of vinyl and plywood at $225, it can purchase them and make up the difference somewhere else, especially in the lack of repair bills in subsequent years. If it wants lounge rooms on each floor, rumpus rooms in the basement, special design for the outside, or single rooms for graduate students, it should make the decision itself. If it appears that costs will mount too high because of the extras, the university itself should either decide what to do without or find the necessary money itself. In the first place it is amazing how suddenly contractors and architects will become interested and economical when they are dealing directly with the user who is also paying the cost, and in the second place what a variety of furniture and equipment can be secured at modest prices when the user purchases and pays for them. Furthermore the user will be more modest in his demands and judicious in their fulfilment when he has to count costs himself. All the efforts should be direct and handled within a small group of people so that there will be a minimum of costs and politics arising from the project, as well as a healthy variety in buildings among a number of campuses receiving funds from the same source.

The inner politics of the university itself requires special provisions for this kind of work and, again, the prevention of an internal bureaucracy. Purchasing agents, accountants, and superintendents of buildings are among the most prolific of empire builders, and they, as well as the university architect, bear careful watching. University building projects have been handled internally in numerous ways. The most expensive have been those of the agents, accountants, and superintendents acting either alone or in charge of a group, and those of large building committees representative of various parts of the university. In both instances interested people either have no voice in the project and dislike the result, or have too much voice and the result is a chaos of conflicting ideas.

It is not difficult to find examples of these phenomena in many universities. Nor, on the other hand, is it difficult to find examples of splendid university buildings, economically constructed and admirably suited to the functions they serve. Almost invariably the latter were the result of a project guided by a small group of three, five or so, led by a layman in the building business who was associated with the university, who had a broad and keen interest in its activities and the ability to ask for advice, select good advice, and make decisions. Any university contains a small number of such people, and they are the ones its authorities should seek out for such a task.

Participatory democracy should be kept to a minimum in this instance. Most professors, including those in the faculties of engineering and architecture, are as unfit for such direction as most administrators and officials, because the task requires entrepreneurial qualities which are not found in most people. Successful direction has come from many university sources, including presidents, chancellors, professors, and students with special interests in such matters. The reason for their success lies not in their knowledge of technical matters, but in their ability to get or use that knowledge; not in their actually doing the work but in selecting the right people to do it; not just in making decisions but in getting ample advice before making them. In almost all instances this service was provided free of charge.

The technical or administrative expert in such projects should be on tap in an advisory role, not on top in a managing one. For a library, for example, the librarians will run up costs, fight among themselves, and ignore other experts. The drama or music departments are the last places to seek final direction on artistic facilities. And most professors and students with special interest in laboratories or sport facilities have little knowledge of how to provide them. Nor should these experts select or elect a committee; they rarely do it well. But every one of these people is capable of giving advice. The advice will usually be conflicting, and the committee will find it more helpful and efficient if it is related to costs, general university policy, and the human considerations mentioned earlier, rather than to the professional dignity and administrative rituals of the professional, from the government engineer to the campus dean of music. We will note the process in detail in chapter 14 on culture. It operates in the same way in universities, particularly when too many participants and experts get in one another's way and responsibility is dispersed.

The impact of administration and its accompanying politics on teaching and studying is increasing sharply, and it can be noted in the work of both professors and students. Participatory democracy requires many committees, and those who serve on them must devote much time to meetings, to becoming acquainted with the business, to manoeuvering opinion and handling details, and to getting results. There arise in this activity the same two groups of people who appear in most other organizations, those who are adept at committee work and are therefore frequently asked to serve, and those, not necessarily adept, who like committee work because they enjoy being involved and therefore take on the duty whenever they cannot be ignored or when others are glad to slough off the responsibility on them.

There is a subtle difference in practice in the attitudes of these groups. To the first committee work tends to be a duty; to the second it is frequently a claim to status or an escape from other work, and it appears justified because it seems important and keeps one busy. The first group usually does sixty minutes work every hour in the committee; the second may do no more than ten, even though each member considers his very presence as worth the time spent. To this time must be added the time taken off from regular work. A few people get their regular work done anyway; but for the big majority committee work cuts deeply into it because they spin out their assumed service by extra talk and politics which waste their own and other people's time. The adept committee man is never seen holding prolonged court in the coffee shop. He knows that every hour spent in committee is in academic terms an hour away from teaching, seeing students, research, and home life, and in student terms an hour away from studies and extra-curricular activities. And since committee work is habit-forming, it does not take long for a professor or student to devote more time to it than to his regular work and to shirk his responsibilities elsewhere. This problem, which is common in many other organizations including government itself, is not so much the result of normal university management as the consequence of an inflated administration, much of which may not have been necessary in the first place. Committee work is directly valuable and fruitful only as long as it is worth the man-hours adept people devote to it and take from their other work. It is also indirectly valuable when, in innocuous committees, it absorbs the energies and satisfies the egos of the more erratic members of the staff and student body. Beyond that, however, it becomes progressively inefficient and expensive.

Two suggestions inevitably follow. One is that an appreciation of the undoubted value of participatory democracy must be accompanied by the recognition that democracy does not thrive on over-participation, especially on the part of those who cannot take participation seriously by being efficient and responsible and those who substitute it for their own work. A small, able, and tough striking committee is soon faced with the fact that some professors and students should never be put on any committees because their participation is simply not worth it, and that others should be on many committees for equally obvious reasons. This fact is familiar to parliamentary leaders. The other suggestion is an understanding that every plan, mechanism, and set of regulations and standards involves talk, routine, an organization, paperwork, money, and resources taken from other activities, and that their value must be weighed against these consequences. Coordination among universities, for example, is a popular idea with government. But its value may not be worth the enormous amount of necessary work and politics, together with the loss of initiative, variation, experimentation, and character, which results from too much coordination. These two suggestions simply mean that, while it is essential for people to mind other people's business, such service becomes ineffective if they cease minding their own or if they thereby increase unduly the business itself.

The reaction to administration also requires attention. If the administration becomes too big and complicated people realize that it is really not worth the effort and slow down, resist, or complain. Even administrators, politicians, and civil servants get to a point where they become slack. As for regulations and procedures, the more there are the more they conflict with one another, the less efficient they become, and the more they are ignored in practice. Indeed every set of regulations invites new sets of politics for interpreting and enforcing them and ultimately for getting around them. Still more of them then appear to shore up the structure, and reactions to them change radically the original reason for them. When communication becomes mere relations between files and encounters between pieces of paper, and people become mere numbers, men wonder what serves whom and react negatively. Like any growing structure, an administrative system requires periodic pruning to simplify it and keep it productive; but it rarely gets it.

Universities have illustrated all these failings of bureaucracy rampant, and a large part of the academic turmoil of the 1960s can be ascribed to it. The reason is not difficult to find. Governmental and business organizations grow without rebellion. In universities, on the other hand, management and business are incidental in importance – necessary, but in a supporting role. The pursuit of knowledge can never be over-administered without being limited, frustrated, or prevented altogether. This pursuit requires the first and commanding place in academic affairs, and the supporting functions should literally be scarcely noticeable. But administration, in universities as elsewhere, is rarely content to blush unseen; indeed it is seldom so shy that it will even blush. It tends to become blatant, pushing, and prominent, and it likes to charge to the front and give the appearance, not only that it is leading, but also that the organization would fail without it. At this point academic leadership retires to the rear, and even there it takes on the colouring of the new managers. Indeed it can do little else when they control the funds.

Meanwhile the administrators paradoxically have less power and influence as administration itself grows. The president, for example, the captain of the ship, must not only give up his commanding position on the bridge and do paperwork in his cabin or negotiate with shore admirals in their distant quarters, but he must also endure the frequent mutinies of his crew, who see their ship on an erratic course determined by too many conflicting signals. The registrar must give up personal contact in favour of IBM cards and machines. Other academic leaders, from vice presidents to department heads, chairmen of important committees, and student officers find it increasingly difficult to give leadership in their preoccupation with housekeeping functions. Meanwhile politicians and civil servants are entangled in the parliamentary and administrative problems that are causing so much concern in government. Thereupon professors, students, and the public wonder about the relevance of it all. Soon they ask if the university is doing its job properly. Then the shore admirals not only retreat while the officers face mutiny, but wonder how the trouble began and send out still more signals to confuse the educational atmosphere.

There is the same cause for wonder and reaction in other organizations. About their problems, however, the customers and the public know relatively little. Who really worries, organizes a protest, or plans a sit-down or teach-in if a government department grows tenfold, or if the cost of management doubles the price of a product? But the student does know when a professor is absorbed in committee work or campus politics. The badly prepared lecture, the rush from a seminar, the lack of office hours, and the postponement of research become obvious. The professor also knows when similar problems beset the student in studies and campus affairs. And the presence of non-academic officials with large staffs is not reassuring when their machines and forms treat professors and students as anonymous statistics. From academic officers students really want evidence of academic leadership and example and interest in them and their affairs, and it is not easy for them to reconcile with these the preoccupation with office work. The public too wants academic leadership and is unimpressed with campus politics. University personnel are too close to those they serve for the consequences of the apparatus to go unnoticed. Compared with similar phenomena in most other organizations, the impact and reaction is immediate and direct.

One remedy for these difficulties, responsible government, suggests itself frequently in universities and in other organizations. It is rarely applied when needed but, sooner or later, it is demanded. People who want to participate should be in a position to handle their own affairs when they can. In a society where increasing numbers of people are administering things instead of producing things, responsible government may be forcibly required in many fields by the breakdown of the apparatus and the discontent of those working in and served by it. The university, where the impact of the problem and its reaction is direct, may illustrate what will happen in other organizations; and the experience of the churches is already a portent. Responsible government is the reform demanded of empires by colonies, their parliaments, and their executives, when distant officials keep a tight rein on their affairs and local ones want freedom to handle their own business. The bogies are always the same – the inability of officials to delegate power, to trust and recognize the abilities of local people, and to resist paper, negotiations, checks and cross-checks, order, accountability, and standardization. An irritating and false premise is usually cited: those who pay the piper call the tune. Piper payers who call tunes ultimately get bad music. Protest and in some places rebellion result, and when responsible government is won everyone is the better for it.

This is not a purely political phenomenon; it is also a psychological one. As most parents know it is stupid to give a child pocket money and tell him how to spend it. He must be given responsibility so that he will learn how to spend it himself, and not be subservient to the nit-picking of an over-dominant parent. Indeed there is no guarantee that the parent knows best how to spend it. The lack of responsible government is just as inefficient in today's government as it is in family life. Large and remote administrative control over society's major activities inevitably means loss of freedom. And it means loss of efficiency and direction as it grows. It also means a decline of initiative and, most serious of all, a loss of spirit. The administrative empire radiating out from a distant capital can be just as exasperating as other empires, and colonialism has the same effects whatever its form. Tune calling by piper payers is as hazardous an operation in administration as it is in music and child rearing. It is at once a paradox and problem that, in the age of collectivism and the welfare state, and at a time when participatory democracy is fashionable, the trends toward responsible government sought and cherished so short a time ago have been reversed, and colonialism and prolonged paternalism have become fashionable in governments and are permitted by those they serve. An undemocratic, inefficient, and discontented society is the inevitable result, now as always, of this lack of trust.

Is there any reason why universities cannot handle their affairs better by themselves than by the constant regulation of the government? Are the ministrations of already busy politicians and civil servants worth all the apparatus and politics? Are a board of governors of responsible citizens and a group of senior university executives and professors less able to handle university policy or less aware of the public interest than distant officials, or less responsible with money than treasury clerks? Acknowledging the undoubted rights of elected representatives of the people to oversee the spending of the taxpayers' money, can they really do it in detail? and is it efficient to set up still another set of apparatus and politics to do it? are the results of their detailed ministrations in the public interest?

My answer to all these questions is 'no,' and I believe that the current unrest in and criticism of the universities are aimed at the wrong place. They should be aimed at the erosion of responsible government which causes a large part of the trouble. Consider, for example, the suggestion of simply mailing out a cheque. The federal government of Canada did it and required no accounting. The total amount was debatable in Parliament and was negotiable between the universities and the government, a formula, also negotiable, determined the detailed distribution of the money, and annual reports indicated how the money was spent. A few universities made a few mistakes, although nothing on the scale of the *Bonaventure,* but the public got excellent value for its money during a challenging period of educational expansion.

The universities furnish an example of yet other consequences of inflated administration and politics: when there are too many authorities no one is in authority, and when too many people are consulted the consultation becomes ineffective. The more impersonal leadership, initiative, example, and opinion become, the less impact they have and the easier it is to bypass or even destroy them. Then a power vacuum occurs and less responsible people rush in to fill it. Moreover the more obstacles there are to authority and the more circuitous the exercise of it, the less readiness there is to use it. A man can scarcely expect to have absolute authority with no checks. On the other hand, if he knows that his action must have the blessing of numerous functionaries and committees, be recorded on many papers, be subject to inevitable criticisms and appeals, be featured in headlines in the press, and be judged as evidence of disorder by government and public, he will tend to hesitate to make decisions at all, seek compromises which will upset no one, waffle on such decisions he does make, or set up committees to assume the responsibility, bury the issue, or fortify him in either acting or not acting. Whatever else may be said about administration, it cannot operate effectively without leadership, and that leadership must be sufficiently localized, identified, personalized, unencumbered, responsible, and accountable. Participatory democracy must be permitted, but talk must eventually make way for clear direction, action, and the assumption of responsibility for the consequences.

Scarcely a commentary on the troubles of modern universities, from that of President Nixon's commission on the subject in 1970 to local assessments of special issues, fails to include an observation that the leadership of administrators, professors, and students has been woefully weak. It is not difficult to find the reasons why. As the universities expanded, as the government got involved, as participatory democracy was carried to extremes, and as procedures multiplied, authority was dispersed and no one could exercise it directly and fearlessly. The people who resent authority of any kind, and there are always some in any activity, were released from responsible direction and enjoyed a heyday of 'freedom.' This freedom was not freedom at all, of course, but the absence of responsibility which readily turned into license. The freedom of others inevitably suffered in the scramble, and fear appeared to cow the rank and file to the point where they became hard to lead. Professors could be pilloried for even the most innocuous discipline, and when they knew that each action had to be backed by forms in triplicate, written authority from a dean, and appeals to a committee, the less hardy of them simply ignored their responsibility. Difficult and unpleasant duties were shirked in numerous cases because they could not be handled without much red tape and a thundering row.

The same problem is evident in student affairs. The principle of student councils is excellent, but their effectiveness depends on the ability of student leaders to lead, to do their work, and to deal with unwise associates. Excess talk and lack of responsibility are no more beneficial to the students' participatory democracy than they are elsewhere. When they arise inflated politics again appears. Everything from Viet Nam to the private life of some professor can provoke a minority of vocal students into a scurry of activity and a heated release of emotions, while at the same time student activities on the campus may die of neglect, a student with five failures may sit on an important policy committee, a neurotic may edit the course-evaluation book, the tenth person approached for the job may head the campus newspaper, the council's treasury may incur a substantial deficit, and the students be able to do very little about it. Few able students will take campus jobs under such circumstances, and the leadership of the weak is largely a waste of time. In this sphere, too, responsible government is a necessary accompaniment to participatory democracy. When it operates able students are attracted by it and, under them, student councils usually operate efficiently and student activities thrive. But when a host of participators, a tangle of apparatus, and a dispersal of leadership appear extra-curricular life disintegrates. We have already noted that much campus unrest is directly caused by failures in student organizations and the decline of student activities.

This dilution of power has yet another cause, a phenomenon that appears in many organizations when the structure becomes too complicated. It is the separation of administration from the body it serves. In normal structures the administration may be called the inner circle, but it is regarded as part, and perhaps the centre, of the structure. In inflated structures the term establishment has appeared, and it generally denotes a special, and perhaps suspect, clique outside and above a devoted group of real members, and with interests different from theirs. The separation of academic and student administrators from professors and students did not take long at universities as both the apparatus and the politics expanded. A dean was once regarded as a professor with administrative duties and a special title; today he is hard pressed to maintain his academic status, and complicated protocol often determines when and how he may mix and negotiate with the faculty. Countless students do not even know the name of their council's president. It is the difference between being part of a team and being 'they,' a difference that has become clear to those who step over the invisible but effective barrier. It is easier for an inner circle to be the executive of a team and to get cooperation, deal with policy, and actually administer than for an establishment, which too often must bridge the barrier every time it acts. Loyalty is weaker between an establishment and the members than it is where there is an inner circle. When trouble arises, as it inevitably does, it is settled more easily and with less acrimony without the barrier; with it protest readily seems like rebellion and rebellion assumes the more sinister characteristics of mutiny. Student officials are subject to the same separation, both within their own ranks and in their relations with administrators and professors, and it wreaks havoc in campus activities.

Certainly the 'we-they' confrontations within universities have darkened the usual image of hot beds of dissension which accompanies higher education anyway, and which can be regarded with a tolerant, 'Well, you know what professors and students are like.' Like 'What can you expect of a politician?', it is a good-natured recognition of natural foibles. But when something that smells of mutiny arises people will not tolerate or forgive it, however justifiable it may be, because the very safety of the organization, and of the service it exists to perform, is at stake. The penalty for mutiny is always severe; for what appears to be academic mutiny it may even be the loss of rights and freedom, caused by public reaction to it. But when one examines celebrated mutinies, one notes that the trouble often arises, not primarily from errors by officers, but from the requirements, mistakes, and perhaps corruption of distant officials, such as the issue of weevily biscuits or regulations providing fifty lashes. Similarly many of the troubles of universities arise from conditions which their officials can do little about because of the growing demands of a distant authority, and which consequently cause and aggravate the 'we-they' divisions in academic life. Just as a domineering or interfering though well-meaning mother-in-law can ruin a marriage and spoil the children by breaking the spirit of a family, so can a government destroy the subtle unions which make up the university community.

This comment is not a criticism of politicians and officials in their personal or official capacities, but of an unnatural alignment of functions. Put a university professor or official in political authority under similar circumstances and the alignment will be no better. Indeed it may be much worse, because he can readily make the old mistake, almost always fatal in administration, of thinking his limited professional experience gives him special licence to dominate. Put a politician in academic life and he will be especially suspicious of governmental control, regardless of whether his political friends or erstwhile opponents are in power.[2] Governmental and university functions, attitudes, and methods simply do not mix well. Both categories contribute more to the interest of higher education if there is between them, not a barrier, but a substantial no-man's-land on which they can meet and negotiate but across which one side cannot dominate the other.

This domination is not all on the government's part. It should not have been supposed that university-government relations would be only one-way. An increased interest in social and political action by university people accompanied the rise of government control. Control always invites demand for a share in it. When the universities directed their eyes and ears toward the government for funds and the resulting regulation, it was only a step further to turn other aspirations in the same direction. This process has been rather rough. It would be a mistake to consider it as ingratitude for government aid: the government is only passing on what the taxpayers contribute minus government costs. Reaction against dependence and control is a more likely cause because, in education as in most things, the more direct and blatant is financial help the more its recipients resent it. Universities have had to become political in dealing with their political patrons to the point where it has become a habit, and it does not take long for this political habit to combine with the reaction against dependence and control to produce a nervous, negative, and perhaps neurotic outlook on public affairs. Theorists exalt the awakening of political interest and activism among professors and young people, which is right, but such an awakening would have been healthier if their institutions were less dependent and if their interest and activism were positive as well as negative. Moreover the prime work of the universities is interest and activism of an intellectual kind which, unfortunately, an excess of politics can change from a creative purpose to a carping, destructive one.

With all its faults the ivory tower is a superb vantage point from which to view the world of knowledge for a short time. It is not a particularly good place from which to till political fields, and most of its denizens cannot work well in the tower and the fields at the same time. Governments, therefore, make a serious mistake in compelling them to run up and down excessively: they will stop half-way and hurl dissatisfactions both upward and downward. It is better to leave them alone so they will stay at the top for a few years, because then flashes from the top will be brighter, and more spectacular, and more useful, and after their descent the denizens will be better equipped to illuminate the fields below.

It may be said on the other hand that there is no reason why universities should not be involved in politics. They can be, provided that the amount of politics is kept to a necessary minimum and that the number of people involved in politics is limited to a reasonably competent few. If the politics which inevitably accompanies administration is expanded too much, too many irrelevant matters are inflated and ultimately handled by too many politically incompetent people. At this point politicians, officials, university administrators, professors, and students lose faith in one another, distrust one another, face too many problems, and make too many mistakes; the remedy for their difficulties will be sought in still more apparatus and talk. As the process spirals less real work is done, the purpose of the organization fades, and *all* the people involved become engaged in peripheral and remote activities.

The quality and nature of such activities are evident in the universities, but they can be seen, upon examination, in all organizations. They are the results of a physical attribute of administration. When there is just enough administration to serve a given number of functions it is a centripetal force tending toward cohesion and coordination. When there is too much administration the nature of the motion changes and it becomes a centrifugal force favouring dispersal. This dispersal not only pulls able people away from the centre of their responsibilities but also hurls the lighter ones into all sorts of places where they have no business to be. Under such circumstances, for example, a professor or student flies off from the work he can do well into dubious participation in things he cannot. The hyperactive and the do-gooders have a hectic time tumbling into other people's business. Or a governmental organization so large that it has a shortage of competent people sends mediocre or incompetent officials to perform important duties or act as vital liaisons with other bodies. It is not fanciful to suggest that the great excess of administration in contemporary society causes this dispersal in many organizations to the point where within that society's orbit numerous whirling organizations are colliding with one another and their lightest people and ideas are colliding most, with disastrous results to the organizations and the society.

The nature of these collisions can be seen everywhere, and again the university furnishes illustrations. The exercise of public financial responsibility, for example, rests in theory with a minister of finance and an auditor general. In practice, however, it is a complaint of universities throughout the world that, as financial responsibility becomes comprehensive and detailed, senior officials do less and less, and it is minor officials with limited knowledge of both finance and education who are, in fact, entrusted with that responsibility, and they cause endless trouble. If the control is too detailed, it is ultimately the 'scrapings of the barrel' that act for government, although 'they regard themselves as of the best.'[3] Relations between universities and churches are often discussed. But if such liaisons are too close and too numerous it is on the weak chaplains and preachers that they in practice depend. If the professions have too large an influence in the university — and law, medicine, theology, music, and others have had in their turn — too much politics is involved, and busy, able professional people have little time for them and tend to entrust the liaisons to their weaker brethren. The government itself has the same experiences with collisions resulting from undue dispersal. The more extensive its meshing with other bodies, the more people it requires to deal with them, and the more people they require to deal with it. Consequently the ultimate clashing of inadequate officials and irrelevant ideas and procedures weakens the impact of the government and the other bodies on one another and dilutes the significance of the work they perform.

Participatory democracy and the responsibility of the people and their government for what is done in the people's name are undoubtedly just. Those who advocate them too often forget, however, that good things often fail because of their own excesses, and that full allowance must be made for the practical abilities and responses of the available people. It is a paradox of our time that the more democratic participation and responsibility are featured in theory, the less they operate in practice, because the participators do not trust one another enough to delegate power responsibly instead of tying it up in a tangle of administration. But they had better learn the ways of trust lest their organizations choke on talk and red tape. The strangled noises of universities everywhere are certainly not triumphant sounds of rampant democracy, but rather the hoarse gasps of compulsive talk produced by constrictive administration and pervasive politics.

The university, like most organizations of people, also illustrates a characteristic of mixing which was mentioned earlier. If one stirs cake batter too much after fruit and nuts are added, or muddles fresh concrete excessively, a chemical breakdown occurs which weakens the cohesive qualities of the mixture. A comparable breakdown in personality takes place in human societies where there is too much togetherness, too much participation and communication. When university affairs get into a swirling state of mix and muddle after countless personalities are added to the educational process, the university shows all the signs of a crumbling cake or a disintegrating wall. The remedy is the same in educational and social matters as in cooking and construction: mix the ingredients separately as thoroughly as possible and then only blend them in institutional affairs.[4]

We may now return to colourful activites and culture as instruments for mixing humans so that they will blend better when they come together to do communal work.

14

The politics of culture

Culture, man's liveliest and most productive field of action, stimulates constructive human sensibilities and absorbs or diverts destructive ones. It includes two categories of action. One, generally visible, embraces performing and creating. The other, usually in the background but no less important, comprises supporting functions like managing, financing, and sponsoring, as well as emotional phenomena such as the exercise of judgment and local and national pride. Actions in both categories may carry the minds and emotions of men to the heights; alone among human endeavours they do not carry them to the depths. They involve the participants in the most complicated of politics with the minimum of harm.

Culture is a major strand in the fabric of a nation and in the bonds which hold people together. This strand is vital because men are not content merely to feed and house themselves and occupy their time with work; they must also create, express themselves, relieve their emotions, and entertain, amuse, impress, and inspire one another. All these activities require politics, and the vitality of a nation's culture depends greatly on how its cultural politics are conducted and on the compensations provided for its peculiarities. As for postures in culture, they are infinite in number and variety. All the strengths and weaknesses of participatory democracy are vividly illustrated in culture and in the reactions to it of those who share the countless opportunities it provides.

We have already noted that culture involves those means of communication by sight, sound, form, colour, and motion which are not limited by time, space, or categories of men. It is as important in relations among people as the other means of communication, and it touches the hearts and stimulates the emotions more effectively. Culture is especially important in international relations; indeed it is the only consistently successful form of communication among different peoples. What politician, diplomat, or businessman from the United States or Russia, for example, has made as powerful and as positive a personal impact on the people of the other country as a writer, a pianist, or an artist? And how much does the average citizen of one country know about the economics or politics of another country in comparison with his knowledge of its music, dance, or architecture? The interest of tourists is largely devoted to the culture of the nations they visit. A ballet or an historic site attracts thousands, a power plant or a ministry of finance, none. This interest is natural because cultural treasures are symbols of man's creative genius, the legacies of civilization.

Within nations culture is the basis of the history, traditions, and spirit of a people because it preserves their cumulative experiences and emotions from one generation to another. No English economics or Chinese trade relations can compare with the culture of Britain or China in fostering a sense of community, even in descendants of emigrants several generations removed from the homeland of their ancestors. Even new African states facing numerous practical problems seek to bolster their nationhood with revivals of their ancient tribal culture. Men tend to be proud of their own culture and responsive to that of others because it is common to all men in its emotional force and yet variable among men in its forms. It is highly individualistic, and yet it encourages maximum tolerance and cooperation among people and classes of people, which is probably the main reason why it is so strong. Somewhere there is recorded an exchange between a 'practical' man and a 'cultural' man; the former favoured 'bands of iron' for preserving national unity over cultural 'moonbeams'; the latter asked, 'did you ever try to cut a moonbeam?'

One feature of the politics of culture is the delicate relationship between freedom and responsibility. Present in all activity, this relationship is somewhat more delicate in culture because in it human sensitivity has more scope, the range of quality, taste, and temperament is wider, and judgment is more tenuous. Freedom of artistic expression is vital. Yet responsibility is also essential because an art tends to thrive best when the artist is prompted and aided by the judgment of others who will excite the creativity which the artist cannot always rouse in himself and who will remind him of the limitations which must restrain his fancy. There are so many variables, and the alignment of them to ensure successful enterprise is so delicate, that the politics of culture requires more reconciliation of the widely different interests and temperaments than any other politics; it requires as well different types of power and different methods of using it. Paradoxically in no other politics is consensus harder to get, yet tolerance the more easily maintained. People fear the incomprehensible in most things; in culture they will tolerate anything.

Participation in culture is endless in its variety and fascination. It involves creators, entrepreneurs, patrons, and the public. The creators operate in a field of ability, imagination, interpretation, and emotion, and anyone concerned with culture must therefore deal with the elusive and insubstantial. The layman must devote infinite patience to his negotiations with artists, while artists must handle laymen and other artists with maximum diplomacy. If the result is good everyone will take credit; but if it is bad no one will take responsibility, because it cannot be fixed, and everyone will lapse into communal silence or support the result as a different interpretation. If, for example, a new building shows physical defects they can be blamed on someone; if it is ugly the architect will say its beauty is an acquired taste and a 'new look,' and the owner will not want to disapprove and admit his inability to appreciate it. A badly painted portrait can be justified as an unusual interpretation displaying the artist's concept of the subject's personality. One can even spill a can of paint on a canvas, frame it and hang it, and be entertained with learned observations on the result and the reticence of those who do not like it but are afraid to say so. Those tempted to make frank appraisals must be careful, however, for today's shock may be tomorrow's treasure and today's triumph a casualty of changing fashion.

The layman must not only tread warily in the artist's domain; he must also inject his own ideas with caution. But he must inject them nevertheless, because the artist needs them. Most creators are rarely able to work without a push; they may be lazy, have little knowledge of finance, need constant reminders of quality, or need to be subjected to the rigours of criticism and encouraged by the comforts of praise. A Michelangelo in any of the arts needs the stimulus of a Pope Julius II who as patron will prod and inspire him to great heights which he himself does not have the confidence to reach for; and lesser artists are in no less need of encouragement. Most writers require the hard and perhaps exasperating ministrations of tough editors to make what they say intelligible. Rarely is an artist a good judge of his own work, and, whether beginner or veteran, he needs the opinions and reactions of others to understand the impact of his medium and his skill. Without interaction with others egoism and temperament can keep an artist from realizing his potential: the promising are rarely as good as they think they are and those at the summit need help and discipline to remain there. The same is true of other activities too, and all experts need to be responsible to someone. But expressing oneself in an art form is a much more elastic process, and talent needs more 'drawing out' than the ordering or supervising more common elsewhere. Expression not drawn out by another tends with rare exceptions to be undisciplined. A combination gives a talent both substance and direction. Moreover much bad art, produced by incompetents and poseurs, requires special obstacles and discouragements in a field where undisciplined expression can easily be foisted off as talent.

Several types of persons perform supporting services in the arts. Lovers are, of course, traditional. If they are wives they marry the art as well as the artist and must regard it as the artist's fulfilment, not theirs. If they are not wives they may play the similar but more delicate role of second mistress to the art — a George Sand or Cosima von Bülow to men like Chopin or Wagner. Some artists need to be loved if they are to serve art, to make practical contact with the realities of life, or, as in the case of Liszt, to turn from performing to creating.

Most patrons are considerably less exotic. The entrepreneur, from Sol Hurok who brought music to every corner of America to the hardworking producer who provokes local people into putting on their own dramatic production, contributes as much to culture as the artists. His job is to act as an irritant which will rouse both the artist and the public from that inertia and indifference which stifle culture and which in new ventures only a tough and dedicated entrepreneur can overcome. There are several equivalents of slaves in the cultural world too — ticket sellers, costume makers, members of the stage crew, and other hewers of wood and drawers of water in the local amateur production or in the ladies' auxiliary of a symphony, as well as those who entertain all these workers at the receptions and parties which make the work bearable and socially attractive and provide opportunities for hero worship of the artists. Because these operations are expensive, individual and collective sponsors fill the same role today that generations of patrons have done before them; they serve the artist by stimulating him and enabling him to live, and the public by encouraging art and keeping down its costs.

The public thus gets its culture from teams of artists and laymen; it makes its contribution by providing the same consumer demand it provides elsewhere. It likes ten Fausts for one Manon, divides its attentions between pop art and old masters, acclaims a Flagstad before a war and jeers her afterwards, makes authors fashionable or consigns them to oblivion, and otherwise brings to culture a touch of collective temperament which matches that of the artists. Thus culture runs the gamut between two groups of prima donnas with many middlemen in between, and emerges in its infinite variety as a rich and powerful expression of individual and collective feeling.

The politics of this remarkable and unpredictable activity starts with an understanding and manipulation of the traditional expert-layman relationship. Generally this relationship relies on the layman to decide what shall be done and the expert to decide how to do it. The ability and judgment of both parties vary greatly, and harmony is secured only when each understands and compensates for both his own limitations and those of the other. This relationship is much more difficult in the arts than it is elsewhere. One goes to a doctor and puts oneself into his hands; his work is technical and one accepts his judgment. To do the same with an architect would be folly; his work is also technical, but artistic concepts and his imagination are variables which require participation by the customer. A patient's observations on the treatment of his liver ailments are usually superfluous; a client's comments on the design of his livingroom are essential. The client contributes something the patient does not have, a set of concepts and an imagination of his own which are as relevant, but in a different way, as those of the architect. A singer may need the suggestions of an entrepreneur in drawing up her programme or her concert may appeal only to other musicians and not to the lay audience whose ticket purchases make her appearance possible. Some of the finest painting and sculpture has been commissioned by patrons who provided both the general specifications and the encouragement, and some of the worst has been produced by artists who consulted their undisciplined imagination alone and then, like the draper in *The King With No Clothes On,* imposed their will by illusion and suggestion. The same trick has been played by writers of books and professional articles in magazines and learned journals, playwrights, interior decorators, and others whose work lacked the discipline of lay judgment and the specifications of intelligent sponsorship.

A brake would be put on such activities in most fields. But brakes are foolish in the arts. They need freedom to create the sublime, and the ridiculous is an inevitable by-product. An artist should welcome his sponsor's judgments as valuable influences. But the artist's decisions should then be free and he should have the final word because the sponsor is not the creator, and his judgment is only an opinion which can be good or bad. Some haggling may be necessary if costs are unsatisfactory or the time for completion is short, but a haggle does both sides good by relating the practical demands of business and the inspirational needs of art.

Artists who neglect this relationship forget that all art involves ideas, and that artists do not have a monopoly on them. Sponsors who neglect it overlook the fact that their judgment is most effective if they lend it rather than command it. People who rage or laugh at the results must remind themselves that their judgment is personal as well as temporary. The waltz was regarded as naughty at its creation, gay when it was accepted, conservative when it was replaced, and finally appropriate for Clark Gable's funeral. The mixture of artistic and lay ideas provides the enchantment of unpredictable results. This is one reason why culture fascinates man; he can never take it for granted.

This fascination is irresistible. But it may develop slowly in a society because of an inertia caused by community shyness and the competition of so-called practical things. The politics of community culture, particularly newly organized culture, is formed by this inertia. Let us illustrate by an example.

If a government in North America constructs a wharf or a grain elevator in a city which does not need it, the public will welcome it unanimously. The bigger it is and the more it costs the more pleased people will be with their local political representatives and others who have provided this morsel from the porkbarrel. Every politician will boast of it at the next election. It will, they say, 'put the city on the map,' provide employment, and ensure a splendid future for business. If there is a large deficit, or if the facility lies idle, not a word will be said by either the government or the public. What a different reception awaits a proposed cultural centre! People speak freely now! 'Aren't there other things which are needed more?' 'Millions for culture to serve only a small segment of the population?' 'Opera and ballet will never go over here!' 'It will be a white elephant.' A politician or city councillor who would be defeated if he opposed the wharf knows he will be regarded as sound if he crusades in headlines against 'culture.' Some clergymen and social activists, silent about the wharf, indulge in tut-tutting and make dire predictions. Every little nuance of the issue is discussed in the press and taken up by the critics, and the fiercest arguments are carried on the national television networks. Meanwhile the wharf getter is being congratulated, while the promoter of the cultural centre is warding off comments like 'Bill's folly' and 'how's the warehouse?' And in every case even the devotees of culture will stand back in the shadows muttering that it will never be built. This difference in attitudes is standard in North America, universal in Canada. Elsewhere it varies; in Rotterdam a new opera house was one of the first buildings constructed after the devastation of World War II; in Sydney, Australia, there was a controversy of world impact over the construction of an opera house.

This situation is one reason for the large deficits of most cultural projects. In the case of the wharf the planners have no reason to be modest about cost; if an election is near they may even exaggerate it. About the centre, on the other hand, woe betide the entrepreneur who states the cost at the beginning. He is forced to be reticent at first so as to ease the inevitable public shock and coax the necessary official consent. He tends, therefore, to mention a low figure and stress what a bargain the project is so as to get acceptance in principle. After the smoke of controversy has partially cleared away he adds other facilities to the original plan and accepts ideas from the numerous committees and experts that suddenly appear when success is suggested. The proposed cost is already much higher when construction begins, but being committed, officialdom consents with reluctance and resignation. As the building rises improvements are made, hidden costs appear, and changes are suggested. The critics, who were silent on the cost of the wharf, now seize on the prospects of a deficit. At this stage they give the project notoriety, but it is too late for them to thwart it. At completion the original cost mentioned has multiplied. There are recriminations, but if the planners have arranged a sufficiently spectacular opening, featuring an appropriate group of celebrities, the criticisms will be overwhelmed for the moment, and both politicians and cultural leaders, hitherto hostile or silent, will now rush forward to profess that they have been favourably disposed all the while and to secure some undeserved credit for the venture.

This kind of financing is not 'bad' or 'irresponsible'; it is natural and necessary to overcome inertia and reluctance. It is evident in other ventures where one must lure the customer and hook and play him before he can be landed. In culture the quarry is much more wary. One reason for this wariness in North America is that the public finds it difficult to see the direct and indirect benefits of culture. It does not appear practical; it does not seem to put money in people's pockets; indeed it always 'loses money.' Supporters appease these doubts with some difficulty by citing construction costs and wages as local benefits, and education and entertainment as valuable for school children and tourists. But it is difficult at the start to convince people of the intangible benefits like artistic appreciation, education, and community spirit which are alleged to be 'flighty' by some and 'irrelevant' by others; and it is next to impossible to mention entertainment, which may appear frivolous, or opportunities for artists, which may be labelled 'privilege for a select few.' It usually takes a major event, such as a centennial or a need for a memorial, to provide sufficient justification for planning a large cultural project, and even then the controversy is so spectacular that deciding on the project itself becomes a public entertainment of greater magnitude than anything the finished project will subsequently provide.

Once in a while such a project has no deficit. Rigorous control is necessary for this result. The entrepreneur must work harder at unfamiliar things than he expects, and exercise judgment over his own ideas. Architects and contractors must be argued with. Many participators with more opinions than experience or financial sense must be warned off. Numerous pessimists must be answered or lured away. Politicians seeking opportunities for patronage must be discouraged. Local businessmen looking for contracts, either directly or through public officials, have to be side-tracked or reminded of the virtues of tendering. And the swarm of favour seekers which always descends must be brushed off. The pressure on the project's entrepreneur is enormous, and the firmness which he must exercise results in much work and criticism for him and controversy for the project. Indeed many negative public reactions to controversy over cultural projects as well as most deficits are not caused by culture, but by segments of the public who seek to participate for the wrong reasons.

Another reason for wariness on the part of politicians and the public is the reputation which cultural suppliers of various kinds have had for being irresponsible in business matters and quarrelsome in seeking what they want. In one respect there is no justification for the reputation of extravagance. Cultural enterprises cost money like everything else and the people concerned must live. The theory that the artist must starve in an attic to do good work does not hold, nor should he be expected to perform for little or nothing any more than anyone else. People in turn get what they pay for in culture, just as in other fields.

In another respect, however, the reputation can be justified because of the tendency of artists, inspired no doubt by a creative sense and a lively imagination, to lose sight of practical things like cost, utility, and broad appeal. This is where judgment is so difficult and fallible. People should not be restrained too much by the cost of a cultural activity because real cost cannot always be assessed in relation to the service performed. Utility rarely inspires the imagination and it is not the chief aim of art. And appeal is as fickle as it is unpredictable. Nevertheless artistic licence cannot go to extremes without undermining the credibility of artists and building up the resistance of patrons. It is to prevent the extremes, not to place restraints on the artists, that a judicious mixture of expert and lay judgment is necessary in cultural ventures. Moreover the lunatic fringe (not the unconventional) need the discipline of criticism, restraint, and perhaps ruin. The politics needed to deal with this kind of judgment must be particularly subtle. When a matter goes beyond the vague limits of artistic integrity into a situation where the artist can be suspected of making work for himself at the expense of both art and his sponsor, the subtlety must be accompanied by firmness. Power in artistic creation needs responsibility no less than other kinds of power.

There is something suspicious, for example about the portrait painter's insistence on having complete freedom in recording his sitter for posterity, perhaps to the point of not showing the canvas to anyone before it is finished. He can plead artistic integrity and the problems arising from the fact that everyone considers himself better looking than a portrait indicates. But the artist may be wrong in his interpretation, or perhaps technically unable to catch the expression or personality of the subject; yet he is unwilling either to admit his inadequacy or to alter or discard his creation. He thus exercises complete power in the transaction because, regardless of the result, the customer must accept the picture, pay for it, and live with it without being allowed to contribute any of his wishes or judgment whatever. It would seem more reasonable for an artist to consult others, submit sketches, and hear his sitter's arguments before making his final and irrevocable interpretation. I do not mean to suggest that there must, or even can, be a vetoing of an artist's skill and judgment before it is committed to canvas. By selecting him to do the job one has made the effective decision. But it seems a disservice to both art and those paying for it to suggest that the artist must be completely unaware of any opinion except his own. His decision should be the final one, but, as with most decisions, it could surely profit from some pre-testing. It is this kind of dictatorship which some artists either impose or attempt to impose that not only results in much bad art but also raises suspicions of 'phoniness' among the public.

Many artists are responsible, cooperative, and sensible in the use of their power, and the results in such instances are usually a credit to them and a source of pride and satisfaction to the patrons. It is often the best artists who are most amenable to advice while being most insistent on making the final decision themselves. But this happy arrangement cannot be taken for granted by patrons. It is interesting, for example, to watch a firm of interior decorators at work. The easy-going customer, having contracted for the furnishing of a building on the advice of his architect, may take no further interest until the job is done. The design consultant's work may result in beauty and practicality at a cost which matches both, and everyone is pleased. On the other hand the consultant may select furniture (perhaps from a favourite dealer) which is beautiful but impractical, practical but ugly, or at a cost which is unrelated to either the function performed or the budget as a whole. His tendency to do this kind of thing increases if there is no one to ask questions and thereby encourage him to select carefully among alternatives. Anyone can test the procedure by purchasing furniture in large quantitites for cultural centres or university residences, especially tables and chairs; this market is an intricate maze to wander around in. Somebody must wander, however, on behalf of the customer, not to make direct decisions but to ask questions and lend opinion.

The customer's judgment cannot be taken for granted either. He may have to be discouraged from furnishing a fine building too cheaply and either spoiling the decor or ensuring himself extra costs for later replacement. Or his wife or some helpful friend who has made a hobby of such things may offer him silly advice. The artist has to be strong enough to argue with the customer and give him expert advice frankly, especially if he is dealing with a sceptical businessman, an unimaginative government official, or a tough board of directors. The meddling customer and the weak artist can do just as much harm as the irresponsible artist. The confrontations in this type of business are often colourful. They seem the more spectacular because of the sensitivity and difficulty of making judgments and because the parties are usually spending someone else's money. The lack of such confrontations and serious preparation by the participants is one of the major reasons for failures in cultural enterprises and deficits in their finances. It is a serious and complicated business, albeit a fascinating and publicly useful one, and the do-gooders must be prepared to do far more than good when they get involved. Their leaders, in particular, must be good ringmasters and referees.

Quarrelling among cultural personnel is common because of clashes of temperament and judgment. Distinguished artists consider themselves experts. Other performers also so fancy themselves. Indeed the artistic outlook tends to make the local amateur painter or drama director readier to offer 'expert' advice and back it with a display of temperament than the most experienced professional. And many amateurs are far more negative than the experts in assessing projects other than their own, as if artistic aggression were necessary to their securing status. The church choir, the drama festival, the artistic competition, and the musical festival are replete with personality problems. On a larger scale such problems have major impacts on cultural projects.

The planning of a new theatre furnishes an excellent example. The building committee and the architect will have to decide on the design, size, seating, cost, facilities, and equipment. The only way they can please the experts is to build six or seven theatres; to build one they should only consult the experts and then be prepared to please no one. The opera expert will plead for 3,000 seats and a huge stage; the drama director, seeking intimacy, will cite 600 seats as ideal and a thrust stage as vital; the concert enthusiast will insist on an orchestra shell and worry about acoustics; the acoustical consultant will throw a web of scientific data around the project and still be unable to guarantee satisfaction; the architect will see a heaven-sent opportunity to create a new wonder of the world and tend to accept every suggestion that raises costs; the manager will measure the suggestions in terms of box-office possibilities; the building committee will have to consider costs and, in the welter of conflicting advice, soon conceives of a multi-purpose hall. Participatory democracy is ineffective in such a scramble because it will produce a hodge-podge of concessions to people who cannot be brought to a consensus. And it will get people involved who are not content with just being consulted; they must have their own way or they will raise controversy. A committee will make a decision; but it requires one person with a probing mind, a sensitive ear, and a thick skin to make the final decision for the committee. With enough advice to keep him responsible and enough criticism to make him cautious, he will be forced more readily than a committee to the best available solution.

Participatory democracy is dangerous in such an enterprise. It must not be frustrated, but it must be subtlely controlled. The appointment of a set of advisory committees is one of the worst tactics, because they create enough confusion to increase enormously the politics involved, or allow a smart architect and contractor to take control by playing the committees off against one another and raising costs by implementing their every request. And they make it very difficult for a building committee to give adequate direction. In theory these committees are supposed to provide participation by interested parties and resulting good will. They do no such thing. They always conflict and rarely offer stable advice, and good will is impossible because conflicting advice is more likely to be rejected than followed. Furthermore if it is too public this activity attracts the large lunatic fringe associated with the arts, because its members see golden opportunities for publicity in the kind of controversy in which they can pose as experts.

The people concerned should be consulted of course. The best way is to appoint no committees, but, when the preliminary designs are prepared, to have everyone view them at a big gathering, with ample refreshments, where the building committee can explain and listen. This event will satisfy the do-gooders and flatter the pseudo-experts, and the building committee may even get some good suggestions. Then the building committee can consult a few sensible advisers and get on with the job. These advisers should be dealt with separately or together on an *ad hoc* basis – never as a standing committee which can become an unstable power bloc. When the model and final plans are ready another big gathering with refreshments (which are vital in making the occasion seem important) will give ample evidence of consultation. No one should be consulted in the construction period; otherwise the extras, those expensive investments in ill will and guarantors of deficits, will multiply like mushrooms. Among the chief causes of the many disputes over cultural centres and festivals has been the concern of too many cooks with the broth.

As for politicians and civil servants, they should be consulted at every stage, but always one at a time. They quarrel in committee like everyone else because the excitements of the project attract their irrelevant responses, and if they do quarrel they are inclined to say 'no' to be safe in a controversial situation. Singly they can be wooed, and they can provide sagacious advice based on experience when their egos get individual attention. Furthermore they do not lose face if they must change a privately expressed opinion. Having said 'yes' individually they are less inclined to say 'no' collectively. 'Divide and conquer' is an essential tactic in culture because divisions among its factions take place naturally, and it is practical to settle them singly while making the concessions to committees as non-commital as possible until the forces are marshalled.

Nowhere is this marshalling more important than in the social functions associated with culture. These functions exist because of the importance of good public relations, support from powerful, influential, or wealthy people, the good will of governments, the efforts of workers who do necessary chores, the needs of artists and workers to be thanked and praised, the urge of admirers to lionize their idols, and the furnishing of opportunities to participate for those who enjoy participating and those who must be kept busy to prevent them making mischief. There is nothing superfluous or snobbish about this activity. It is a welcome diversion for members of the public who are frustrated as artists in an age when opportunities for personal involvement, as distinct from armchair spectatorship, have declined with the colourful community activities of other years. Those who cannot sing in a barroom or play in an orchestra can feel they are participating, albeit indirectly, by rubbing shoulders with those who perform. Moreover a good time at a party can be a better means of opening pocketbooks or getting tickets sold than a fine performance of a sonata. And nothing will win the support of a patron or politician like an introduction to a ballerina or a chat with a conductor. Indeed many people patronize the arts, as they do other activities, because they like to be seen and appreciated, or simply because it is the thing to do. It is better still to get cultural activities beyond social events and out into the streets, parks, and other public places where many people can see and hear them. 'Indoors' causes a psychological barrier which can be broken down by outdoor introductions which were once common, like a painting in a store window, or a song by a beautiful soprano in a tavern or a dashing tenor in a high school. In a TV age people have to be coaxed out of their homes, and they require the same enticement that Barnum and Bailey provided through the circus parade.

It is easy to be cynical about social activity. But it performs a valuable function, not only in providing assistance to the arts, but also in spreading their influence and educational and entertainment value, and in providing many people with something to do which they feel helps them and the community. The whole community benefits because of the increase in community spirit. There are literally thousands of people from tough businessmen and prominent politicians to little known and lonely men and women for whom this auxilliary cultural activity provides a refreshing change from practical affairs, or perhaps the only opportunity to get involved in something or meet and mingle with interesting people. The need of numerous lonely people for this kind of involvement is evident everywhere; it was illustrated in dramatic fashion in Toronto in 1972 when there was an exposure of the dance lesson racket, in which pathetic lonely people have been getting involved in expensive programmes of dance lessons, perhaps committing themselves to fees of thousands of dollars, in the search for social outlets.

Far from being snobbish, the cultural gathering is probably the most democratic of all social affairs in that it mixes people from every walk of life. It is participatory democracy at its best because there is something for everyone to do. Nowhere are there to be found harder workers. It is astonishing how much time and effort people will devote to fund raising, ticket selling, entertaining, and washing dishes. And for every one who does it for publicity or for personal contacts there are ten who do it to help the cause or to be part of something they consider worth while. These people do not just help themselves and the cause materially; they also add a sense of spirit and an element of appreciation to the arts which backs up the creative work of the artists and swells the impact of culture on the community. A symphony, therefore, is not just the collective effort of a group of musicians; it is also the women's committee addressing envelopes, the service club members soliciting advertising and selling tickets, and perhaps the daughter of the piccollo player proudly watching her father receiving compliments while she passes sandwiches at a post-concert reception.

The organizing of cultural activities is a major service in any community. It takes a few skilful persons to marshal all the participants, put them to work, and get results. A community's leaders must be careful to keep cultural leadership from falling into the wrong hands. The habitual do-gooder who bumbles into worthwhile work, the dictatorial type who likes to run things, or the permanent patroness or personality who absorbs offices can make names for themselves, but wreck quickly a project or an organization because they do not know what they are doing or they do it for the wrong reasons. Stupid leadership of promotional and supporting services is as big a factor in the failure of cultural enterprises as artistic incompetence, governmental negligence, or public indifference. Good causes and good intentions are not enough. And yet, for example, cultural organizations will often send their stupidest enthusiasts to interview government officials, attend conventions, or sit on boards of directors, a practice which no doubt spawned the phrase 'culture vultures.'

A mixture of these people and the so-called 'arty' types, plus the lunatic fringe, is a potent brew which culture must bear. Much effort is required to shunt such people aside into relatively harmless activity lest they wreck an important community asset. It may also be necessary to break up the cliques that do gooders like to form; cliques obstruct culture which thrives best with wide identification and support. A cultural endeavour with which a limited few are associated to the point where it becomes exclusive soon declines because it discourages those who would like to contribute to it and gives the public the impression that culture is the handmaiden of the few. It takes skill, however, to keep enthusiastic and committed workers from regarding a venture as 'our project' and rebuffing the interest of others not of 'our crowd.' There must be a core of dependable people to provide leadership and continuity, but they need to cast their nets widely to enjoy the confidence and appreciation of the public.

The marshalling of forces in culture must therefore be effective if the opportunities for culture are to be appreciated. Unlimited opportunities must exist for individual and group participation. But the marshalling must, by the very nature of the activities, be subtle because it requires skilled politics and appropriate postures. If it is not subtle cultural activity is destroyed, and much more quickly than the other activities of man. Temperament is less readily controlled than economic self-interest, talent than political loyalty, and taste and judgment than doctrinal affiliation. People cannot be browbeaten into being amused, coaxed into appreciating Brahms, or told they must like ballet – or else. They must respond to cultural stimuli themselves. The more participatory and democratic this response is, and the more subtle the control of its peculiarities, the stronger and more lasting culture will be.

It must not be supposed that culture is confined to activities in galleries, museums, concert halls, and educational institutions. Much of it is a vital component in life outside such centres. Parades and dancing in the streets, reading and singing in the homes, folk arts and variety entertainments at community festivals, all have the beneficial attributes of culture. They also provide recreation and good fun. They have, too, an element of community which is more pronounced than that of other forms of culture when they are properly managed and widely supported. A festival or fair, for example, mixes people and brings them together more than any other large-scale effort if it is organized as a participatory event, not just a spectators' entertainment. Neglect of this distinction has been the cause of much of the decline in this form of community culture.

All citizens are able to participate if the opportunity and encouragement are provided. And their communities benefit from every opportunity, large or small. Various activities come to mind: dancing in the streets on Saturday nights and holidays, even in the biggest cities; street corner performances at strategic locations by an adult with an unusual talent or a teenager with a guitar; exhibitions of handicrafts in display areas on the streets or in the main rotundas of public buildings; visits to homes for the aged by any group or individual with a hobby or talent; parades for bands and the numerous organizations for both young and old that otherwise the public may never see or hear; entertainment which ethnic groups treasure and would like to share; and community singsongs in stadiums and parks or round the campfire in fields and vacant lots in the suburbs.

The facilities for such activities are everywhere numerous. City streets which close down at night in most places, school buildings, arenas and rinks, parks and playgrounds, and even the steps in front of buildings can provide platforms for a great variety of activities. The participators and the audiences can also be numerous; there are thousands of bored or lonely people with nothing to do or see (including drug addicts who need something to 'turn them on'). The incentives are many in a society which states in theory that its denizens need to know, understand, and appreciate one another. These they cannot do through the communications media alone; personal contact is essential.

The pragmatist might deem this kind of contact frivolous in an age of serious social problems. It is not a question of 'fiddling while Rome burns,' but rather of fiddling to prevent men from setting more fires. Crime in the streets, for example, may well decrease if there is more to do and see in the streets. Poverty is not just a question of income, but of happiness and relevance. Discrimination, persecution, and class conflict require means of association among people as well as regulations. Education needs creativity along with knowledge. Health is an attribute of mind and spirit as well as of body. The welfare state, the just society, or whatever other concept the pragmatist advocates, is not to be achieved unless material satisfactions are accompanied by emotional contentments.

The pragmatist is not the only questioner. The puritan will ask if cultural activities will interfere with people's work, perhaps even with their dignity. If it does it will be doing a great service in many directions. Hard workers need an occasional change because work tends to be limited in significance, particularly if it becomes an obsession. An increasing number of bureaucrats need opportunities for getting their 'kicks' elsewhere than in their offices – simply to protect the rest of society. People who do not know or understand other people are narrow in their service. People without a sense of humour rarely have a healthy sense of duty. The effectiveness of work is not to be calculated only by the time spent at it. Indeed much work, especially administrative paperwork, is unnecessary, unproductive, expensive, and irritating, and a man must get away from it into contrasting activities to appreciate its limitations and its significance. As for dignity, there are two kinds of it. That which denotes over-seriousness, stuffiness, and dullness is already in too great a supply among men, as their discontents and quarrels indicate, and any activity is to be welcomed that diminishes it. The other kind of dignity, that which denotes respect among men for themselves and others and the use and enlargement of their talents, is never under any circumstances achieved by puritanism. On the contrary both individual and collective dignity are splendidly encouraged and preserved by culture.

Both pragmatist and puritan may not consider cultural activities to be very efficient. Nevertheless there is every indication that the productivity of man in relation to his happiness is increased more, and thereby made more efficient, by culture than by anything else. By most so-called practical standards man is not very efficient, as the dangers of pollution and ill will so eloquently testify. In economics his efforts become more, instead of less, costly as mass production, collective enterprise, and labour-saving devices increase and natural resources diminish. His wants are not satisfied; they spiral. In politics and international relations he caters to the worship of ideologies rather than to his individual and collective happiness. Much of his work is not creative; he spends as much time administering other people and preventing them from doing things as he does in positive work. And much of this activity, from filling out forms to waging wars, is unnecessary. Cultural activities, creative and stimulating, should prove healthy alternatives to much of this waste of human energy and happiness.

The politics of this kind of community effort is simple. It involves, first, action by people as people, not as members of governments and professions. Public authorities and the professions *provide* events; to *put them on* is much more effective. Second, the effort must be spontaneous, not contrived. People should be encouraged to get out and make the effort, without all the fuss and red tape of planners who ritualize it. Provided and contrived events last for a while, but they eventually die out when the people who have participated feel impersonal about them and spectators see them as just other kinds of routine. For example, a program arranged for a school band by a department of education or a local school board involves enough organizing and administration by official worthies to render the project impersonal and short-lived. A program put on by the band itself, or a few members of it, in a park one noon will delight the public and not be a duty to the members.

Leadership is needed, however, and it provides further scope for participation by the people. Countless individuals have gained much interest and satisfaction from their activities as entrepreneurs for community events. Indeed staging a YMCA variety concert can bring more happiness to a man and meaning to his life than most activities in his daily work. For many service club members community projects are the highlights of their lives. Life assumes large proportions for the Rotarian or Shriner who visits and entertains crippled children, or joins in singing Christmas carols at a home for the aged. There is so much talent and good will among men that seeking it out and encouraging the sharing of it are among the most satisfying and important activities in culture and in community affairs.

The success of a community's culture depends greatly on the kind of leadership. The do-gooders and the lunatic fringe kill most activities they try to direct because they are concerned with self-indulgence rather than service, and they cannot command the support of others for long. Big committees are usually ineffective too, because there is responsibility involved, and it takes a small group headed by hard workers to discharge it effectively. University productions provide good examples. One year a musical is a great success because one or two persistent students seek out the talent, do the necessary work, and command support. Another year a musical fails because it gets into the wrong hands, or because too much talk and interference from a students' council or administrative office discourage initiative. It is not surprising that community culture has suffered a decline as society has become increasingly organized. Excessive planning gives an air of contrivance to matters of the mind and spirit; it discourages the spontaneous and individual leadership and enjoyment on which they depend.

Spontaneity is also vital for participation in citizenship, and it is not unreasonable to state that community culture is the best medium for encouraging it. Over-serious individuals and groups take not only themselves, but also other people, too seriously. Ultimately they make boring, perhaps even belligerent, company for one another. Democracy needs emotional and creative expression if its business is to be effective, and participatory democracy needs the sharing of pleasure as well as duty. Square dancing in Main Street, baking a cake for the mayor's New Year's reception, singing folk songs at an orphanage, exhibiting a collection of ship's models at a high school, producing *Mikado*, or wheeling a paraplegic to an event are just as important in their own ways in a democracy as voting, paying taxes, and obeying regulations. Indeed the latter category of activity means far more when the first is encouraged. A collectivity can never be successful unless it is also a community.

15

The state and culture

Relations among performers, entrepreneurs, sponsors, and the public are altered greatly when the chief sponsor is the state. As a society becomes collectivized culture becomes more dependent on the state, and a whole new structure of politics is thereby added to the already complicated politics of culture. The resulting mixture is volatile for two reasons. Politicians and civil servants have all the abilities, limitations, and temperaments of artists and other sponsors. And governments can readily go to extremes of interest and neglect, or throttle the arts by confining them to the standards used in politics. Artists can go to extremes too by reacting negatively to all state interference, or by catering to the state's whims by political fawning which serves in the long run the interests of neither culture nor the state.

Extremes are not frequent in most countries, but there are many perplexing problems caused by financial relationships. Government funds have supplied increasingly larger proportions of the resources of culture because taxation has limited the help which rich sponsors can offer, and cultural organizations have had to turn from the private sponsor to the government, something they are encouraged to do anyway by the welfare state. This change has had two far reaching results.

It has altered the role of sponsorship mentioned earlier. As in education there is in culture a great difference between the influence of several sponsors as distinct from that of one sponsor. If an activity needs the encouragement or discipline of laymen it will get them much more readily from several sponsors than from the state alone. Private sponsors help because they are interested; the state helps because it has to. Participants do more themselves at less cost if projects depend on them alone than if they rely on the public purse. As soon as a government helps an artistic organization, other organizations, however deserving or undeserving, also expect support, and other sponsors and those who could be relied on for free services are inclined to back off or impose charges; costs then soar. The quality of presentation changes too, as does the tendency to adventurous innovation. The state's participation may encourage safe projects, the repetition of popular stand-bys, and the sponsorship of nationalistic entertainments. A civil servant is much more interested in subsidizing the tried *Aïda* than the esoteric *Mid-summer Night's Dream,* the homey *I Remember Mama* than the more contro-versial *Chalk Garden,* Shakespeare than Fanny Burney, a pageant than a ballet. A private sponsor is less concerned with the popular, especially if a shrewd entrepreneur convinces him that he is being daring and *avant garde.* A Joseph Duveen can hoodwink the top businessmen of the United States into providing the finest and most expensive art, first for their own homes, and then for museums, on a scale which no government could be coaxed into doing unless, like Hitler's Germany, it does it by conquest. Local counter-parts of Duveen share his experience in even the most limited projects helped by neighborhood sponsors, and they are inevitably more successful than local public authorities.

State involvement in cultural activities may also encourage irresponsibility. In the absence of influence by knowledgeable laymen and sponsors and of direct interest and knowledge on the part of state officials, the professionals may exercise exclusive control over an enterprise. Trouble nearly always results. Costs mount and artists go to extremes of conservatism or adven-turousness. Artists need to be argued with and told when they are either stuck in a rut or over-indulging in fancy. Interested lay sponsors are the only people who can tell them. Other artists cannot do it because of tendencies either to professional protection which condones the problem or to pro-fessional jealousy which compounds it. The state cannot do it in practice: if it will not it is lax, and if it does it tends to meddle. It is a sponsor but not an interested sponsor.

The second far-reaching result of increasing state sponsorship of culture is a change in the consuming public's interest and in its responsibility to that interest. The public now exerts its influence, not just through its response to cultural activities and through the participation of interested laymen, but also through the sponsorship of the government. The first method is practical; the second is theoretical. There is a big difference between the old combination of the box office and a sponsor's pocket book and the new combination of the box office and the public treasury, with the private sponsor and volunteer entrepreneurs playing a diminishing part. There is also a big difference between people as ticket buyers and people as taxpayers. There are many advantages in the change, such as the dispersal of cultural assets over a wider area or their introduction into remote places, the encouragement of large-scale enterprises such as operas or ballets which only the state could afford to sponsor, and the expensive display of national culture abroad. There are disadvantages, too, such as periodic interference in artistic activity for purely political reasons; the disadvantages need special compensations to protect the advantages.

What concerns us here is the fact that the politics of culture has shifted with the double public influence. If, for example, an art gallery wished to secure a great or controversial painting, its entrepreneurs used to persuade its benefactors to purchase and donate it; the public would accept it, or at least tolerate it, and perhaps later appreciate it. The entrepreneur soon learned the tricks of making and keeping happy his prospective donors, or of retaining a group of influential contacts who could be relied upon to pressure the donors, especially when a sudden opportunity for an important purchase occurred. He also learned how to please the public. With the state as sponsor, the entrepreneur must pursue different tactics by cultivating civil servants and making explanations publicly and to a public accounts committee who in turn are naturally suspicious of public reaction rather than informed about it. Moreover the public is far more inclined to be critical of a picture and less grateful for it if it pays out of its own taxes than if it pays out of the profits it provides its businessmen. On the other hand the gallery too is much happier to take 'no' from an interested sponsor than from an impersonal department.

The situation is similar in music. After repeated visits to a well known European opera house I wondered at the narrow repertoire and the comparatively old singers. A distinguished authority told me that the government department on which the house was dependent favoured works by national composers, and that the artists regarded themselves as civil servants whose rights to tenure and political connections outlasted their voices. Because the governmental influence intruded on the cultural interest, the reputation of the company declined, audiences fell off, costs rose, and the government's grants spiralled – all the result of governmental policy, not cultural problems or public response.

The impact of government on the arts helps to turn entrepreneurs into bureaucrats. The organizations concerned, whether they be galleries, cultural centres, theatres, or museums, tend to set up hierarchies modelled on the civil service, with departments of this and directors of that, and like all such structures they eventually operate under Parkinson's Law. A vast administrative labyrinth has grown up in the arts and is a first and fixed charge on expanding budgets. It is also a source of much politics, because the relationships among the staff multiply as rapidly as those between the staff on the one hand and the artists, the government, and the public on the other. New inner professional groups form, from unionized support staff to sophisticated public relations experts. Management must cater to non-artistic prima donnas, and the efforts of the performers must be presented to the public in accordance with the ideas of many administrative middlemen. 'The intramural politics of the Metropolitan [Museum of Art],' writes one observer, 'have been lively and cutthroat from the beginning, directors resenting trustees and curators resenting directors, experts venomously challenging one another's scholarship, the public often adding its two cents worth.'[1]

Its efficiencies notwithstanding, this structure tends to make cultural activities complicated, expensive, and impersonal. The effect is deadening as it becomes political and administrative. 'Government control,' says Sanche de Gramont of French culture, 'with its insistence on non-creative, administrative formations, is a heavy handicap to art. It is no accident that what is most fertile in French art is precisely what revolts against the bureaucracy of the Ministry of Culture ... Even when the nationalized cultural program attracts talented artists, they soon grow impatient with the lack of available funds, the red tape, and the climate of mediocrity generated by run-of-the-mill civil servants who worry about paper clips and pastepots ... The result of the government's cultural control is that the best men leave or are evicted ... while those who shine by their subservience are elevated to important posts. When the state considers that taste and style fall within its jurisdiction and links culture to the preservation of national values, it does not create, it embalms.'[2]

As for the performers, they differ in their responses to a public institution, a private institution with public support, and a private institution. Fees and other expenses were once negotiable and smart sponsors knew how to bargain; they are now high and fixed and they are arranged by a director of programs or some such official with public funds or the expectation of public funds behind him. Once performers or producers get government grants they expect to keep on getting them, sometimes regardless of the quality of their contributions or of public support. Thus the admission-paying public may disagree with itself as a taxpaying public, while the performers and producers may operate for political rather than cultural reasons. A theatre company, festival, or symphony orchestra will be, for example, far more sensitive to the demands of its art, the support of its friends, and the response of the public if it knows that its very existence depends on whether it continues to be good than it will be if it knows that it exists because its city sponsors and maintains it for political reasons and on the basis of automatic government grants. Dependence on state sponsorship may reduce the need to live dangerously, but it also reduces the stimulus provided by reliance on self-motivation backed by direct lay influence and public response.

As for the members of the public, their response to culture is also altered in subtle ways by state involvement. You do not 'put on' something any more, you 'provide' it, and the public's feeling for it and response to it are therefore less intimate. This fact aggravates the inertia and resistance to culture that must be overcome by those who would appreciate it. Many cultural activities are dependent on an acquired taste, an accustomed as distinct from a trained eye or ear, and a spontaneous reaction, each of which is at first hindered by awe, shyness, or hostility as distinct from ignorance. Some people in North America think of opera, for example, as 'high brow' (which it certainly is not since it is the only form of communication able to feature unashamedly all the sins and vices by singing them), and ballet as 'sissy' (although dancing is one of the most rigorous forms of athletics). In contrast, the opera in Italy and the ballet in Russia are a part of everyone's heritage, loved and enjoyed by people of all ages and classes. This inertia is particularly noticeable in financial matters in countries without long cultural traditions. Most of their voters would not hesitate to support a multi-million dollar expenditure for a highway in a doubtful constituency, yet they quarrel furiously over supporting at much less cost a symphony orchestra.

Governments are sensitive about this inertia and resistance when sponsoring the arts. They know that cultural activities bring few votes, that negative reactions are inevitable, and that crises always blow up, especially over deficits and quarrels among interested parties. A row accompanied the construction of almost all cultural centres and the beginning of most major festivals in Canada, and even relatively innocent projects, like the sculpture commissioned for Toronto's City Hall, provide titillating *causes célèbres* on a national scale. The label 'white elephant' is so vigorously attached to new cultural centres that it takes years of public relations to overcome it. Meanwhile governments either shy away from too much contact with the problem or become annoyed at repeated calls for help because there are more popular things to do with the money. The public, in North America at least, takes a long time to regard a centre or festival as 'theirs' and to give it the support it needs, because their natural inertia is reinforced by controversy and encouraged by the state's lack of enthusiasm. It is a strange phenomenon that in our society all the cultural enterprises together may cost less than one scarcely noticed, and perhaps quickly obsolete, fighter plane.

A recent method of securing leadership, providing participation, and making special provisions for increasing state patronage of the arts is the development of arts councils. The complicated politics of culture, and particularly the problems of standards, need, and availability of funds, were considered rightly in many places beyond the competence of most politicians and civil servants. Some governments thereupon set up bodies of men and women interested in cultural matters, and allotted them powers and funds with which to deal with groups and individuals on behalf of the state. These councils varied in composition and character depending on the ratio of professionals and laymen and on the degrees of independence given by their charters and recognized in practice.

Other governments preferred ministries of culture to arts councils. They established departments of culture with a minister, deputy minister, heads of divisions, and other officials who were part of the civil service. Committees and consultants were often appointed to provide professional and lay advice for the department. The chief difference between these types of bodies lies in the nature of their decisions. In the one decision making was delegated by the state to the council; in the other this power was retained by the state.

The authority delegated to an arts council includes responsibility for making contacts with the field of culture, for evaluating requests for funds, and for deciding on and applying the standards on which grants are based. The council also becomes a buffer between political and artistic pressures and deals with the inevitable criticisms. To handle all this the council itself assumes responsibility for broad policy, gives administrative and advisory functions to its staff, and delegates responsibility for recommendations on grants to advisory committees.

The politics of the arts council begins when the government appoints members to it. Four classes of prospective members generally appear, and some minister will either select from among them himself or sound out the opinions of politicians and cultural leaders. The first group comprises men and women who have provided leadership as promoters or sponsors, or as professionals, but whose interest is much broader than their own specialties. These are generally the best people for such work because they know something of the cultural network and its problems, and it does not take long for what naivety they do possess to be disciplined by the realities of cultural politics, or for them to take responsibility for decisions. They are neither so close to the government that they are constantly looking for political guidance nor so close to one set of artistic circles that they may be regarded as lobbyists.

In the second class are the professionals whose experience has been confined largely to one field. A few of these quickly learn to take the broad view, but many are lost in discussions of fields other than their own, overenthusiastic and inclined to meddle in their own fields, or too technical and impractical in their approach. The third group, and these are the people most inclined to press for their own appointment, is composed of the 'culture vultures' mentioned earlier — persons who are motivated by their own interests and egos, especially the do-gooders who look on appointment as a deserved reward for their services. Such people are to be avoided, for they will be of little value to the council but will secure enough recognition to enable them to meddle with increased ferocity in the cultural activities of their home areas. The fourth class consists of defeated political candidates, party officials and supporters, and others whom the government may wish to recognize or reward. A few of these make excellent members when they combine an interest in cultural matters with successful experience in public affairs. Most make poor members, either because they lack ability and experience or because they, and everyone else, know that they were appointed for the wrong reasons. In either case they enjoy the confidence of neither the government which appointed them nor the people with whom the council must deal.

The appointment of the chairman is a major task for the government. He will be expected to play the role of a cultural statesman, to be a shrewd negotiator for funds with the government and yet independent of it, to be an effective chairman of an able board and director of a dedicated staff, to present a respected and sympathetic image to the cultural world, and to be a diplomat in solving sensitive problems. These are the attributes of any good board chairman, but it is the sensitivity needed which makes the chairmanship of an arts council such a difficult role. He must deal with people in controversial fields where judgment is intangible and elusive, give businesslike direction in matters in which it is hard to be businesslike, and often explain the incomprehensible both to the government and the public.

Like most public bodies the council requires an administrative staff. The council itself holds a few meetings a year and has time for only a general policy. The details are the staff's business. The relationship between the two requires careful management in any organization, but in a cultural body this management is most difficult. If either group does too much it does harm; if either does too little it permits the other to get into mischief. A cultural czar may appear, and governments do not take kindly to czars in areas where they delegate power, while cultural groups resent czars who may impose' themselves rather than render services. Or the council may either meddle in details which are always tempting but usually beyond the members' competence, or not be aware of the details at all and decide policy on faulty bases. Or the staff may assume too much power and turn the council into a bureaucracy immersed in rules and regulations for their own sake rather than that of the people they are supposed to serve. The politics of an arts council involves keeping a balance among these temptations in endeavours that can never be successfully *administered*, but only supported, patronized, and encouraged. The staff members, therefore, should not be administratively inclined; they should be entrepreneurs.

The difference in outlook between these two kinds of staff accounts for differences in approach between an arts council and a ministry of culture. The staff of the ministry tends to be administrative in its outlook because of its civil service connection, and, consequently, its decisions are more inclined to be regarded as directives than are those of arts council staffs. It tends also to absorb the ideas which the government of the day is currently pushing even when they are irrelevant to the cultural needs of the state. In extreme form these ideas may conform to party ideology and propaganda; in their more common form they vary from concepts of nationalism to personal favouritism. It is more difficult for a staff of a ministry to sponsor unusual or controversial projects than it is for an arts council, because, while a government always likes to take credit for successful ventures, it does not as readily assume responsibility when the outcome may be doubtful. It is also harder for a ministry to single out the able from the mediocre for support, to refuse or limit aid to influential groups or individuals, and, in other ways, to follow cultural standards rather than political ones. The arts council on the other hand is in a more independent position to act on the basis of its own decisions and to absorb and render comparatively harmless the pressures of claimants.

Consider, for example, the allocation of money for symphony orchestras in a country with several orchestras. There are four ways of dividing the money: 1 / equally among the orchestras regardless of their size, quality, or location; 2 / among them all according to a formula based on their needs; 3 / among them all but with the major share granted to the better orchestras and only token amounts to the others; and 4 / among only the better orchestras, those which have achieved a certain standard, with nothing granted to the others. Many complications arise in deciding on the policy, such as whether to subsidize quality only in the hope that it will percolate down by example from major orchestras to other musical levels; whether to let the prestigious orchestras fend for themselves and encourage weaker or newer ones; how to make grants conditional on local enterprise; how to support culture in central cities while also encouraging efforts in smaller places and outlying areas; how to bring the arts to the people by sponsoring travelling companies and how to pick the best companies for such support; and how to project the nation's culture abroad by arranging for the best companies to travel and paying the enormous expenses involved, as well as saying a firm 'no' to companies which are not good enough to travel.

Orchestras also illustrate cultural politics at the individual level and point to the limitations of participatory democracy. It is obvious that an orchestra must achieve certain standards if it is to deserve and get public support. What happens, however, when an orchestra which is the pride of some city includes some mediocre musicians who are perhaps dedicated music teachers, whose lives are involved with the orchestra, who are perhaps even among those who founded it? There are two alternatives: allow the orchestra to remain mediocre and lose support, or remove inadequate players and incur accusations of ingratitude. The implications of either policy can be numerous and distressing, especially if outsiders are hired because of a scarcity of local talent. Such a situation is impossible for any elected authority to deal with. It takes highly skilled politics of a cultural rather than a political kind to initiate solutions and soothe injured feelings. It also requires all kinds of attractive busywork and social endeavour to keep the various factions and individuals associated with the enterprise and happy with their roles in it.

Problems and controversies in this one field invite sensitive discussion and negotiation and require tough decisions. A council is in a much better position than a ministry to reach and stand by a sensible policy because, although it must consider political factors, it will be motivated primarily by cultural ones. The ministry will also consider cultural factors, but the political ones will influence it more than the council, and those it serves will be tempted in turn to exercise a degree of undesirable political pressure which would be severely rejected by an arts council.

The subtle effects of standards and politics on grants by governments and public councils is evident in awards generally. Despite the fact that the funds may come from the public purse, much of the impact of the awards depends on how, and through whom, they are given. Both recipients and the public tend to respect awards bestowed by the Crown or bodies associated directly with the activity concerned more than those given by the government itself. The government can never escape the feeling of political patronage no matter how hard it tries. It is simply the government, not the state, and, aside from whether or not it is a popular or successful administration, its patronage is not good enough as backing for public recognition. Thus a minister of culture's gold medal for achievement does not carry the prestige of a similar medal from an arts council or the Crown advised by an arts council; a council grant gives more of an impression of professional and cultural standing than does that of a government department. This difference in impact between the two types of recognition is also evident in most other awards, from a school prize to the Victoria Cross. An aura of distinction surrounds both medals and grants bestowed by the Crown, a national research or science council, a foundation or an institute, which no disposition from a prime minister or minister of science, education, or industry can possibly claim. The government gives prizes, favours, or grants; the other bodies make awards.

Culture is very dependent on awards for prestige as distinct from financial support. The biographies of artists are as full of such recognitions as the list of ribbons and trophies associated with athletes and the obituaries of Russian generals. That the artists covet them and use them for professional advancement and publicity purposes is obvious to anyone who has selected winners of competitions or read the programmes at concerts and plays. It is as impossible to please everyone in the giving of awards in the cultural setting as it is to please pupils, and especially their parents, on prize day at school, or to satisfy politicians when patronage is dispensed. The recipients are concerned, of course, with the financial benefits of the award they get, but they are especially excited by the recognition which their awards bestow, particularly in comparison with the awards won by others. A writer who receives an award may turn it back because another writer got a more valuable distinction. He may even reject it to avoid association with a particular level of government. Invariably he will reject it publicly to make professional or political capital out of it. The farther away from government the award giving is located the less frequent such issues become and the more the judgment of the donor is accepted and respected.

The intervention of government in cultural affairs is therefore more effective and more democratic when indirect. Once it has decided how much money it can give, much cultural politics is avoided if the decisions on the distribution of the money are delegated to politically independent bodies which stand midway between the government and the recipients. Of all the kinds of politics in human affairs, with the exception of church politics, the politics of culture mixes least well with the politics of government. The combination of freedom and responsibility so important to culture can be achieved only if cultural politics operate by means of interactions between the participants and their patrons. As for democratic responsibility to the people, culture does not need to be accountable to government because, more than in most fields, it operates in full view of the people and their media, and the people themselves participate directly as observers, patrons, and performers. The culture of a state is therefore healthier and more democratic if the people exercise this direct influence themselves without reliance on the detailed intervention of the government.

16

Man's only unlimited asset

There is something in a society's culture for everybody from a Joan Suther-land on the stage to a washer of dishes at a 'gathering.' Culture pro-vides more opportunities for participation by more people in more ways than any other field. Its challenge to those with talent, from a Pavlova to a Grandma Moses, is obvious. But even those with no talent in any branch of culture can participate in countless activities associated with it and feel a part of it. And the rest of the people can participate simply by watching, listening, or reading at their own discretion and on their own initiative, and having a grand time doing it.

The people – all people throughout the world, collectively and individ-ually – are the creators and the beneficiaries of culture. What they want from culture determines its character. They want to be educated, trained, amused, laughed at, listened to, mystified, mesmerized, frightened, inspired, inform-ed, aroused, soothed, deceived, and even remembered by posterity. What other field offers such a variety of accepted ways of influencing people? And what a dull creature man would be without them!

Indeed trouble arises in any state or community if there is not enough culture and other fields are relied on to provide these effects, or if leaders of other fields control the culture so that they can do their will with the people for non-cultural reasons. Mozart's music and Bavarian dances are a more efficient focus of emotion and action than Nazi theory. Comic and tragic dramas are healthier outlets than the emotional disturbances of ecclesiastical conflict. Entertaining people is more productive than managing them. Supply-ing the demand for cultural goods and services is more economical than manufacturing weapons for war. Cultural assets bring more happiness to their possessors than an excess of wealth or power, not just because people respect them more, but also because they fear them less. On the international scene a country that wishes to impress another will find a ballet company a more effective, happier, and more permanent instrument than a fleet, its best literature more efficient than propaganda, and its artists more popular and influential than diplomats. No spy in history did as much good for his own or other countries as did Verdi, who reached countless homes and institutions; no missionary could match Caruso in touching the hearts of men of other lands and creeds; no tome on international law or conqueror's code has had the impact of a volume of Shakespeare. On the local scene political, economic, and ecclesiastical groups and leaders may perform essential services, but they can never fill men's needs adequately or well without cultural groups and leaders to touch men's hearts and cater to their emotions. And they can rarely handle cultural functions themselves without debasing them, ultimately by subordinating them to their own interests.

Direct involvement in culture is, therefore, a healthy means of self-expression for people, from whole populations of states or villages to families and individuals. Men have little enough opportunity for expression in life; yet without it they turn in upon themselves and are stifled and crippled because of the confinement and the pressures which build up. 'The mind,' wrote Louis XIV, whose cultural sponsorship was the greatest and most lasting benefit of his reign, 'perfects its own thoughts by expressing them and until then it holds them in a confused, imperfect and sketchy manner.'[1] People without culture, whether nations or individuals, are narrow and confused. People with it are much surer of who they are and what they think and feel because they appreciate their opportunities to make a judgment and express an emotion every time they exercise them. To participate in, watch, hear, or work for a cultural activity is to be carried out of oneself, to participate in a complete episode of life, to be part of a natural sensation, and to make a decision about the experience and like or dislike it. Someone who has watched Nijinsky dance or heard his own small daughter sing in public will never forget the experience. One who reads sees life far beyond his narrow personal existence. A person projects and shares himself every time he acts in a play or participates in a square dance. A whole population relates to its traditions when it hears the drums of Africa, the bagpipes of Scotland, or the waltzes of Vienna, and recognizes the significance of Tolstoi, Tagore, Goya, or Wren. And the very instincts of man are aroused by an acquaintance with aboriginal culture or the discovery of the lost traditions of prehistoric civilizations.

Culture may therefore be an answer to the problem of relying too much on education as the instrument for human communication. Mass education can be effective, but it is limited because all men cannot be expected to become scholars, because it costs so much, and because even the most educated of people can be stupid or unhappy. Cultural activities, on the other hand, are available to everyone on both an individual and a mass scale. Even the most illiterate tribesman can express and enjoy himself in dancing, and the most unhappy child can find expression in handicrafts. Culture certainly must accompany education to give it perspective, a requirement as true today as when Plato advocated it. There is a big difference, for example, between a carpenter who is a mere technician and one who is also an artist in wood, and between an historian who is just a chronicler of events and one who also appreciates the traditions of men. Cultural activites do not inevitably bring instant happiness and usefulness, as the lives of some narrow professionals in the field indicate; rather they provide a sense of creativity, of quality, and of feeling, and an experience in performing primary functions which may not be provided by even the most extensive education.

Beside cultural forces the political, economic, and ecclesiastical activities of man seem selfish and divisive. Culture can be shared across the most restrictive boundaries and through time, and it is therefore the most effective stimulus of the brotherhood of man. It is his only universal language. Indeed culture and colour are the only assets of man which can unify people who have nothing else in common. Political philosophies and practices, economic activities, and religious beliefs are, on the other hand, hard to share because they are, or have so often been used as, the weapons of self-assurance and aggrandizement. This is one reason why leaders of other activities so often use culture to give substance and strength to their own purposes. A conqueror will borrow a philosophy to serve as an instrument of aggression, and the first thing he censors is the philosophy of his victims. The economic tycoon, surfeited with wealth and power, often turns to art collecting as an assurance of immortality. A church makes liberal use of its organ pipes and decorations to put people in a reverential mood and of symbols to remind them of their loyalty. It is the cultural assets of political, economic, and church groups that are most easily shared with other groups and appreciated by posterity, and it is cultural feelings that best encourage the sharing.

Cultural activities are also the safest things to disagree on, because it is the one field where difference in interpretation, argument, and violent opposition are expected and even welcomed. In politics disagreement is often considered obstructionist; in business, retrogressive; and in church matters, insulting; and much conflict in these fields results from the inability to bear criticism. In culture however people can say what they like, and this freedom is both a useful check on it and a healthy means by which people release passions. Indeed this tolerance of controversy is so natural that people who fear intolerance in other fields flock to see or hear something controversial in culture, partly out of curiosity and partly to air their own views. Officialdom can ban a political or economic practice or a church dogma and thus bind and frighten people. If it bans a book or theatrical production it ensures its success, and if it expresses an opinion on art or music it invites derision or a contrary reaction. A Hindu, a Christian, and a Jew can have a wonderful time arguing, even insulting one another, over the merits of Dali or *Hair*, and part the best of friends; if they discuss frankly foreign aid, imperialism, transubstantiation, the cow or the pig, however, they will likely break up as enemies.

It may seem strange that this tolerance should be natural in such sensitive activities as the arts – that people should be attracted to other people's expressions and yet readily accept other people's disagreements. The reason lies in the fact that culture is the best and safest vehicle for man's greatest interests – his interest in himself, his expressions of himself, and other people and other people's expressions of themselves. When people use political, economic, or denominational instruments for influencing others both the influence and the tolerance are less effective because the instruments are featured, not the people; the instruments may become obstacles to natural relationships. It is such instruments that cause wars, not hatred among people. Indeed the instruments create the hatred. In local disagreements it generally happens that groups quarrel because their instruments clash; they may not even know one another. One cannot resist concluding that if Jews and Arabs, Catholics and Protestants, Germans and French, communists and conservatives, and blacks and whites, projected themselves more by singing, dancing, eating and drinking with one another, exchanging art objects and viewpoints on them, reading one another's literature, attending one another's plays, they would understand one another better and would enjoy their relationships more.

Non-cultural relationships, which are all much less natural than cultural ones, are easier when the cultural ones are paramount, because relations have never been and cannot be successful if people are subordinated to instruments. The theoretician and the dogmatist will say that people *should* be subordinate to the right, to the truth, or to God. 'What profit a man if he gain the whole world and lose his soul?' This is precisely the point. The evidence of history is surely overwhelmingly in favour of culture as the nearest expression man has to the right or the truth, to the soul and to God. Culture caters to love, beauty, knowledge, feeling, and joy in people and among people and does it more effectively because it does it directly. The theoretician and dogmatist propound, not the right or the way to God, but their own special interpretations of them which have proved lamentably unreliable. 'Dictatorship of the proletariat,' 'free trade,' 'down with the infidel' are traditional means of proclaiming right. A Beethoven sonata, a tribal dance, or a great book seem to be nearer to right and truth and better evidence of God and his will toward men.

Pragmatists repeat again and again the tragic error of regarding culture as impractical. They see the extensions of man as being practical and emphasize his housing and transportation, his social and administrative structures, his accumulations of power, his creeds and his wars. These extensions are important in limited ways, but they are secondary, and they have always proved unsatisfactory unless man himself is given inner resources and permitted direct expression. This is a lesson of history, and the problems of contemporary urban society, pollution, revolution, and war continue to teach it. Social services illustrate the same lesson. They are important but insufficient, because they usually ask that man share the extensions of himself, his standard of living instead of his standard of life, his comfort rather than his self-fulfillment. The rich society of the twentieth century may well earn the title 'the age of complaint' because of this emphasis on extensions. Man is bound to complain when his own self-expression and fulfillment are considered less practical than the development of his extensions. He becomes frustrated and ultimately looks with doubt on the extensions when they overwhelm him, as they are now everywhere threatening to do. He cannot 'do his own thing' if he has no 'thing' to do.

The great highway is practical, but no more so than the splendid concert hall. The automobile may be necessary to a family, but so is a library of books in the home. The poor man must have food, clothing, and shelter for his body, but he also needs nourishment and outlets for his mind and emotions. A whole society needs resources and government, but it will find a Stephen Leacock, a Gilbert and Sullivan, a series of winter carnivals or summer festivals, and a host of barbershop quartets, parades, and folk dances just as practical, far cheaper, and more lasting in impact and enjoyment because they touch the creative and expressive needs of people. These needs tend to be overlooked in the pragmatist's ordering of priorities, which are consequently miscalculated. A society needs, not one set of priorities, but at least two – one set for the mind and one for the body. Contrary to the pragmatic view, the second set will never operate effectively unless the first has equal, and sometimes greater, status.

The pragmatists make another mistake when they emphasize the costs of culture, underestimate the returns, and perhaps raise every obstacle they can to it. They overlook the much greater costs of the extensions. They forget that what they regard as a frill or a luxury may be both immediately and permanently productive of intangible, but nevertheless real, benefits. Indeed it is often the most practical things in life that turn out to be the most costly and least beneficial. A large bureaucracy, a factory, a subsidy for an industry are considered practical and money for them well spent. Beside them a Versailles would be considered extravagant.[2] Yet they are instruments of economics which, essential as they may be, touch no one's heart and soon pass into oblivion, while the other is a creation which has become part of the permanent glory of a nation. Even if this kind of creation and glory should disappear, as six of the seven wonders of the world have done, it remains in records and in memory a part of the traditions of all nations and men which successive generations will go to any lengths to rediscover and preserve. 'That which gave most pleasure and ornament to the city of Athens,' records Plutarch, 'and the greatest admiration and even astonishment to all strangers, and that which now is Greece's only evidence that the power she boasts of and her ancient wealth are no romance or idle story, was Pericles' construction of the public and sacred buildings. Yet this was that of all his actions in the government which his enemies most looked askance upon and cavilled at in the popular assemblies ...'[3] At the individual level a carpenter who works on a beautiful building or a splendid room will boast of it afterwards; a child who has had music lessons adds an extra dimension to his mind; an old man will proudly recite poems or tell stories long after he retired from productive work. The creativity and the store of emotions in both mass and individual minds are practical, productive, and rich dividends of culture which are priceless, though sometimes invisible, assets on the balance sheets of a people.

Another asset of culture is valuable but again not visibly practical. The pragmatist might call it innocence, and distrust it as being fanciful. A civilization ignores innocence at its peril, however, because it is a vital ingredient in those most important aspirations of man: love, pleasure and trust.

Another practical value of cultural projects is the extent to which they fulfil the excessive ambitions of leaders and drain off public emotions which might otherwise cause mischief. Many leaders are anxious to create glory for themselves, and often they do it by sponsoring expensive works of temporary significance, rearranging their administration's apparatus, engaging in power plays with their rivals and with other governments, and provoking and waging war. Such leaders rarely observe how costly are such ventures in money and lives and how tiny is the proportion of leaders who won lasting fame in this way. The public in turn is easily roused to support these projects without assessing the cost or the bloodshed of many previous ventings of collective emotion. Leaders simply get into mischief and get their people into trouble if they do not have enough to do or sufficient outlets for their sensitivities.

Leaders stand a better chance of contemporary approbation and future honour if they allocate skills and resources to governing and direct ambitions for glory to culture. The people in turn will find happiness in being part of a colourful era, and their international neighbours will be glad they have enough to do without meddling in their affairs. Occupying leaders in this way is also useful at local levels where over-busy or over-serious officials can do as much harm as good. If a community keeps its authorities busy attending functions, sponsoring cultural matters, even cutting ribbons and sitting at head tables, they will be happy to see and be seen and will have less time for mischief. People who think leaders should not devote time to what might be called irrelevant frivolity neglect the consequences of over-serious and narrow leadership. No less an authority than the president of the American Psychological Association proposed that leaders be given drugs 'to subdue hostility and aggression and, thereby, allow more humane and intelligent behaviour to emerge.'[4] History confirms the need for some remedy, but surely the stimulations and satisfaction of colour and culture is safer than the hallucinations and sedation of drugs.

Similar stimulation permits more humane and intelligent behaviour on the part of citizens. The average person is happier and less inclined to bully, gossip, and meddle if he uses his spare time in creative activities wider in scope and significance than his routine experience. Pressing contemporary problems may also be diminished or solved by these activities. People are devoting so much time and ability to increasing their material wealth that they are wasting resources and polluting the atmosphere in a spiral of escalating wants and planned obsolescence. Culture is an excellent means of diverting citizens from this costly, and now dangerous, pursuit into activities more productive of happiness.

The increase in leisure time in contemporary society furnishes still another reason for culture. People need significant things to do and see if they are to enjoy shorter working hours. Indeed they should be able to *use* their leisure time rather than fill it up with unnecessary routine which always tends to expand and fill the time made available by labour-saving devices. Even recreation will not serve this need entirely, because people can get bored and mentally soft with excess activity on the golf links or at the bridge table or too much relaxation before the television set. Equally important is the usefulness of culture in diverting some of the titillators, tinkerers, and tamperers of society into colourful activities where they can express themselves comparatively harmlessly. If participation is to be a feature of democracy, it must be varied to fill the many needs of citizens. There is not enough variety and primary activity in contemporary political, economic, or social affairs to satisfy the demands of participatory democracy and the abilities and limitations of people who have increasing amounts of time to devote to either boredom or happiness. If leisure time is not taken up with culture, the vacuum will be filled by the paraphernalia of collectivized administration, and the sounds of music will be drowned out by the rattle of paper. Then men will not be men any more because they will have lost their natural dimensions.

Culture is the dimension of man which now offers the greatest potential for development and for group and individual participation. If he wants to be brotherly, cooperative, neighbourly, and ecumenical, man should put more emphasis on culture than on theories and institutions. If he wants to be active, creative, colourful, and happy, culture offers endless possibilities. If he wants to be human, it offers scope for his talents and individuality. According to the zoologist man is the only species that makes a habit of killing his own kind; according to the ecologist he is the only species that lives off earth's natural capital in addition to its yield; according to many scientists he had better make some quick adjustments or he will become extinct. Cultural postures and politics among men are the one kind of activity that has never caused death. Cultural capital is the only kind which is unlimited. As for the individual, man has never made the most of his potential through exclusive devotion to material wealth, management, theories and dogmas. His brain and his body, still more wondrous than his computers and his structures, have endless scope for satisfying all his instincts and releasing all his emotions, if he would direct his efforts to the vast field of culture which has already yielded splendid treasures, and which can be the source of yet untold riches. It is time man became less reckless with the earth's resources and more generous with his own.

Acknowledgments

I appreciate greatly the cooperation of numerous people with whom I have discussed this subject, especially those who have talked frankly of difficult matters in their jurisdictions, including politicians, bishops, and officials of professional, educational, and cultural organizations. My children, energetic and penetrating in family discussions, my students, interested in examining both historic and contemporary problems in seminars, Professor Norman Ward of the University of Saskatchewan, who read an early draft and made helpful comments, Miss Joan Bulger of the editorial department of University of Toronto Press who edited the manuscript – all these contributed to the book and I thank them warmly. I also appreciate the financial help of the Canada Council and the Social Science Research Council of Canada, and the courtesy of the British Council. As always, my wife encouraged me during that period when 'the book' was an entertaining but demanding visitor at our house.

Notes

CHAPTER ONE

1 Lewis Richardson, quoted and discussed in J.D. Carthy and F.J. Ebling, eds., *The Natural History of Aggression* (London and New York: Academic Press, 1966), p. 110. The period cited was 1820–1945, since which time the slaughter has continued.
2 *The Times*, London, 16 September 1971. The figures were released by UNESCO. They do not include money spent by mainland China, North Vietnam, and North Korea.
3 Sir Kenneth Clark, *Civilisation* (London: BBC and John Murray, 1971), p. 347.
4 'Change the Constitution,' exclaimed former Premier Pierre-Etienne Flandin on proposals to end the third republic of France. 'But why? What need is there to change our institutions? The reproach is that we did not respect them.' William L. Shirer, *The Collapse of the Third Republic* (Richmond Hill, Ont.: Simon and Schuster, 1971), p. 935. 'The constitution died,' said Senator Boivin-Champeaux, 'less from its imperfections than from the faults of men who were charged with guarding it and making it work.' Ibid., p. 943.
5 *Life*, 15 October 1971.
6 Frank MacKinnon, *The Politics of Education* (Toronto: The University of Toronto Press, 1960).
7 Don Schollander, Olympic gold medalist in swimming, *Readers' Digest*, June 1971, p. 255.
8 Patience Thoms of Brisbane, Australia, President of the International Federation of Business and Professional Women, *Globe and Mail*, Toronto 7 July 1971.
9 Many writers and activists consider man's problems to be the result of not taking theories and institutions seriously enough. Actually they seem to be the consequences of taking them far too seriously. There is much evidence to support the latter view in numerous contemporary accounts; among the most vivid of these are William L. Shirer, *The Rise and Fall of the Third Reich* (Greenwich, Conn.: Crest, 1962); Shirer, *The Collapse of the Third Republic;* and John Toland, *The Rising Sun* (New York: Bantam, 1971). Every chapter in these books and many assessments of man's virtues and problems indicate what a belligerent collection of 'stuffed shirts' the species has become, and how much need there is for a collective sense of humour.

CHAPTER TWO

1 Laurier in an address on parliamentary life, 14 May 1884, published in William Toye, *A Book of Canada* (London: Collins, 1968), p. 338.
2 An experiment in the New School for Behavioural Studies in Grand Forks, North Dakota, revealed that a piece of tulle as a net draped over the heads of both teachers and pupils 'encourages even introverted children to talk.' *Life*, 1 October 1971.
3 See report in *New York Times*, 29 August 1971.
4 Sir Kenneth Clark, *Civilisation* (London: BBC and John Murray, 1971), p. 347.

5 'I think,' Premier Alexei Kosygin is reported as saying about 'the virtues of conviviality,' 'it would be best if ministers could meet more often, have lunch together, maybe drink vodka together and maybe think less about fighting. I think this would be cheaper for everyone.' Report of speech to the Canadian Manufacturers Association in Toronto, 25 October 1971, in *The Star-Phoenix*, Saskatoon, 26 October 1971.

6 *Ross's Weekly*, Charlottetown, 15 September 1864, and *Examiner*, Charlottetown, 31 October 1864. These reports are contained in P.B. Waite, *Confederation, 1854–1867* (Toronto: Holt, Rinehart and Winston, 1972), pp. 81, 85.

7 It is a notorious fact that faculty and committee meetings take up far too much time in universities, as similar bodies do in government. Part of the reason may well be the informality, comfortable clothing and chairs, and the provision of coffee. It is not unreasonable to suggest that if an earlier practice were followed, professors in gowns and hoods, seated on hard, formal, high-backed chairs and presided over by a dean in heavy robe would take one another more seriously, be better prepared for meetings, be sufficiently uncomfortable to spend less time in unnecessary talk, and, if a suitable supply of food and drink was promised in a commonroom *after* the meeting, make their decisions with laudable dispatch. And the dean would be much more credible and efficient as chairman than he would be in shirt sleeves with a cup of coffee in one hand and a cigarette in the other. One may also suggest that the committee's collective work would be done better, that its members would enjoy it more, and their participatory institutions be more efficient than they are now. Academic, no less than governmental, responsibilities never placed a man above the natural advantages of a little Pavlovian treatment.

8 P.M. Kendall, *Louis XI, The Universal Spider*, quoted in *Time*, 22 February 1971.

9 'Why did I escape the fate which they suffered?' he is cited as asking in reference to his friends who were purged; '... Nadya's reports helped determine Stalin's attitude toward me ... It was because of her that Stalin trusted me.' *Khrushchev Remembers* (Boston: Little, Brown, 1971), p. 44.

10 Duff Cooper, *Tallyrand* (London: Cape, 1947), p. 19.

11 Examples of people whose useful talents were allowed to diminish are legion. The chauffeur illustrates several aspects of the matter. The idea of a chauffeur driving an official may seem ostentatious, unproductive, and undemocratic. Yet it is none of these. The busy official with heavy responsibilities may get some necessary rest during a long drive through heavy traffic or be able to read documents or just think over a policy quietly. He avoids the risk of an accident which for him always attracts more publicity by way of gossip or blame than that incurred by ordinary citizens. He may even use the car to meet the convenience or tickle the vanity of visitors and thereby facilitate business. The chauffeur, usually an older person, a retired war veteran, or someone who cannot do heavy labour, is performing useful and interesting work. He preserves his pride and serves society instead of sitting at home with nothing to do but draw social service benefits. Furthermore he is a much needed example of good driving on the streets, and he increases directly the amount of work his boss is able to do. Indeed for these and other reasons that come to mind the decline of the chauffeur has been a most costly and inefficient event. I discussed this matter fully with an English professional chauffeur and an RCMP traffic expert, both of whom support these conclusions and give many examples which indicate that cabinet ministers, party leaders, judges, mayors, and the like should not drive when on duty.

12 J.B. Priestly, *The Prince of Pleasure* (London: Sphere Books, 1971), p. 293.

13 W.H. Lewis, *The Splendid Century* (New York: Anchor, 1957), p. 26.

14 Fred Davison, 'The Henry Lawson Myth,' *Australia*, February 1924, quoted and discussed in Denton Prout, *Henry Lawson, The Grey Dreamer* (London: Angus and Robertson, 1963), pp. 298–9.

15 For those professors who may say 'Oh no! not us!' I can produce ample evidence. I have taught in three academic institutions over twenty-six years. By chance I was, for twenty-five of those years, chairman of committees that brought distinguished speakers to the universities. Invariably it was the celebrity, not the eminent visiting scholar, who drew

the attendance of professors, and prompted the requests for opportunities to meet the visitor or for invitations to the entertainments which accompanied the events.
16 Plutarch, *Lives* (New York: Collier, 1909), p. 48.
17 Sanche de Gramont, *The French* (New York: Bantam, 1970), p. 295.
18 Clem Whitaker, quoted by Irwin Ross, 'The Image Makers,' in R.M. Christenson and R.O. McWilliams, *Voice of the People* (New York: McGraw-Hill, 1967), p. 49.

CHAPTER THREE
1 Julian Critchley, 'Keeping MP's Out of Mischief,' *The Times,* London, 20 February 1971.
2 Winston Churchill, *Great Contemporaries* (London: Fontana, 1959), p. 222.
3 The reliability of public diagnosis was illustrated by a poll during one of Eisenhower's illnesses. To the question, 'Do you think President Eisenhower will have another heart attack?' one-third said 'yes,' one-third said 'no,' and only one-third gave the reasonable answer, 'don't know.'
4 Anthony Storr, 'Possible Substitutes for War,' in J.D. Carthy and F.J. Ebling, eds., *The Natural History of Aggression* (London and New York: Academic Press, 1966, pp. 139–40.

CHAPTER FOUR
1 Some of the material in this section was published earlier in my 'The Crown in a Democracy,' *Dalhousie Review,* 49: 2 (1969), and *Commonwealth Journal,* December 1969.
2 Sir Robert Borden to John W. Dafoe, 12 July 1935, in Sir Robert Borden, *Letters to Limbo,* ed. Henry Borden (Toronto: University of Toronto Press, 1971), p. 219.
3 Edward R. Murrow, quoted in Harry Golden, *The Right Time* (New York: Pyramid, 1971), p. 276.
4 'There are,' testified Prime Minister Baldwin, 'only three or four people whom I can take into my complete confidence.' Quoted in James Stuart, *Within the Fringe* (London: Bodley Head, 1967), p. 75. Mr (later Viscount) Stuart was, as chief whip of the Conservative Party, fully aware of the practical significance of this limitation.

CHAPTER FIVE
1 Aline B. Saarinen, *The Proud Possessors* (New York: Vintage, 1968), p. xx.
2 Stephen Birmingham, *Our Crowd* (New York: Harper and Row, 1967), pp. 294–5.

CHAPTER SIX
1 Stephen Birmingham, *Our Crowd* (New York: Harper and Row, 1967), p. 306.
2 *The London Times,* 17 June 1971.
3 Donald Wilson, in *The Financial Post,* 15 May 1971.
4 For a detailed discussion of this point see Frank MacKinnon, *Responsibility and Relevance in Education,* Quance Lectures, University of Saskatchewan, 1968 (Toronto: Gage, 1968).

CHAPTER SEVEN
1 A.P. Ryan, 'The Marquis of Salisbury,' Duff Cooper, ed., *British Prime Ministers* (New York: Roy Publishers, 1951), p. 143.
2 A common example is the erratic selection of national officers in some organizations. A president, chosen by a system of geographic and other calculations may be, not the ablest candidate, but just the local president or representative on the national executive

who happens to be in office at the particular moment when his area or group has its turn. Incompetent leadership is often the result. The situation is similar in local organizations. I have been on numerous speaking tours and have had many opportunities to observe and hear about the health of organizations. Almost invariably both the activity and spirit of an organization reflect the ability and initiative of its leadership. In one city a group may thrive under a stimulating president or secretary; in the next city the same society may be weak, or indeed dying, because the officers do little more than hold office and send out notices. The same difference can be noticed in one club over a short period of time. The idea of many 'dear souls' having a turn in office is splendid in theory, but it does not work in practice. Groups that know this and do something about it are generally the healthy ones.

3   Rt Rev. R.W. Dean, Anglican Bishop of Caribou, reported in *Calgary Herald*, 7 November 1970.

CHAPTER EIGHT

1   Marshall McLuhan, with Wilfred Watson, *From Cliché to Archetype* (New York: Polet Books, 1971), pp. 12–13.
2   Irving Stone, 'Horace Greeley,' in *They Also Ran* (Toronto: New American Library, 1966), p. 21.
3   Dwight D. Eisenhower, *At Ease* (New York: Avon, 1967), p. 249.
4   B.M. Montgomery, *The Memoirs of Field Marshal Montgomery* (New York: Fontana, 1960), p. 38.
5   James Reston, *New York Times*, 17 October 1971.
6   'I am an old newspaperman,' said Senator Allister Grosart, 'and I do not remember a single occasion in the reporting of any story at any time over a period of many years when all the facts on either side, on a pro and con basis, were presented.' *Calgary Herald*, 23 December 1971.
7   C.R. Attlee, *As It Happened* (London: Heinemann, 1954), p. 86.
8   Richard M. Nixon, *Six Crises* (New York: Pyramid, 1968), p. 319.
9   *New York Times*, 29 March 1970.
10 James Stuart, *Within the Fringe* (London: Bodley Head, 1967), p. 146. Mr (later Viscount) Stuart was chief whip of the Conservative Party from 1941 to 1951 and later Secretary of State for Scotland.
11 Peyton Lyon, in S. Clarkson, ed., *An Independent Foreign Policy for Canada?* (Toronto: McClelland and Stewart, 1968), p. 35.
12 For example, when some students booed, jeered, and threw eggs and rotten fruit at a member of their provincial legislature and prevented him from speaking when he attempted to explain why he changed his party affiliation, they endangered and rendered unbelievable students' allegiance to free speech, however popular or fashionable an opinion may be, and, in the worst tradition of *trahison des clercs*, invited official and public reaction (Hugh Shea at Memorial University of Newfoundland, *Calgary Herald*, 2 February 1972). There have been many such episodes.
13 William L. Shirer lists members of the intelligentsia who rationalized both the Vichy regime and the returning De Gaulle in his *The Collapse of the Third Republic* (Richmond Hill, Ont.: Simon and Schuster, 1971), p. 902.
14 Lord Balniel, MP, 'The Upper Class,' in Richard Rose, ed., *Studies in British Politics* (London: Macmillan, 1967), p. 76.

CHAPTER NINE

1   I must emphasize that I have the highest regard for the study of theology and political theory. They are essential and valuable. But few men can understand them and use them effectively without rigorous practical experience with life or training in practical subjects in the university. With rare exceptions the inexperienced specialist in them is usually a

bad philosopher because he tends to get hallucinations rather than inspirations. If he acts on hallucinations he becomes a nuisance.
2 Martin Luther King, Jr, 'The Future of Integration,' in W.W. Boyer, ed., *Issues 1968*, The Alfred M. Landon Lectures and Convocation Addresses, Kansas State University (Lawrence: University Press of Kansas, 1968), p. 48.
3 A.P. Ryan, 'The Marquis of Salisbury,' in Duff Cooper, ed., *British Prime Ministers* (New York: Roy, 1951), p. 139.
4 J. Christopher Herold, *Mistress to an Age*, (London: Readers Union, 1960), pp. 463–4.
5 Eric Hoffer, 'Thoughts of Eric Hoffer,' *New York Times Magazine*, 25 April 1971.
6 William von Humboldt, *The Limits of State Action*, ed. J.W. Burrow (Cambridge: Cambridge University Press, 1969), pp. 69–70.
7 Obituary in *The Albertan* and other newspapers, 3 November 1970.
8 Violet Bonham Carter, *Winston Churchill As I Knew Him* (London: Pan, 1965), p. 154.

CHAPTER TEN
1 Quoted and discussed in Gunnar Myrdal, *Asian Drama* (New York: Pantheon, 1968), I, 107.
2 *New York Times*, 22 August 1971.
3 F.C. Engelmann and M.A. Schwartz, *Political Parties and the Canadian Social Structure* (Scarborough: Prentice-Hall, 1967), p. 58. For a detailed discussion of the 'religious influence in Canadian society,' see S.D. Clark, *The Developing Canadian Community* (Toronto: University of Toronto Press, 1968), X.
4 Richard Crossman, MP, in Gordon Hawkins, ed., *Order and Good Government*, Proceedings of 33rd Couchiching Conference of the Canadian Institute of Public Affairs (Toronto: University of Toronto Press, 1965), 1. 13.
5 P.S. O'Connor, 'Sectarian Conflict in New Zealand 1911–1920,' *Political Science* (Wellington, NZ), 19: 1 (July 1967), 3–16.
6 *The Times*, London, 27 February 1970.
7 C.E. Bryant, reported by CP, *Edmonton Journal*, 7 August 1971.
8 Will and Ariel Durant, *The Age of Voltaire, The Story of Civilization:* Part IX (New York, Simon and Schuster, 1965), pp. 152–3.
9 Ibid., p. 119.
10 The *Calgary Herald*, reported by AP, 4 April 1970.
11 The Aga Khan, *Memoirs of Aga Khan* (London: Cassell, 1954), p. 277.
12 Ibid., p. 17
13 Rabbi Abraham L. Feinberg, in foreword to Rev. R.D. Horsburgh, *From Pulpit to Prison* (Toronto: Methuen, 1969), p. v.
14 Bishop F.R. Barry, *The Times*, London, 26 September 1970.
15 Duff Cooper, *Tallyrand* (London: Cape, 1947), p. 330.
16 Canadian Press, 11 April 1970.
17 *Kingston Whig-Standard*, 30 January 1969.
18 Harry Golden, *For 2¢ Plain* (Montreal: Permabrooks, 1960), p. 198.
19 Principal, Rev. G. Tolley, *The Times*, London, 1 October 1970.
20 A.N. Whitehead, *Adventures of Ideas* (Harmondsworth: Penguin, 1948), p. 201.
21 Myrdal, *Asian Drama* I, 103.
22 See, for example, A.C. Lewis, former dean, Ontario College of Education, Toronto, in *Globe and Mail*, Toronto, 11 March 1971; Archbishop Philip Pocock of Toronto, in *Globe and Mail*, Toronto, 20 May 1971; a call for the defeat of government, *Globe and Mail*, Toronto, 22 May 1971; and an editorial assessment, 'The Pulpit and Politics,' in *Globe and Mail*, Toronto, 2 October 1971.
23 See, for example, the question of seating at state functions of representatives of episcopal and non-episcopal churches in Ottawa, in *Public Servant: The Memoirs of Sir Joseph Pope* (Toronto: Oxford, 1960), pp. 159–60, and the seating of representatives of the Anglican Church in Charlottetown, in a series of letters and reports in *The Guardian* and *The Evening Patriot*, Charlottetown, November and December 1951.

24 Gervase Duffield in *The Christian* quoted in *Signs of the Times* (Seventh Day Adventists), May 1969.
25 Ian Grey, *Peter the Great* (New York: Lippincott, 1960), pp. 399, 402.
26 Hugh MacLennan, 'Two Solitudes that Meet and Greet in Hope and Hate,' *MacLeans Magazine*, August 1971, p. 23. See also Clark, *The Developing Canadian Community*, for the influences of the denominations in Canadian politics.
27 David Howarth, *The Desert King, A Life of Ibn Saud*, (London: Collins, 1964), pp. 69–70.
28 Carl J. Burckhardt, *Richelieu, His Rise to Power* (New York: Vintage, 1964), p. 20.
29 Stefan Zweig, *Joseph Fouché* (New York: Blue Ribbon Books, 1932), pp. 43–4.
30 Ibid., p. 54.
31 *Globe and Mail*, Toronto, 8 November 1971.
32 'Passer-by, is it not a strange thing that a demon should be next to an angel.' Aldous Huxley, *Grey Eminence* (Cleveland: World, 1962), p. 330.
33 Rabbi Lewis Ginsburg of Calgary, *The Albertan*, 26 February 1971.
34 *The Times*, London, 5 February 1971.
35 *Globe and Mail*, Toronto, 7 December 1968.

CHAPTER ELEVEN
1 Louis L. Snyder, *The Blood and Iron Chancellor* (Princeton: Van Nostrand, 1967), p. 322.
2 Sigmund Freud and William C. Bullitt, *Thomas Woodrow Wilson, A Psychological Study* (Boston: Houghton Mifflin, 1967), p. xi.
3 Rabbi Abraham L. Feinberg, in forward to R.D. Horsburgh, *From Pulpit to Prison* (Toronto: Methuen, 1969), p. vi.
4 'The entire political edifice of Lebanon continues to depend on a compromise representation of the confessional and regional forces operating in Lebanese politics. While there is widespread recognition that this apparent harmony could suddenly break down, the dangers of introducing change are so enormous that they presently act as a deterrent to any meddling with the constitutional and electoral system of the country.' Maurice Harari, *Government and Politics of the Middle East* (Englewood Cliffs, NJ: Prentice-Hall, 1962), p. 114.
5 Theodore H. White, *The Making of the President 1960* (Montreal: Cardinal, 1962), p. 288.
6 Richard M. Nixon, *Six Crises* (New York: Pyramid, 1968), p. 396.
7 Uluschak, *Edmonton Journal*.
8 Gunnar Myrdal, *Asian Drama* (New York: Pantheon, 1968), I, 108.
9 Hector Bolitho, *Albert Prince Consort* (London: Max Parrish, 1964), pp. 106–7. Queen Victoria who created bishops had more forceful views. 'A very ugly party,' she said of a reception for bishops attending the Lambeth Conference; 'I do not like bishops ... I like the man but *not* the bishop.' Elizabeth Longford, *Victoria R.I.* (London: Weidenfield and Nicholson, 1964), p. 549.
10 Edward Gibbon, *The Decline and Fall of the Roman Empire* (New York: Collier, 1899), I, 680.
11 Horsburgh, *From Pulpit to Prison*. For a poignant description of the issue see *Globe and Mail*, Toronto, 6 October 1971.
12 Roy Jenkins, *Victorian Scandal, A Biography of the Right Honourable Gentleman Sir Charles Dilke* (New York: Chilmark, 1965), p. 409.
13 Most Rev. H.H. Clark, quoted in *Globe and Mail*, Toronto, 22 August 1970.
14 William S. White, *Majesty and Mischief* (New York: MacFadden, 1963), p. 64.
15 Quoted by John Buchan, Lord Tweedsmuir, in *Memory Hold the Door* (Toronto: Musson, 1940), p. 138.
16 Archbishop Teopisto Alberto y Valderrama of the Phillipines, quoted in *The Star-Phoenix*, Saskatoon, 26 October 1971.

17   Arnold Brown, Chief of Staff of the Salvation Army, *Weekend Magazine,* Montreal, 27
     November 1971. The full quotation is 'No man in any of our hostels is forced to pray or
     attend any kind of meeting or devotional exercise. He gets the shelter, the food, the job
     found for him, just because he needs it. If, out of gratitude, he says he'd like to go to a
     meeting, then that is there for his taking. But no one will say: "Look Bud. You've had
     a month here and we've done all this for you, don't you think you ought to ..." That
     would be considered immoral as far as we are concerned.'
18   R.C. Suggs, *The Hidden Worlds of Polynesia* (Toronto: Mentor, 1962), pp. 58–60.
19   Ibid., p. 60.
20   Vilhjalmur Stefansson, *My Life With the Eskimo* (New York: Collier, 1966), pp. 28, 30,
     32, 35, 44–5. See also C. Hogg, 'Christianity Root of Indians' Trouble,' *Calgary Herald,*
     12 October 1968.
21   Helmut de Terra, *Humboldt* (New York, 1955), p. 111.
22   Alan Moorhead, *The Fatal Impact* (New York: Harper, 1966), pp. 87, 92.
23   J.K. Fairbank, E.O. Reischauer, and A.M. Craig, *East Asia, The Modern Transformation*
     (Boston: Houghton Mifflin, 1965), pp. 332–3.
24   Peter Calvocoressi, *International Politics since 1945* (New York: Praeger, 1968), p. 335.
25   A. MacArthur and H.K. Long, *No Mean City* (London: Corgi, 1967), p. 57.
26   C.E. Bryant, reported by CP, *Edmonton Journal,* 7 August 1971.
27   James A. Michener, 'A Lament For Pakistan,' *New York Times Magazine,* 9 January
     1972, p. 58.
28   Aldous Huxley, *Grey Eminence* (Cleveland: World, 1962), p. 221.

CHAPTER TWELVE
1   *New York Times Magazine,* 23 August 1970.
2   For example, a frequently noted student power group in a big city university is a number
    of associates from a large local high school who act together in campus politics.
3   How governmental administration affects education I have discussed in detail in *The
    Politics of Education* (Toronto: University of Toronto Press, 1960), and *Responsibility
    and Relevance in Education,* Quance Lectures, University of Saskatchewan, 1968
    (Toronto: Gage, 1968).
4   *The Globe and Mail,* Toronto, 3 November 1971.
5   Ottawa: University of Ottawa Press, 1970.
6   Toronto: Newton, 1968.
7   The extent to which politicians actually 'represent the people' varies greatly. Some use
    the responsibility well and really know the people's interests and desires. Others do not.
    One can almost always tell the difference. The first exercise judgment, act, take responsi-
    bility, and let others do the same; the second generally sniff the political wind, talk
    much, seek publicity, and interfere incessantly. The first are really interested in the
    people's business; the second are concerned with their own, and use 'the people' as an
    excuse for advancing it. One can always be suspicious of an official who talks too much
    about his democratic sensibilities. Like Bacon's judge, he is ill-tuned.

CHAPTER THIRTEEN
1   On 'bureaucratic interference and meddling of the silliest kind' from Public Works, see
    the report of the vice chancellors of Australian universities to Australian Universities
    Commission, *The Australian,* 22 August 1968.
2   See the remarks on academic freedom and independent audits in universities by Lord
    Butler of Saffron Walden, Master of Trinity College, Cambridge, and former Chancellor
    of the Exchequer and Minister of Education, in *Special Report from the Committee of
    Public Accounts on Parliament and Control of University Expenditure;* Session 1966–7,
    London, HM Stationery Office, pp. 76–90.

3 J. de V. Allen, in *The Straits Times*, Singapore, 9 August 1968.
4 The art of cooking suggests another parallel. If fruit and nuts are simply mixed together and put in a batter, they sink to the bottom in the baking, and the cake lacks cohesion. The cook prevents this by first dredging the fruit and nuts thoroughly in flour; this ensures that they will be evenly distributed throughout the cake. In terms of social organization individuality among citizens, encouraged by special interests, and not a mass of undifferentiated people clinging together, appears to be the strongest characteristic of an effective society. It is my view that individual *cultural* interests are the best and safest medium for both stimulating the lives of individuals in a society and ensuring the unity of the resulting group, regardless of the place each man occupies, the work he does, the ability he has, or the education he has received.

CHAPTER FIFTEEN
1 Jean Stafford reviewing Calvin Tomkins, *The Story of the Metropolitan Museum of Art* (New York: Dutton, 1970), in *New York Times*, 12 April 1970.
2 Sanche de Gramont, *The French* (New York: Putnams, 1970), pp. 343–7.

CHAPTER SIXTEEN
1 Discussed in Gabriel Borssy, *Les Pensées des Roi de France* (Paris, 1949), p. 216; and Vincent Buranelli, *Louis XIV* (New York: Twayne, 1966), p. 34.
2 Those who think of Versailles and other such structures as extravagant housing for monarchs should recall that a large part of the government of the day was housed there; they should also consider the extent, cost, and architecture of the structures which accommodate modern governments.
3 Plutarch, *Lives* (New York: Collier, 1909), p. 49.
4 *New York Times*, 5 September 1971.

Index

Aberhart, William, 66, 162
Académie Française, 38
Accommodation, 44, 45, 50-4
Acton, Lord, 81
Adenauer, Conrad, 66, 162
Administration: efficiency limited
    in, 58; compensations in, 58-9;
    postures in, 75-87; categories of work
    in, 76; committees in, 82-3, 84; ec-
    centricity in, 88-98; egoism in, 88-9;
    'buck passing' in, 91-4; saying 'no'
    in, 92; lay-profession in, 102-5, 120,
    128, 228-9, 233; universities
    and, 206-24
Aga Khan, 150
Aggression, 56
Albert, Prince Consort, 172
Allen, J. de V., 223n
Architecture, 103-4
Aristocracy, 40
Art collecting, 79
Arts councils, 246-51
Attlee, Clement, 49, 70, 125
Austen, Jane, 152
Australian Universities Commission,
    212n
Awards, 250

Bacon, Francis, 81
Bagnold, Enid, 34
Baldwin, Stanley, 72n
Balniel, Lord, 127n
Baptist World Alliance, 149, 175, 181
Barnum, P.T., 85, 209
Barry, Rt. Rev. F.H., 151n
Bends, the, 44, 45, 46-50
Birmingham, Stephen, 83n, 89n
Bolitho, Hector, 172n
Bonaventure, the, 219

Borden, Robert, 69
Borssy, Gabriel, 253n
Bowin-Champeaux, Senator, 5n
Brown, Arnold, 179n
Bryant, C.E., 149n, 181n
Bryant, William Jennings, 162
Buchan, John, 178n
'Buck passing,' 88, 91-4
Bullitt, W.C., 168n
Buranelli, Vincent, 253n
Burckhardt, C.J., 162n
Butler, Lord, 221n

Calvert affair, 157
Canada: federal provincial relations
    in, 28-9; women in public life in, 32;
    Crown in, 65-7; university grants
    in, 200-3; science policy in, 202
Canada Council, and Calvert affair,
    157
Calvocoressi, Peter, 180n
Carlyle, Thomas, 178
Carnarvon, 33
Carter, Violet B., 142n
Castro, Fidel, 63
Chalk Garden, The, 34
Chaplains, 164-5
Charity, 83-4
Charles, Prince, 33
Chiltern, Mabel, 32
Church politics, 145-83
Churchill, Winston, 13, 48, 63, 142
Civil rights. See Rights
Civilization, 5
Clark, Most Rev. H.H., 176n
Clark, Sir Kenneth, 5, 24n
Clergymen, 145-83
Clerical work, 79-80
Clothes, fashion in, 10, 22-4, 29-30

Cocktail parties, 27, 100
Colour: definition of, 6; in institutions, 20; in democracy, 22-43; relevance of, 22; in economics, 31; and women, 32-3; and sensitivity, 55; Crown and, 61-7; as dilution of power, 90; and universities, 208-9
Committees, 82-3, 84, 214-15, 234-5
Communications, 3, 188, 226-7
Conventions, 100
Confidence, 5
Convocations, 208-9
Cooper, Duff, 33, 152n
Coughlin, Father, 162
Courtesy, 23-6
Cowardice, 121-2
Craig, A.M., 180n
Critchley, Julian, 47n
Crossman, Richard, 48n
Crown, the, 57, 61-7
Cultural centres: lay-professional relations in, 104; construction of, 229-36
Culture: definition of, 6; as human asset, 52, 225, 253-9; politics of, 225-41; public and, 238-41; and the state, 242-51
Curzon, Lord, 48, 49
Cushing, Cardinal, 142

Dance lessons racket, 236
Davison, Fred, 40n
Dean, Rt. Rev. R.W., 108n
De Gaulle, Charles, 33, 62
de Staël, Madame, 111, 138
de Terra, Helmut, 180n
Democracy: drabness in, 22-43; honours in,36-43; elites in, 63; leadership in, 108. See also Participatory democracy
Diderot, Denis, 182
Diefenbaker, John, 63
Dilke, Sir Charles, 175
Disraeli, Benjamin, 33
Divine auspices, 6, 7
Do-gooders, 111-29, 237, 240-1
Dominion Drama Festival, 157
Drabness, 22-43
Dreyfus affair, 172
Duffield, Gervaise, 160n
Duplessis, Maurice, 66
Durant, Will and Ariel, 149
Duvalier, François, 63
Duveen, Joseph, 243

Eccentricity, 94-7
Ecumenical movement, 149, 151

Egoism, 88-91, 117-18
Eisenhower, Dwight, 49, 114
Election, 46, 51, 67
Elizabeth II, Queen, 33
Engelmann, F.C., 148n
Enmity, 31

Fairbank, J.K., 180n
Faith, 139-40
Fashion, 10
Fathers of Confederation, 29
Federal-provincial relations, 28-9
Feinberg, Rabbi Abraham, 151, 168
Flagstad, Kirsten, 228
Flandin, P.E., 5n
Fly-tying, 101-2
Forsyte Saga, The, 95
Fouché, Joseph, 162
France: la gloire in, 33, 35, 42, 43; culture and government in, 245
Franco, General, 63
Freud, Sigmund, 168n

Garter, the, 38
Gauntlet, running the, 46
Gibbon, Edward, 172
Gilbert, W.S., 16
Ginsburg, Rabbi L., 165n
Gladstone, W.E., 38, 49
Glasgow, 180
Golden, Harry, 154
Government: and mistake remedying, 9; power and, 16-19; compensations in, 17; the people and, 17-18; colour in, 22-43; public spirit and, 35; honours in, 36-43; political ailments in, 44-60; fools and misfits in, 48; image of, 65; and professions, 105; and other governments, 116; and intellectuals, 127-8; and universities, 199-203, 206-24; 'odd balls' in, 205; and culture, 242-51; and awards, 250
Governor-General, 35
Gramont, Sanche de, 245
Gresham's Law, 114, 153
Grey, Ian, 161
Grouchiness, 55-6
Group activity, 105-10

Hampden, John, 74
Harari, Maurice, 169n
Harriman, E.H., 89
Heath, Edward, 89
Heenan, Cardinal, 149
Herold, J.C., 138n

Hertzberg, Gerhard, 202
History, 52
Hitler, Adolph, 49
Hoffer, Eric, 139
Hogg, C., 180n
Home, Sir Alex D., 49
Honours, 36-43
Horsburgh, R.D., 175
Hotels, conventions in, 100
Howarth, David, 161n
Hugo, Victor, 154
Humboldt, Wilhelm von, 141, 180
Hurok, Sol, 228
Huxley, Aldous, 163n, 181

Iconoclasm, 22, 30
Ideal Husband, The, 32
Ideologies. *See* Theories
Imagination, 11
Institutions: man's dependence on, vii;
    excessive growth of, 3; failure of, 4;
    scrutiny of, 7; control of, 18; assess-
    ment of, 19; refraction in, 56-7;
    complexity of, 75; postures in, 76,
    99-110; interdisciplinary activity
    in, 101; intellectuals in, 124

Jenkins, Roy, 175n
Jesters, 29

Kahn, Otto, 89
Kendall, P.M., 31n
Kennedys, the, 33, 63
King, Martin Luther, 132
King, W.L.M., 49
Killing, man's record in, 5
Kosygin, Alexei, 26n
Krushchev, Nikita, 32

Landers, Ann, 15
Lambeth Conference, 172n
Latitudinarianism, 22
Laurier, Sir Wilfrid, 22
Lawson, H.L., 39-40
Leadership, 9
Lebanon, 169
Legislatures. *See* Parliaments
Lewis, W.H., 35
Lhevinne, Rosina, 126
Long, H.K., 180n
Longford, Elizabeth, 172n
Lords, House of, 68
Louis XI, 31
Louis XIV, 86, 253
Lunatic fringe, 32; dabbling among,
    12; diversions for, 13; among

professors, 193-5; among stu-
    dents, 197-8; among politi-
    cians, 205; in the arts, 235
Lyon, Peyton, 126n
Lyre birds, 75

McArthur, A., 180n
McGill, W.J., 193
McLennan, Hugh, 161
McLuhan, Marshall, 111
Macmillan, Harold, 47
Makarios, Archbishop, 162
Manners, 24-6
Manning, Cardinal H.E., 177
Mao, Chairman, 63
Maritime Provinces, 29, 168
Marquesa Islands, 179
Maugham, Somerset, 176
Mayflower syndrome, 40
Mazarin, Cardinal, 162
Meddling, 12, 51-2, 111-29
Meetings, 26-7
Melbourne, Lord, 38
Ministries of culture, 246-51
Missionary Societies Act, 1962,
    Lebanon, 180
Michener, James A., 181
Montgomery, B.M., 119n
Moorhead, Alan, 180
Moran, Lord, 49
Muggeridge, Malcolm, 154
Murrow, E.R., 70
Musante, Giovanni, 150
Myrdal, Gunner, 145n, 155, 172n

Napoleon I, Emperor, 41, 62
Nasser, Abdul, 49
National Day, Singapore, 35
Nehru, Prime Minister, 145
Neurosis, 44, 45-6, 54-6
Nixon, Richard, 125, 171n
Non-conformism, 22
Nuisances, 32, 111-29

O'Connor, P.S., 148n
Olympics, 19
Opposition, the: colour and, 30;
    over-seriousness in, 30, 55-6;
    disappearance of, 64

Parkinson, Northcote, 28, 77, 244
Parliaments: theory of, 47; refraction
    in, 56; second chambers in, 61,
    67-74, 68; changes in, 64, 68; and
    principles, 135; favourable con-
    struction in, 140, 182; church school

bills in, 148; state and government in, 158
Participatory democracy: dialogue in, ix; definition of, 5; kinds of, 6; motives in, 6; qualifications in, 6-16; credentials in, 7; scrutiny of, 8; fashion in, 10; opportunity for, 13; displacement in, 14; politization in, 14; categories of participation in, 14-15; freedom of speech in, 15; voluntary and involuntary action in, 18; manners in, 24-6; apathy and, 35-6; and colourful activities, 35; committees in, 82-3, 84; eccentricity in, 94-7; group activity in, 105-10; meddling in, 111-29; perception in, 119; cowardice in, 121-2; in universities, 190-2; in culture, 236-7, 252, 254; culture and, 253-9
Patronage, 70, 169
Pavlova, 252
Pavlovian treatment: for professors, 30n; for officials, 36
PEI confederation conference, 29
Pericles, 257
Peter the Great, 161
Peter Principle, the, 37
Pitt, William, 50
Planning, 50-1, 54
Plato, 254
Plutarch, 257
Politics, definition of, 3
Politization, 14
Postures: definition of, 3; in religion and war, 4; in making love, 4; in social reform, 5; in government, 5; misplaced, 76; collectivized, 99-110
Power: assessment of, 16; levels of, 48; and postures, 76; and administration, 76-81; impacts of, 85; delegation of, 88, 91-4; and church politics, 90; dilution of, 90; accumulations of, 91; eccentricity and, 94-7; and principles, 136; in churches, 177-80; in universities, 219-20
Press, the, 123-4
Priestley, J.B., 34
Principles: dependence on, 6; committment to, 11; assessment of, 130-44
Professions, 99-101; and lay participation, 102-5; clerical, 159
Professors: and gowns, 23; and celebrities, 41; and saying 'no,' 92; and professionalism, 102; and

intellectualism, 124; and pseudo-intellectualism, 124-8; variety of, 187-95; and convocations, 208-9
Prout, Denis, 40n
Pseudo-intellectuals, 124-8
Public opinion, 87
Punishment, 143, 155
Puritanism, 20, 22, 27, 30, 36, 40-1, 142
Pym, John, 74

Quebec confederation conference, 29

Rain, 176
Ratisbon pamphleteers, 181
Refraction, 44, 45, 56-9, 72-3
Regency, the, 34
Reischauer, E.O., 180n
Relevance, 9-12
Responsible government, 71, 217-8
Reston, James, 122n
Richardson, Lewis, 5n
Richlieu, Cardinal, 160
Rights: and responsibility, 8; and courtesy, 24, 25; abuse of, 192-3
Roosevelt, Franklin, 38, 49
Russian Orthodox Church, 161
Ryan, A.P., 103n, 132n

Saarinen, Aline B., 79
Sabatini, Raphael, 152
Saint Andrew's Day, 35
Salisbury, Lord, 103, 132
Santa Claus parades, 35
Saud, King Ibn, 161
Schollander, Don, 19n
Schwartz, M.A., 148n
Second chambers, 61, 67-74, 68. See also Valhallas
Senate of Canada: appointments to, 37, 68; effectiveness of, 69
Sensitivity, 54-5
Shaw, G.B., 99, 150
Shirer, W.L., 127n
Singapore, 35
Smallwood, Joseph, 66
Snobbery, 22, 24, 38-9
Snyder, Louis L., 168n
Stafford, Jean, 245n
Stalin, Joseph, 33, 49, 63
Status seeking, 106-10
Stefansson, Vilhjalmur, 179
Stevenson, Adlai, 70
Stone, Irving, 113n
Storr, Anthony, 56n
Stuart, James, 126n

Sudan, 180
Suggs, R.C., 179
Supreme Court of the United States, 15
Sydney Opera House, 230
Symphony orchestras, 249-50

Tallyrand, J.M., de Perigord, 33, 111, 152, 162
Tantrums, 10, 20, 123
Temperament, 54
Theories: man's dependence on, vii; auspices of, 6; compensations for, 46, 51; fanaticism and, 60; as labels, 76; and reality, 131
Thoms, Patience, 19n
Tolley, G., 154n
Toscanini, Arturo, 54
Turnbull, Agnes, 152

Uluschak, 172n
United States diplomatic service, 37
Universities: puritanism in, 36; student newspapers in, 36, 39; joiners in, 84; presidents of as 'wailing walls,' 86; departmentalism in, 101, 128; inter-disciplinary activity in, 101; residences in, 104; student activists in, 112-13; meddlers in, 114, 115; intellectuals in, 124; pseudo-intellectuals in, 124-8; and study of theology, 153-4, 165; personnel of, 184-205; board of governors of, 185-7; president of, 186-7, 203-6; variety of professors in, 187-95; faculty council of, 190-1; participatory democracy in, 190-2; students in, 195-8; unrest in, 195-7; administration of, 199-203; and government, 199-203, 205, 206-24; convocations in, 208-9; committees in, 214-15

Valderrama, Archbishop T.A., 178n
Valhallas, 30, 53-4, 57-8, 61, 67-74
Versailles, 256
Victoria, Queen, 172n
Voluntary action, 18

Waite, Peter, 29n
Ward, Norman, 261
White, Theodore H., 171n
White, William S., 178n
Whitehead, A.N., 154
Wilde, Oscar, 32, 152
William II, Kaiser, 168
Wilson, Donald, 95n
Wilson, Woodrow, 49, 168
Whitaker, Clem, 42n
Women, colour and, 32-3

Zweig, Stefan, 162